MW01421086

Praise for All the Way to the Top

"Exceptional in its depth, this is a business book with particular relevance. Books about business leadership are almost uniformly 'light' in the sense that they mostly offer strategic platitudes but few implementation guidelines.

Calloway, an executive coach and former operations executive, takes the opposite approach, providing a leadership playbook that is comprehensive and textbook-like.

The book begins with an overview of leadership, which includes a solid definition, a brief explanation of leadership models, a discussion of "leadership levers" (teams, feedback, and coaching), emotional aspects of leadership, leadership credibility, and leadership psychology and behavior. The author presents all of this information in a single chapter that is peppered with numerous scholarly references, suggesting that he not only painstakingly researched the topic but also provided a strong, supportable platform for the material.

The manner in which the author describes the fictional company is quite impressive: Calloway provides a financial snapshot and an organization chart and, even more remarkably, plays out the backgrounds and roles of seven specific employees.

As a leadership manual for teaching MBA students or a guidebook for business leaders who want their executives to excel, All the Way to the Top should be ideal."

~ Foreword Clarion

"Calloway's academically oriented work presents leadership strategies and tactics from a number of sources, including his own models. He provides a detailed description of his own leadership improvement model – the 5C LIM and explains how to use it.

Calloway gives a number of public-speaking tips and explains the 5P model for building and delivering presentations. In this book…Calloway's detailed stories about his fictional managers are entertaining and help to provide real-world examples of common leadership dilemmas.

The author finishes with several useful appendices. For those looking for an introduction to the technical side of leadership, this book delivers an engrossing…read."

~ Kirkus Indie

"Climbing the corporate ladder, based on its very image, is a journey linked to terra firma…but author Jesse Calloway, in All the Way to the Top, takes exception to this metaphor…readers will find useful guidance here.

An adjunct faculty member at the Batten College of Engineering and Technology at Old Dominion University in Norfolk Virginia, Calloway is no stranger to 'textbook-ese' …fortunately he also finds ways to break that mold by using charts and diagrams to illustrate his concepts."

~ Blueink Review

ALL THE WAY TO THE TOP

ALL THE WAY TO THE TOP

A Practical Guide for Corporate and Business Leadership

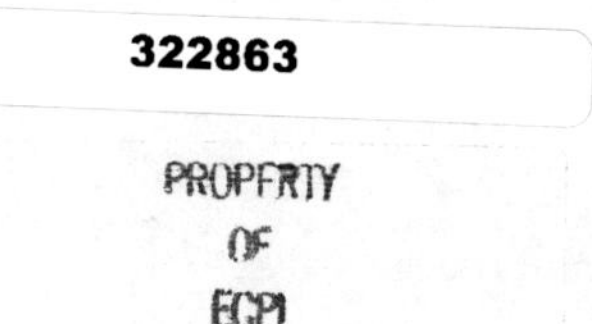

Jesse L. Calloway, PhD

Library of Congress Control Number: 2016909861

ISBN:	Hardcover	978-1-5245-1007-7
	Softcover	978-1-5245-1006-0
	eBook	978-1-5245-1005-3

Print information available on the last page.

Rev. date: 03/30/2017

To order additional copies of this book, contact:
Xlibris
1-888-795-4274
www.Xlibris.com
Orders@Xlibris.com
732259

CONTENTS

PREFACE

BEGINNING HIS CORPORATE career as a blue-collar worker before rising to prominence as an operations executive at a top Fortune 500 corporation, Dr. Jesse Calloway, currently president of Leadership and Motivation Consultants, certified executive coach, adjunct faculty member at Old Dominion University in Norfolk Virginia, and recipient of the prestigious TMCF Corporate Leadership Award, presents key easy-to-understand strategies for individual growth in the corporate, business, and nonprofit sectors.

Complementing his thirty-plus years of experience in the corporate sector, Dr. Calloway has conducted scholarly research in the area of leadership theory. Now, using empirical methods and simulated corporate scenarios, he details the practical application of such theory.

General Colin Powell stated: "There are no secrets to success. It is the result of preparation, hard work, and learning from failure." And while Dr. Calloway fundamentally concurs with these sentiments, he also believes strongly in the tremendous value, particularly in the area of empirical leadership, afforded the reader upon completion and subsequent implementation of strategies in this book, with particular focus on a business process termed the Leadership Improvement Model (LIM), which comprises 5Cs: conversation, calculation, collaboration, communication, and cognizance.

Aimed at facilitating and further solidifying your understanding of key concepts presented, six simulated corporate scenarios using leadership positions in manufacturing operations, procurement, sales, marketing, information technology, and customer relations are explored. In addition to buttressing the theoretical leadership perspectives shared early on in this book, these corporate scenarios are also predicated to a large degree on real-world experiences. Further leveraging both empirical and theoretical methods, Dr. Calloway introduces a unique leadership-oriented model for developing and executing effective presentations that encompasses 5Ps: purpose, preparation, perception, persuasion and power.

Who might benefit from the lessons to be learned in this book? The answer is simple: anyone who has a boss, is a boss, or aspires to be a boss; anyone who receives or delivers a performance appraisal; or anyone who may have succumbed to current organization role complacency. To this end, college students (particularly those majoring in business), sole contributing professionals, supervisors, managers, directors (in all fields and disciplines, such as operations, marketing, sales, engineering, accounting, IT, health administration, education, and not for profit), and, yes, even executives will do well to read and implement the concepts and strategies presented.

Addressed in this book are renowned leadership and management theories (transformational and transactional leadership, emotional intelligence, psychometric modeling, LMX, path goal, and teams), and argumentation methods (deductive and inductive logic). Easy-to-follow corporate and business operations topics include finance, accounting, economics, statistics, marketing, information systems, project management, quality, continuous improvement (including Six Sigma), and more.

ABOUT THE DESIGN OF THIS BOOK

In support of the information contained herein, various references are provided reflecting the extensiveness of the scholarly research and topic review. Thus, you will observe frequent citations and source identifiers in the form: "(author year, page)". Additionally, as key business and technical concepts are discussed, such as capital budgeting, analytical marketing, and statistical applications, tutorial information will be provided to assure reader comprehension. And finally, key leadership insights are offered to solidify understanding of character execution of the presented strategies and theory.

Author and journalist Ernest Hemingway wrote: "Show the readers everything, tell them nothing." Thus, you will note I have liberally used diagrams, charts, and graphs, as my intent is to take advantage of Hemingway's sentiments to aid you in comprehending the concepts and strategies presented.

The first chapter focuses on leadership definitions, theories, and principles. Building on this foundation, discussion of a key piece of corporate and organizational infrastructure (the performance appraisal) follows, which is linked to the theory presented. An overview of corporate structure follows, with emphasis on corporate initiation, implementation, and operation. You are then introduced to the simulated corporation: Summit Consumables Incorporated.

Next comes a systematized discussion of inputs, processing, and outputs (IPO). Then I introduce my leadership improvement model (the 5C LIM). This model is applied by a simulation that demonstrates how to handle corporate and business scenarios, seen in the examples of six Summit Consumables employees as they respond to performance evaluation results.

Bolstered by previously reviewed leadership strategies, the book then offers leadership-oriented approaches: *purpose, preparation, perception, persuasion*, and *power*—the 5Ps—for development and delivery of individual presentations leveraging the previously introduced Summit Consumables employees.

The final chapter demonstrates how stages of the 5C LIM may be used as a stand-alone model to circumvent issues and opportunities occurring in the typical world of leaders.

ACKNOWLEDGEMENTS

IN HIS POEM "Ulysses," Alfred, Lord Tennyson wrote: "I am a part of all that I have met." Likewise, this book would not be possible were it not for the tremendous contributions of my family, friends, and colleagues. The unbiased feedback offered by my wonderful daughter and the patience exhibited by my wife of more than thirty years deserve special recognition.

In loving memory of my two sisters, I am donating twenty percent of all proceeds from sales of this book to charitable organizations, including dementia and cancer research centers.

CHAPTER 1

Introduction

I'M FREQUENTLY ASKED two questions regarding this book. 1) What does it mean to go all the way to the top? 2) What prompted you to write this book? The answer to the first question is—philosophically speaking—it depends. In 1978, I began my career as a blue-collar electrical apprentice. For me back then, the top was simply achieving the A-class certification while concurrently receiving a certificate in electrical electronics. From there the proverbial top for me became receiving an AAS degree in electronics technology and moving from blue-collar worker to white-collar employee as an engineering aide. After that the top became receiving my BS degree and advancing to the position of electrical engineer. As the foregoing comments imply, "the top" could very well mean different things (such as positions) to different people.

Consider the following question: What is the first month of a calendar year in the United States? The answer is quite clear, and anyone who either resides in the United States, or is aware of the usual twelve-month calendar, would offer January as the proper response. There are, however, many questions to which we are exposed that are not so black and white, requiring consideration of applicable contingencies.

Next, consider the case where you are presented with two corporate job offers and must decide which one to accept. Let's assume that one job is located outside the geographical area in which you reside, and the other is located within drivable proximity of your current residence. All other things being equal, most might perceive the local job to be the slam dunk choice; however, another job seeker (local to the area) presented with the same two opportunities, but who prefers to relocate, might see the local job as less appealing.

The contrasting perceptions offered by these two cases might be best characterized by considering the effect of relativism. Thus, what is viewed as acceptable, correct, or an endgame by one individual may be viewed differently by another. Kobel and Zeman concur with this perspective, stating: "the view that it depends on certain features of the thinker whether it is correct to believe such and such is sometimes called 'relativism' or 'relativism about such and such'" (2012, 529).

My view of the proverbial top changed from one job to the next. Adding fuel to the fire, despite having become an executive at a Fortune 500 company, it could be argued that because this position was not the highest job in the organization, I hadn't reached the top. But academicians might argue that despite the level achieved in a corporate or business setting, only roughly 2 percent of the U.S. population age 25 and over possess a doctorate degree, and because approximately "57 percent of doctoral students will get their degree within lo years of starting," anyone on whom this diploma has been conferred has indeed reached the top (census.gov; cbsnews.com). Consequently, this discussion becomes somewhat circular, leading us to support ideals espoused by Kobel and Zeman regarding the relative nature of belief.

Returning to the job offer example, another explanation for the contrasting behavior is the result of mind dependence, that is, a belief driven solely by how one perceives the world and all things in it. Viewed in this manner, one job seeker's perception of a job offer (local or otherwise) may be inconsistent with that of another's. Thus, unlike more objective forms of knowledge or belief, the designation of a job offer as acceptable or not acceptable is dependent upon decisions made in an individual's mind. This contrasts with comments offered by Bertrand, who writes in reference to the preference of a table being mind-independent, "to the eye it is oblong … to the touch it is smooth and cool and hard … anyone else who sees and feels the table will agree with this description …" (1812, 1). Aggregating the comments regarding relativism and mind dependence, it is logical to assume that determining what the top means rests with you—the reader.

Let's visit the second question regarding my decision to write this book. Over the course of my career, I longed for a book that presents key lessons from certain theories akin to what would be acquired by pursuing higher level education (such as getting an MBA) but without committing the time to do so. My thinking was that such a book would facilitate my growth in the corporate sector and assist me in navigating the corporate ladder.

What do you mean "navigate the corporate ladder," you ask? Let's begin here: *Merriam-Webster* defines *navigate* as follows: "to sail on or through ... to steer or direct the course of a ship or aircraft ..." (2007). Consider the concept of traveling the ocean. If the objective is to traverse the ocean with the intent of moving from point A to point B, and such a course is in the direction of the current and winds are consistent, the journey might be greatly facilitated. In this case, and analogous to John Masefield's poem "Sea Fever," the only thing required to sail the seas "is a tall ship and a star to steer her by." Such was not the case, however, for the ill-fated *Titanic*. Even though Martin and Schlinzinger said the *Titanic* "was proclaimed the greatest engineering achievement ever," in April 1912, the ship, thought to be unsinkable, sank when it collided with an iceberg, killing "1522 out of the 2227 on board" (2010, 77).

It is known that an ocean's current is continuous and flows for great distances. Moreover, "the average ocean depth is 2.65 miles" (waterencyclopedia.com). It is also known that "currents exist at all depths in the ocean; in some regions, two or more currents flow in different directions at different depths" (waterencyclopedia.com). Indeed, the oceans can embody a formidable adversary. Yet Masefield's poem, despite its reference to "seas [which] are found on the margins of the ocean," implies that this formidable adversary is easily conquered (oceanservice.noaa.gov).

Analogously to the oceans, organizational culture, bureaucratic barriers, and performance management systems may offer opposing currents and tremendous headwinds to employees seeking to advance beyond present levels. So the question becomes: How do we transcend these figurative oceanic currents and headwinds? In other words, how in a practical sense do we give credence to Masefield's poetic and perhaps prophetic writing? The answer lies in the manner in which we anticipate, approach, and respond to corporate challenges and concerns. Metaphorically speaking—it's about how we navigate the corporate seas. Thus, the aim of this book is to offer strategies for facilitating your journey across the corporate seas.

Now, let us begin the journey of not simply following the path of the existing current but, instead, leading the way into the headwinds to a new place—a place to which we arrive free of apprehension and fear. In order to do this, let us first peel back the onion a bit by defining the most important prerequisite attribute for corporate advancement—the capacity to lead.

1.1 What Is Leadership?

Let's now discuss the notion of leadership, which has been described and defined at length in textbooks and literature of all types. One such descriptor is provided by Katz and Kahn (1966), as cited by Johns and Moser, characterizing leadership as "any act of influence on a matter of organizational relevance" (1989, 115). This would imply that one of the principle responsibilities of a leader is to move an organization forward in a manner consistent with the best interests of the business.

This notion of consistency should not be understated. All too often, instances have been documented of leadership application in a manner inconsistent with an organization's stated relevance, as happened with Enron and Global Crossings. Burns (1979), as also cited by Johns and Moser, said: "I define leadership as leaders inducing followers to act for certain goals that represent the values and the motivations of both leaders and followers" (1989, 115). This descriptor implies that there exists a sort of connectedness between and among the leaders and followers. Perhaps this is the intent of the following comments offered by Boyatzis et al.: "great leaders are awake, aware, and attuned to themselves, to others and to the world around them" (2005, 3). Chemers (2001), as cited by Kark and Yaffe, defines leadership as "a process of social influence through which an individual enlists and mobilizes the aid of others in the attainment of a collective goal" (2011, 806).

This perspective, similar to the preceding comments, suggests that leadership involves not only the leader but also the stalwart participation of those to whom the leader is looked to for guidance and direction. A key distinction here is the reference to "social influence," which could suggest that the leader's actions and behaviors are somehow swayed by those with whom the leader interacts. Another key distinction in this leadership characterization is reference to "a collective goal." Focusing for a moment on the two words *social* and *collective* warrants some discussion regarding cultural influences on leadership. That a leader may be influenced by or at a minimum consider perceptions and priorities of others (such as social and collective aspects) might also suggest that such a leader values *allocentrism* ("viewing oneself in terms of the in-groups to which one belongs [this versus the contrasting perspective *idiocentrism* which is] viewing oneself as the basic social unit where individual goals have primacy over in-group goals") (Avolio, Lawler, & Walumba 2007, 214).

Given its synonymous attributes with the word *collective,* Kark and Yaffe would most likely adopt *allocentrism* as a surrogate for *collective* in the process description of leadership. Expanding discussions regarding the cultural influences on leadership behavior in the context of social and collective leadership suggests a further link to allocentrism.

According to Christopher & Weber, "individualism emphasizes personal freedom and responsibility; collectivism endorses social relatedness and interdependence with others in one's family or social group" (1998, 1209).

Interestingly, collectivism and individualism, as is the case with allocentrism and idiocentrism, suggest contrasting styles or behaviors which, in the context of the previously discussed leadership process, might offer clues as to how one leader interacts with his followers. For example, leaders who are closely aligned with a culture of collectivism may engage in a more participative style of leadership when compared to those more aligned with an individualist culture. Therefore, leadership culture "may play an important role in predicting how followers respond to different leadership styles/orientations" (Triandis, Chan, Bhawuk, Iwao, & Sinha 1995, as cited by Avolio et al. 2007, 214).

Leadership, according to Northouse, "is a process whereby an individual influences a group of individuals to achieve a common goal" (2013, 5). This definition attempts to transform leadership from the psychological realm to a sort of interdependent network. *Merriam-Webster* defines *process* as follows: "a forward or onward movement … something going on … a natural phenomenon marked by gradual changes that lead toward a particular result" (2007). With this definition in mind, it may be inferred that leadership, viewed as a process, is about a leader providing direction or inputs to the followers who, in turn, move forward with that direction (transform it into a qualitative or quantitative deliverable), seeking consistency of the output with the initially provided direction (input). Systematizing this thinking (see figure 1-1) would yield a codependence characterized by inputs, processing, and outputs, with the addition of a feedback mechanism to close the loop.

Figure 1-1: Leadership Systemization

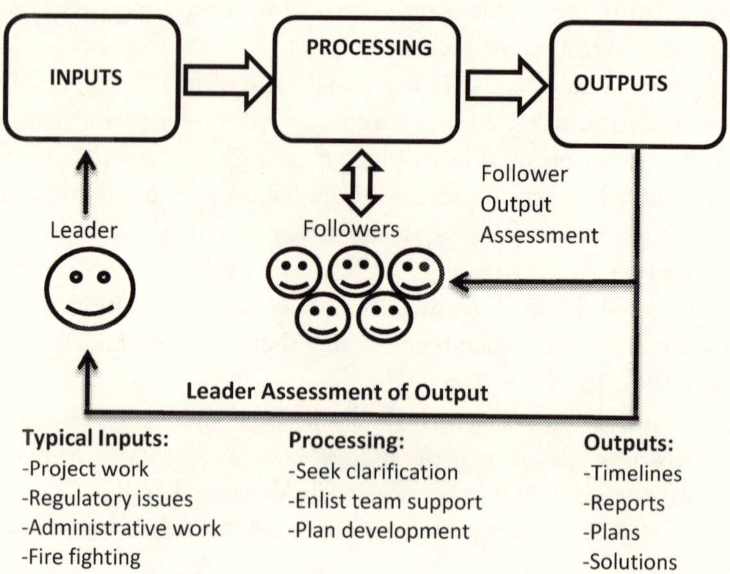

Focusing on figure 1-1, you can see the leader provides direction in the form of inputs to the followers who in turn process that direction to develop an output. The initial output is reviewed by followers and modified to fit their interpretation of leader inputs. Follower output is submitted to the leader for assessment. Upon assessment by the leader, the output is either reworked by the followers, or it is accepted by the leader who then provides a new input for processing. (The topic of inputs, processing, and outputs will be discussed further in chapter 4.)

Hesburgh (1971), as cited by Johns and Moser, "gave an inspiring definition of leadership, 'the mystic of leadership, be it educations, political, religious, commercial or whatever, is next to impossible to describe, but wherever it exists, morale flourishes, people pull together toward common goals, spirits soar, order is maintained, not as an end in itself, but as a means to move forward together it requires courage as well as wisdom.'" (1989, 115). This leadership characterization suggests that almost in a supernatural manner a leader is able to galvanize the team, the organization, and perhaps a nation. Further, those who receive the message all march with one accord, en route to accomplishing the unimaginable.

Nowhere was this perspective more evident than in the following passage provided by Burton, quoting then President Kennedy: "We choose to go to the moon in this decade and do the other things … not because they are easy, but because they are hard" (2009, 29). Such direction provided in the twenty-first century would not be unexpected and may seem quite trivial. However, this proclamation was issued at a time when those accountable for the ultimate deliverable were asking fundamental questions regarding how to make it happen. This perspective was evidenced by the comments written by Burton: "Immediately following Kennedy's announcement, NASA managers asked themselves, 'how do you get to the moon'" (2009, 29).

Despite having touched on several leadership perspectives, it was not my intent in the foregoing discussion to present exhaustive commentary in this area. Indeed, as written by Burns (1978), and cited by Johns & Moser, "the list of well-reasoned definitions of leadership could go on and on" (1989, 116).

With these comments, discussion now shifts toward reviewing attempts to prototype leader functions and behaviors.

1.2 Theoretical Leadership Models

Modeling leadership approaches and patterns has proven quite useful, particularly in an academic setting where the students have yet to experience firsthand the joys and pains of leadership. Among the many leadership models is "contingency theory" which is, according to Fiedler & Garcia (1987) as cited by Northouse, "the most widely recognized [contingency theory model]" (2013, 123). As the name implies, the model posits that leadership styles and responses are contingent on various situations and, based on these situations, characterizes the leader as either "relationship motivated" or "task motivated." Specific situations may be characterized in terms of "leader-member relations, task structure, and position power."

As an example regarding leader-member relations in an environment where trust and good overall perception of the leader is experienced, such relations are "defined as good." Task structure refers to "the degree to which requirements of a task are clear and spelled out," while position power has to do with "the amount of authority a leader has to reward or to punish followers [both of which, to some degree, parallel transactional leadership, which we will discuss later]" (Northouse 2013, 124–25).

From these comments, it should be clear that the contingency theory model suggests certain paths be embarked on, driven by the situation at hand. For example, if the situation to be addressed is "moderately favorable or moderately unfavorable," the model suggested approach is one that is "relationship oriented." Further, "if a leader is moderately liked and possesses some power" under somewhat ambiguous job conditions for subordinates, a "relationship orientation" should provide the best chance for success.

The underlying premise for this contingency approach is that leaders must be perceptive enough to recognize certain situations and circumstances that, in turn, will prompt them to adjust that environment to better match their leadership approach. Another way to interpret this is: "when leaders can recognize the situations in which they are most successful, they can then begin to modify their own situations" (Ivancevich & Matteson 1993, 444). This approach may seem a bit counterintuitive as it suggests that rather than exhibit leadership flexibility the leader should modify the situation to one more compatible with personal style. The premise for this approach was that "Fiedler [was] not particularly optimistic that leaders [could] be retrained successfully to change their preferred leadership style" (Ivancevich & Matteson 1993, 444).

Path-goal theory, expanding upon the contingency theory approach, "suggests that a leader must adapt to the development level of subordinates [emphasizing] the relationship between the leader's style and the characteristics of the subordinates and work setting" (Northouse 2013, 137). An important point to be made regarding path-goal theory is that it is based on subordinate perceptions of their leaders' work, and how to achieve goals within their particular work environment. Similar to "other situational or contingency leadership approaches, the path-goal attempts to predict leadership effectiveness in different [leadership] situations" (Ivancevich & Matteson 1993, 451).

House and Mitchell (1974), as cited by Northouse, offers four leadership behaviors applicable to the path-goal theory: "directive, supportive, participative, and achievement-oriented" (2013, 139). As the stated behaviors would suggest, the directive style focuses more on providing direction, whereas the supportive and participative approaches tend to enlist collaboration from subordinates while achievement orientation seeks to build capability among subordinates. The key takeaway from this approach is that the leader must be fully aware of the capability of his or her subordinate staff as well as their motivational needs and the overall work environment. It is only after such analysis that the leader will be positioned to apply the appropriate leadership style.

Although it is not my intent here to address all possible theoretical leadership models, two remaining theoretical models have garnered quite a bit of support: "leader-member exchange theory" and the "Vroom-Jago model of leadership." Leader-member exchange (LMX) is predicated not simply on the style of the leader or subordinates or even the specific situation at hand. Instead, it "takes still another approach and conceptualizes the leadership as a process that is centered on the interactions between leaders and followers" (Northouse 2012, 161).

To this point, we have assumed a degree of universality among subordinates. Leader-member exchange by design seeks to segregate subordinates into two distinct groups—the "in group" or the "out group," contingent on the leader to subordinate relationships (Northouse 2012, 163). Generally speaking, the more collaborative and ambitious the subordinate, the greater the likelihood that this person will be aligned with the in-group. Those falling outside this area would obviously be more closely aligned with the out-group. And depending on the group allocation, the leader-subordinate interaction varies accordingly. For example, as noted by Dansereau et al. (1975), as cited by Northouse, "subordinates in the in-group receive more information, influence, confidence, and concern from their leaders than do out-group subordinates" (2012, 163).

Barge and Schlueter suggested that LMX theory is predicated on the notion that "in-group relationships will be associated with higher levels of employee satisfaction and productivity" (1991, 544). The effectiveness of LMX has been empirically confirmed as "in-group relationships are not only positively associated with increased employee satisfaction (Ferris, 1985; Graen & Ginsburgh, 1977), but with employee performance as well (Liden & Graen, 1980; Tjosvold, 1984; Vecchio, 1982)", as also cited by Barge and Schlueter (1991).

This perspective of employee effectiveness is shared by Dubrin, who wrote, based on study results, "the quality of the relationship with the leader had an impact on the effectiveness of influence tactics…a poor relationship with the leader resulted in less [co-worker to co-worker assistance while] a positive relationship with the leader positively related to helping behavior" (2010, 247). While LMX can result in positive contributions by certain team members, there are some negative implications as well. This is principally due to the variations in business relationships. Indeed, Dockery & Steiner (1990), as cited by Suleyman, stated that, "in high-quality interactions, leaders establish closer relations with only a few key subordinates, the (in-group) due to limited resources [consequently] they provide (in-group) members with support and resources beyond the employment contract" (2011, 1494).

The Vroom-Jago model has to do with decision making and the degree to which subordinate involvement should be taken into account when making such decisions. The fundamental assumption for use of this model was that "no single leadership style was appropriate" and that leaders must exhibit flexibility even if doing so requires the leader to modify her style to fit the situation at hand. The model, by design, also considers the types of decisions with which leaders are faced, namely "individual and group." As implied by the terms *individual* and *group*, the former decisions have to do with leader decisions that affect only one member of the team while the latter addresses decisions that "affect several followers." Due to the complexity associated with use of this model (driven by the highly variable nature of decisions to be made), "decision making heuristics, or rules of thumb, have been developed" (Ivancevich & Matteson 1993, 446–48).

As previously mentioned, leadership models aimed at improving leader effectiveness, be it through subordinate motivation, performance management, decision efficiency, or otherwise, abound in the related literature. While it was not my intent in this section to comprehensively address all such theoretical approaches, those mentioned should adequately introduce the topic and possibly precipitate additional enquiry, which is left to you to pursue at will.

1.3 Leadership Levers

Thus far our discussion of leadership has considered for the most part leadership characterizations, theories, and models. Yet there are other mechanisms at the leader's disposal that may also be of assistance in moving the needle of organizational effectiveness. Three such critical tools are leveraging *teams* and their associated infrastructure, receiving and delivering f*eedback*, and leadership *coaching*.

Regarding teams, there is much to be said of the progress that can be made working in a collaborative group versus flying solo. Strength in numbers is perhaps nowhere more evidenced than by nature's wolves. Wolves, like humans, achieve even the most critical and fundamental goals (such as hunting) in packs or groups. Operating in a sort of hierarchy, wolves are pack animals that communicate by gestures of head, body, and limbs, thus maintaining order in the pack. In the same way that a father wolf obtains food for the family, the leader of a human team removes barriers to effectiveness and quenches the members' hunger for challenge (Funk & Wagnalls 1995, 2802–3).

One way to view a team of people interacting interdependently is to consider them in a systems context. Doing so is consistent with the perspective described by Kets et al., who suggest that "a system is a set of interacting units with relationships among them" (2007, 31). Human teams, particularly when operating at optimum efficiency, provide such a relationship. Teams may be formed formally (such as when designated by a leader or sponsor) or informally, whereby a group of employees with a common goal recognize the benefits of operating collectively.

Despite the motivation for group formation, formal and specific stages of behavior occur before optimization. Bateman and Zeithaml describe these stages as "forming, storming, norming and performing [then] adjourning" (1993, 477). Although each stage is relatively self-explanatory, *storming* is perhaps the most controversial aspect of group and team development, where each member seeks to define him or herself and lobby for respective contributions to the team. While conflict may be minimal when each team member is perceived as bringing different yet valued skill sets to the team, such is not necessarily the case where one or more members appear to exhibit expertise in the same area. It is this situation that may give rise to conflict over such matters as how to decide which team member is most suitable for a needed role.

The team leader, formal or informal, is most often looked to for deciding and allocating team member roles and contributions. The leader is also accountable to ensure a clear understanding of *team potency*, which is, according to Champion et al. (1993), as cited by Hu and Liden, "team members' shared beliefs about their collective capabilities" (2011, 852). This is a critical aspect of team evolution and effectiveness. If team resource capabilities are either underutilized or overstated, the result will be team suboptimization. So the team must trust that the leader is best positioned to make such determinations while concurrently fully making use of and valuing whatever a team member has to offer. This perspective is supported by Lam, Peng, and Schaubroeck in the statement, "members' trust in their leaders is critical for effective team performance and potency" (2011, 870).

It is also important to note the leaders' influence on the team given certain cultural and social settings. Earlier, we discussed allocentrism and collectivism and the role that such approaches might play in leader-team dynamics. Further, according to Yukl (2010), as cited by Chang, Johnson, Mao, and Venus, "leadership is a social process of exerting influence over the thoughts, feelings, and actions of others" (2012, 1). With this in mind, it was also noted in the same report that "leaders' group based identities have also been found to spill over to their followers" (2012, 1). Thus, collective consideration should, in turn, promote healthy member collaboration.

Although providing team leadership, recognizing the unique contributions of each member, and appropriately allocating resources among team members allow a team to progress toward optimization, *empowerment* can accelerate such optimization. Indeed, according to a study implemented by Leach (1998), as cited by Clegg, Cordery, and Wall, which also considered enhanced feedback, "system performance improved considerably following empowerment" (2002, 159). The essential goal of empowerment is for the leader to provide the team with needed resources and then get out of the way and serve the team. Said differently, empowerment is simply "a means of granting work-related decision-making authority to employees as a means of enhancing performance" (Menon 2001, 154). Through empowerment, team members derive a sense of ownership for goals and accomplishments. In this way, they execute with passion and quality.

While charged with providing direction to the team and steering them along the correct courses of action, the leader must nonetheless be careful about advocacy of certain actions. Granted, the team must take certain paths, and the de facto decision maker in such situations is the team leader. However, when opportunities exist to engage the team in making decisions or plotting future courses of action, there is a somewhat tacit expectation among the team that they are expected to participate. The astute team leader recognizes these opportunities as well as the possibility of a disengaged team if such opportunities are not appropriately pursued or if team members perceive their input to be of little value. Indeed, according to Vroom, "strong advocacy by the leader of a particular course of action along with critical judgments of alternatives proposed by others, might reasonably be expected to decrease [team] participation" (1997, 423). More often than not, the team's success or failure rests with the team leader. Consequently, the team leader's strengths and development opportunities are often ultimately measured by overall team performance.

A frequently used tool aimed at honing a leader's effectiveness is the *360-degree feedback* instrument. Although the emphasis of this section, for the purposes of reviewing 360-degree feedback, has to do with individual improvement, it may also be used "for succession planning, merit raises, performance appraisals, and downsizing" (Capritella 2002, as cited by Crispo & Sysinger 2012, 2). Throughout this writing, reference has been made to leader-to-group interactions and their importance in the leadership arsenal. Here, we delve a bit deeper into a formal feedback instrument, the 360-degree form, as well as review aspects of its supporting infrastructure.

We begin with an efficient definition of the instrument as follows: "The 360 degree feedback is a questionnaire that is completed by the participant, participant's supervisors, coworkers, peers, and subordinates" (Crispo & Sysinger 2012, 2). Hence, reference to the tool as being "360 degree" feedback adequately articulates the extent to which organizational feedback (participants' strengths and weaknesses) is provided. In fact, in some instances, the word *weaknesses* is often supplanted with "development opportunities" to assure the highest chance for success in the leader's acceptance of such feedback. (The latter descriptor may be viewed as less critical.) This is an important property of the 360-degree process as the intent is to receive balanced feedback from the organizational levels with which the participant most frequently interacts. This perspective is shared by Hellervik, Hazucha, and Schneider (1992), as cited by Carless, Mann, and Wearing as follows: "Obtaining information on an individual's performance from multiple sources enhances the credibility of the information and therefore, presumably the individual's motivation to change his or her behavior" (1998, 482).

Aimed at providing a more coherent review of the 360-degree feedback questionnaire composition, we will focus on the "global executive leadership inventory (GELI)" described by Kets et al. (2007), which includes the following key components for inventory: "visioning, empowering, energizing, designing and aligning, rewarding and giving feedback, team-building, outside stakeholder orientation, global mindset, tenacity, emotional intelligence, life balance [and] resilience to stress" (2007, 83–84). The significance of the balanced approach, coupled with use of the feedback circle, cannot be overstated and offers the best chance for success in elevating behavior to the desired state.

Those in the feedback circle (the raters) assess each of these components and provide information to the one being rated about how well that person scores within the component (for example in team-building) and also how those scores compare to an average score. This feedback helps leaders to understand better the emotional lives of the ones being rated.

The feedback might be supplemented with a *personality audit*. It may focus on a person's motivation and emotional management (such as trustful versus vigilant or extroverted versus introverted). *Archetypes feedback* reveals how the one being rated deals with people and situations (such as whether he or she is a strategist or a coach), (Kets et al. 2007, 85–96). In the end, the comprehensive nature of this feedback is expected to fully convey those personality characteristics that, if modified, would facilitate increased individual and organizational effectiveness. (Beginning in chapter 5, reference will be made to the Multifactor Leadership Questionnaire (MLQ). Similar to the GELI, it may be used for receiving feedback on a 360-degree basis.)

The final leadership tool I wish to discuss in this section is *executive coaching*. How often have we seen the underdog team miraculously execute an amazing come-from-behind victory or heard about an impoverished elementary school that succeeded against all odds in meeting testing score requirements? These stories convey the essence of the power behind coaching. Yet, effective coaching is not confined to circumstances offering low probability for success. Today, many executives depend on coaching, either formally or informally, to buttress their success. Indeed, according to the Chartered Institute of Personnel and Development (2010), as cited by Baban and Ratiu, "two-thirds of organizations report using coaching ..." (2012, 140).

You might wonder how effective executive coaching can be, given that managers are seasoned and to some degree unyielding. A metaphorical adage says: "you can't teach an old dog new tricks." Nonetheless, retraining seasoned executives by coaching them is quite doable and beneficial. According to Kets et al., "people whose personality characteristics have been largely formed (this includes most people over 30) can still make significant changes in their behavior" (2007, 13). While coaching strategies vary depending on a client's operating environment, this book assumes the typical corporate or business environment with a leader who has no lineage ties within that organization.

Although a great deal of coaching efficacy may depend on the one being coached, Nelson and Hogan (2009), as cited by Baban and Ratiu, stated that "coaching in general can be a more productive and impactful process if coaches engage in a well-planned and intentional manner" (2012, 141). One of the first steps used in executive coaching is to provide the client with unbiased feedback such as that offered via 360-degree instruments discussed previously.

Such an approach is extremely valuable given that effective coaching has to be as objective as possible—a sort of reality check. According to de Berg et al., "feedback is particularly relevant in coaching practices where it is provided to support self-awareness, learning, and to improve performance" (2012, 14). Indeed, many executives have a differing perspective of their interactions and, given their positions of power, often face little resistance regarding their beliefs about themselves. This view is shared by Kets et al. as they comment, "although few would admit it, many business leaders are ... like the mythical narcissus they see the person they love most in the world roughly 70% of executives believe they are in the top 25% of their profession in terms of performance" (2007, 76).

With this in mind, the need for coaching is clear as is the need to approach this task in a manner most effective for the client. Therefore, in addition to implementation of 360-degree feedback, effective coaching should include time for *reflection*—allocating time for the leader to freely assimilate information about his or her leadership challenges without the stresses of day-to-day operations. Effective coaching should also use *group coaching*, whereby all members of the session share their perspectives about themselves and their respective coaching opportunities.

My final point on the subject of coaching is *follow-up*—an attempt to have group participants follow up with each another on the progress they have or have not made relative to feedback they received (Kets et al. 2007, 111–15). Often participants don't follow through on something they learned in a coaching classroom when they return to the workplace, particularly when it involves self-reflection and improvement. While some responsibility for lack of follow-through may be attributed to a person's resistance to self-change, according to Goldsmith (2009), as cited by Baban and Ratiu, "some studies suggest that not all individuals are coachable [and that] coachable individuals are committed to change, [and] have strong motivation to improve their competencies" (2012, 142).

Another contributing factor to the lack of follow-through is the leader's return to day-to-day operations and the issues that doing so poses. It is not at all unusual for an executive to return to the proverbial office with the intent of executing certain plans only to find that, when getting there, the picture has changed significantly: sales forecasts just went south, a quality issue has occurred in a major manufacturing facility, or a rumor of divestiture has spawned a precipitous company stock sell-off. Although seemingly a bit extreme, these issues come with the territory of executive leadership and cannot be put on the back burner while less threatening concerns are addressed, such as reflecting on received 360-degree feedback.

Despite the commoditized nature of executive coaching and organizational openness to engaging in such developmental processes, there are those who view the need for coaching as a sign of failure or weakness, which may be driven by their introspective views of self-competencies. While superficial coaching may provide a path for leadership style changes, more visceral behavior modifications require additional insights. And given the personal nature of coaching, it is imperative that coaches be adept in discerning the source of improvement opportunities presented by those being coached. Berglas (2002), as cited by Ellam-Dyson and Palmer, also noted this perspective by "emphasizing how important it is that coaches have the ability to be able to recognize when clients may have deep seated psychological difficulties" (2011, 115).

Viewed in a "clinical paradigm" context, an individual's "inner theater" plays a crucial role, not only in how the individual is coached, but also in how he or she interprets and responds to such coaching. The "transferential patterns" (actions linked to our past lives) can be powerful and controlling as we are, in essence, forced to relive our past behaviors perpetually (Kets et al. 2007, 6).

As the next section shows, dealing with one's past demons and ghosts often requires much more than external influences. Indeed, a comprehensive understanding of one's operating environment (and the role of emotions in that environment) is a prerequisite for effective leadership.

1.4 Emotional Intelligence and Leadership

It is no secret that intelligence is a fundamental requirement for executive leadership. However, while the technical aspect of intelligence no doubt facilitates critical decision making, personal or emotional intelligence (EI) enables leaders to make the best critical decisions.

Ability to motivate followers to contribute their best in every situation and in all cases is a fundamental property of successful leadership. Often, in order to accomplish this goal, a profound emotional connection between leaders and followers is required. According to Boyatzis et al., "the emotional task of the leader is primal ... it is both the original and most important act of leadership ... [thus] the leader acts as the group's emotional guide" (2002, 5). This notion that the leader serves as an emotional guide is key given that, also according to Boyatzis et al., "we rely on connections with other people for our own emotional stability" (6).

It would logically follow, then, that leaders who possess the capacity to connect at this level are best positioned for success. The importance of employee emotional satisfaction cannot be understated as it links directly to job performance. In fact, Boyatzis et al. suggest that "employees who feel upbeat will likely go the extra mile to please customers and therefore improve the bottom line" (15).

Given the significant role that EI plays in a leader's overall organizational effectiveness, it is appropriate that we seek to define EI through the lens of various writers. Salovey and Mayer (1990), as cited by Brackett, Rivers, and Salovey, described EI as "the ability to monitor one's own and others' feelings and emotions, to discriminate among them and to use this information to guide one's thinking and actions" (2011, 89). This definition suggests the capacity to be in touch not only with the vicissitudes of your thoughts and impressions but also to control how you react to them. Goleman (2000), as cited by Hosein and Yousefi, stated: "the emotional intelligence is an inherent ability and the genes have [an] important role in its creation, but emotional intelligence can grow by training and it needs many efforts and practices" (2012, 57). This would suggest that while EI may be attributed to lineage, it is not bound by innate qualities and can therefore be acquired via learned behavior based methodologies (such as in seminars).

Kets et al. say that "emotional intelligence focuses fundamentally on one's capacity to manage in a social and emotional climate" (2007, 18). Within this definition, we are once again reminded of the importance of recognizing the interdependencies of individuals and, perhaps more importantly, the leader's awareness of such need for connectedness. Northouse offers the following comments regarding EI: "as the two words suggest, emotional intelligence has to do with our emotions (affective domain) and thinking (cognitive domain), and the interplay between the two" (2013, 27). This definition distinguishes between the two words *emotional* and *intelligence*, suggesting that effective use or implementation of EI be predicated on an understanding of emotions resulting from user intellect.

There are "four domains of EI, self-awareness, self-management, social awareness, and relationship management" (Boyatzis et al. 2002, 30). Self-awareness, as the name implies, suggests that leaders first be cognizant of their emotions and feelings.

Demonstration of proficiency in the area of EI is given by the following example. Assume that an employee named Jack was disappointed with his end-of-year performance review. Such a situation might precipitate a fight, flee, or freeze reaction. Certainly one response, as damaging as it might be in this situation, would be for him to fight, to respond with anger and dissention. While this may seem to be a natural response in this situation, it is not a response consistent with the notion of self-awareness.

An alternative action, in the context of self-awareness, might be to first recognize that the different perspectives regarding performance may have resulted from a lack of calibration between subordinate and superior. With this in mind, the conversation may be shifted to how to circumvent a similar situation in the future. The key point here is that the first step for an emotionally intelligent individual is to recognize personal doldrums and to proactively respond (self-manage) in such a manner as to eliminate any further erosion, in the negative sense, of the situation at hand. It is only after Jack is able to be in tune with his emotions (self-awareness) that he will be able to self-manage and subsequently resonate with others.

This perspective is shared by Boyatzis et al. in the following statement: "self-awareness also plays a crucial role in empathy or sensing how someone else sees a situation" (2002, 30). Expanding a bit on empathy, it is important to understand what it is not. It is not about trying to modify your actions such that the masses are sure to like you or, for that matter, taking on another's feelings as your own. It is about appropriately processing the feelings of others. Boyatzis et al. address the topic of empathy as follows: "empathy means taking employees' feelings into thoughtful consideration and then making intelligent decisions that work those feelings into the response" (2002, 50).

Social awareness, as we have discussed in relation to allocentrism, takes into account the emotions of those around us. The leader, in this case having first developed competencies in self-awareness as well as empathy and self-management, is now positioned to perceive and appropriately acknowledge the feelings of others.

Having an awareness of and capacity to manage one's own feelings as well as being able to empathize and connect with others' feelings positions the leader to implement effective relationship management—our last of the four EI domains. More specifically, relationship management is about "authenticity" and how its use may serve to strengthen a leader's connectedness, not only with employees, but also those with whom the leader interacts on a 360-degree basis.

Thus far, we have discussed the four domains of EI and how each might be effectively implemented. However, simply mastering the domains of EI without fully addressing their integration within the leadership realm is incomplete. So leaders should continue to build on existing EI skills and seek to expand the strengths associated with these skills, such as organizational awareness and collaboration. "Having a larger repertoire of emotional intelligence strengths can make a leader more effective because it means that leader is flexible enough to handle the wide-ranging demands of running an organization" (Boyatzis et al. 2002, 51, 85).

There still remains an open question in the area of EI: How does one develop EI competency? According to Boyatzis et al., "to begin or sustain real development in emotional intelligence, you must first engage that power of your ideal self" (2002, 116). This, of course, means to contemplate the person that you want to be, which should comprise the elements that invoke the most passion. This profound change requires crafting of a vision reflecting 360-degree interactions and feedback. It is not simply what you, the leader, will be doing but also how you interact with those with whom you make daily contact.

Unfortunately, accurate feedback is often elusive. No one likes to be the bearer of bad news. Subordinates prefer to convey messages that make the boss feel good; peers sometimes refrain from candor in pursuit of their own agendas; and bosses, believe it or not, often avoid messages that precipitate conflict. Boyatzis et al. offered the following comments in this area: "Rare are those who dare to tell the commanding leader he is too harsh, or to let a leader know he could be more visionary, or more democratic" (2002, 133).

With this in mind, it is only through the leader's use of EI skills, namely empathy and awareness, that he is able to discover the brutal feedback regarding his behavior and how it affects others. The reference to "brutal feedback" may appear a bit harsh and inconsiderate. In fact, providing or receiving such feedback may not be in the best interest of either party if the goal is to appear friendly and unwaveringly collaborative. Viewing it as a sort of hard tactic, Knippenberg and Steensma stated that "tactics that may be assumed to place a strain on the relationship between agent and target are less frequently employed" (2003, 63). This is an important point from a leadership perspective as, although leaders are tasked with motivating workers, which is often viewed synonymously with making everyone feel happy, they should not refrain from providing brutally honest feedback. Important though is that doing so be accomplished with an eye toward empathy, as previously discussed. Also important here is awareness and openness to feeling, listening and thinking, and appropriately acting on the inputs received.

Thus far, our discussion regarding EI has focused on the individual level. However, in order to transform the organization, a leader must go beyond self-transformation; she is also responsible for transformation of the team. Key attributes of EI, such as self-awareness, are also applicable at the team level.

Effective use of EI at the team level begins with each member of the team acknowledging the feelings and emotions of every other member. Actions in this area "might also mean creating norms such as listening to everyone's perspective—including that of a lone dissenter—before a decision is made" (Boyatzis et al. 2002, 179). Leaders must master the art of listening to experience organization connectedness and resonance, as will be discussed in the next section.

1.5 Resonant Leadership

A not-so-subtle relationship exists between resonant leaders and emotionally intelligent leaders. To an extent, resonant leadership is all about connecting or being in tune with those with whom the leader interacts (for example subordinates, peers, and other constituents). Said differently, "when leaders drive emotions positively they bring out everyone's best we call this effect resonance [and EI is] how leaders handle themselves and their relationship" (Boyatzis et al. 2002, 5–6).

In the lexical sense, resonance is defined as "a reinforcement of sound in a vibrating body caused by waves from another body vibrating at nearly the same rate" (*Merriam-Webster* 2007). From the foregoing definition, the relationship between resonance and EI should be lucid relative to leadership. By definition, motivation is, "the act or process of motivating … a motivating force, stimulus, or influence" (*Merriam-Webster* 2007).

Leadership would be so much easier if all employees showed up motivated to accomplish any assigned task. Unfortunately, the job of employee motivation most often rests with the leader and must be externally sourced. Sure, some help is available to the leader in the form of intrinsic motivation. Yet, according to Ivancevich & Matteson (1993), intrinsic rewards typically align with one or more of the following categories: "completion—the ability to start and finish [something], achievement—derived when a person reaches a challenging goal, autonomy—right and privilege to make decisions,

[and] personal growth—expansion of capabilities" (1993, 208–9). However, what happens in instances where, resulting from job design (for example), the employee is not allowed to complete an assignment or goal before being reallocated to another task, or when decisions are handed down rather than allowed, or when job stagnation exists? Under these circumstances, the challenge of motivation, and thus resonance, falls upon the shoulders of the leader.

As I discussed previously, feedback is one tool available to leaders that has served as an enabler for boss subordinate calibration regarding work performance. Indeed, according to DeNisi and Kluger (2000) and Gregory, Levy, and Jeffers (2008), as cited by DeBerg, Jarzebowski and Palermo, "feedback, which is information regarding individuals' current levels of performance, has been shown to influence motivation, job satisfaction and performance" (2012, 14). Implemented correctly, feedback, particularly if collected on a 360-degree basis, can offer tremendous returns. According to Wimer and Nowack (1998), as cited by Crispo and Sysinger, "when 360 degree feedback is used appropriately, it can be a very effective tool that can lead to behavioral changes and effectiveness of an individual, group, and organization" (2012, 2).

While it is not my intent in this section to discuss the 360-degree feedback instrument in detail (it was discussed earlier in this book), certainly its use may facilitate leadership resonance. Whether resonance is enabled through motivation or otherwise, tuning in to the resonant frequency of multiple followers, while certainly doable, is not accomplished without tremendous effort and persistence, which can be extremely exhausting, and if left unaddressed, leader burnout is inevitable.

How, then, should a leader continuously replenish the well—the source of motivation, guidance and emotional drain? Boyatzis and McKee believe that this is accomplished via a "cycle of sacrifice and renewal that must be regulated to maintain resonance" (2005 7). The type of stress precipitating the need for renewal is termed "power stress" and is the source for dissonance. Contributions to this stress type are provided by ambiguity and requirements for complex decision making. "Fire-fighting" is another source of this type of stress and in some situations leaders may become physically ill as a result of the day-to-day battles.

The principal issue with power stress is not necessarily the effect experienced while in the heat of the battle. It is, instead, "too little recovery time" which results from leaders "failing to manage the cycle of sacrifice and renewal" (Boyatzis & McKee 2005, 7). It is this process of renewal that allows leaders to sustain connectedness within and among the organization.

Leaders are continually being assessed, analyzed and scrutinized. Not only are company owners (shareholders) seeking optimal returns, boards of directors are also demanding unprecedented results while employees are looking to be coached, promoted, complimented and supported, not to mention given clemency regarding mistakes.

It is not unrealistic to assume that leaders contemplate the antagonizing aspects of these events ahead of their occurrence. This perspective is supported by Martin (1997), as cited by Boyatzis and McKee in the following comment: "humans have what many consider a unique ability to create their own stress by merely anticipating stress-inducing situations" (2005, 206). In the most fundamental sense, the cycle of sacrifice and renewal has been presented to each of us from day one. As infants, we might be encouraged to accomplish a goal or task only later to be rewarded with something worthy of the sacrifice—a sort of renewal, if you will, for our efforts.

Another similar example is the typical sports drink commercial depicting an athlete accomplishing a feat through physical exertion only to later be rewarded with a bottle of colored liquid consumed while in a position symbolic of achievement and gratification. In leadership, mental stress, unlike physical stress as described above, may be directly related to psychological health and well-being. Under the conditions of power stress, the "sympathetic nervous system (SNS)" is aroused which precipitates the "fight or flight" response as discussed in the section regarding EI.

Combinations of certain types of stress encountered in the day-to-day leadership circle are "said to increase the allostatic load" which can result in severe health issues. Under these stressful conditions, increases in "multiple neurotransmitters" occur which may also result in increased blood pressure (Boyatzis & McKee 2005, 207). While power stress implications may be most profoundly realized in the SNS, the "parasympathetic nervous system (PSNS)," when appropriately stimulated, is the system responsible for recovery from any such stressful condition. Such renewing stimulants may include "hope," "compassion" and "meditation" acting as a sort of "antidote to stress" (Boyatzis & McKee 2005, 211).

Leadership is not a job for the meek at heart. Not only are sacrifice and renewal integral to long-term effectiveness, the leadership responsibility also requires self-discipline; a willingness to make the tough calls; an almost uncanny knack for providing brutally honest feedback; and, perhaps most importantly, the ability to feel comfortable feeling uncomfortable. However, despite the vastness of a leader's soft and hard skill repertoire, nothing precipitates more respect from a leader than his or her credibility, as I discuss in the next section.

1.6 Transformational Leadership and Credibility

Despite the best business school preparation, only experience in the field can prepare an executive for the vicissitudes of leadership. Transcending these ups and downs of leadership is earned credibility that often serves as a prerequisite for leadership effectiveness. While the principal goal of this section is to discuss leadership credibility through transformational applications, primarily to allow for reader comprehension, I also briefly address the transactional leadership (XL) and transformational leadership (TL) styles.

Nystedt (1997), as cited by Korner and Nordvik, suggests that "behavioral styles have been elaborated into constructs such as charismatic, transactional, transformational and visionary leadership" (2004, 49). Focusing on XL and TL styles, we find, according to Cilliers et al., the following distinguishing characteristics: "[TL]—idealized influence, implies that followers respect, admire, and trust the leader and emulate his or her behavior, assume his or her values, and are committed to achieving his or her vision and making sacrifices in this regard … [XL]—involves a social exchange process where the leader clarifies what the followers need to do as their part of a transaction (successfully complete the task) to receive a reward or avoidance of punishment (satisfaction of the followers' needs) that is contingent on the fulfillment of the transaction (satisfying the leader's needs) …" (2008, 255). It might be argued that the characterization of XL is predicated on certain aspects of Maslow's needs hierarchy, as I will discuss in a subsequent section.

Referring once more to TL, which is built on openness and engagement, Lo, Min, and Ramayah wrote, "transformational leaders [have] a more significant relationship with organizational commitment" (2009, 137). Through motivation and workforce engagement, TL builds equity in the form of employee loyalty, which serves the entire organization and its constituents.

One very simple yet often illusive TL practice that facilitates organizational engagement is listening to the employees. This in turn enables four dimensions of effectiveness. First, the leader is able to gain an understanding of how employees view the world around them and thus, how they might interpret direction provided to them. Second, the leader is able to begin the process of connectedness (previously discussed), which enables the engagement process. Third, the leader gains the respect of employees because they now feel that someone—one quite powerful in the eyes of the organization—cares about what they have to say. Finally, the leader gains insight as to what is really happening within the organization and, depending on the employee's organizational hierarchy, critical operational details that might otherwise be overlooked are now made available to the leader. Listening to and engaging employees also sets the groundwork for the leader to execute the "five practices of exemplary leadership: model the way, inspire a shared vision, challenge the process, enable others to act, and encourage the heart" (Kouzes & Posner 2007, 14).

To this point, we have discussed benefits resulting from leader engagement with the organization. However, engagement alone is not the panacea for leadership effectiveness. Such interactions, particularly when considering TL, are assumed to be authentic. With this in mind, resulting from the leader's behavior, an increased level of organizational integrity and morality should be realized and thus, leadership credibility. Indeed, according to leadership attribute survey results referenced by Kouzes and Posner, "for people to follow someone, the majority of constituents believe the leader must be honest" (2007, 29, 32). This perspective is appropriately aligned with characteristics of transformational leaders. Indeed, according to Burns (1978), as cited by Plinio, "in transforming leadership, persons engage with others in such a way that leaders and followers raise one another to higher levels of motivation and morality" (2010, 279).

Integrity and honesty are the building blocks for leadership credibility which, according to Kouzes and Posner, requires leaders to "practice what they preach, walk the talk, actions are consistent with their words, put their money where their mouth is, follow through on promises, and do what they say they will do" (2007, 40).

Another key attribute of TL, as mentioned above, has to do with creating a shared vision. As viewed here, a shared vision is one whereby the organization doesn't simply march to the drumbeat but also picks up and carries the torch in one accord with ownership as though the vision was crafted from the bottom up. Kouzes and Posner suggest that "visions are ideals" and as such, "they're expressions of optimism" that should "appeal to common ideals" (2007, 133).

If TL attributes are correctly imparted, the organization should assume the leader's values. The focus here is on shared and synchronized values, which "are the foundations for building productive and genuine working relationships." As a result of this approach, "tremendous energy is generated when individual, group, and organizational values are in synch" (Kouzes & Posner 2007, 60–61).

Still another attribute of the transformational leader is *trust.* This important leadership attribute serves as a critical factor for leadership efficiency and resource optimization. Viewed in this way, when a leader assigns work within an organization, that leader can do so with utter reliance on the worker to accomplish the task or, conversely, with follow-up and questioning in such a way as to micromanage the worker. In the latter case, work efficiency is reduced in two areas. First, the leader is now allocating time that could otherwise be used to accomplish other more strategic activities, and second, the worker is now focused on the next intervening moment initiated by the leader and reverts to a sort of wait-for-direction mode, effectively slowing down the processing of the received input. (Refer to figure 1-1, a description of leadership systematization.)

Trust in either direction (trusting others or being trusted by others) is an essential component of effective leadership. Kouzes and Posner share this perspective with the following comments: "At the heart of collaboration is trust … without trust you cannot lead … you cannot get extraordinary things done" (2007, 224).

Trust and engagement add to the list of leader credentials and aid a leader in moving toward the state of credibility. However, new leaders are often expected to manage more than the status quo. They are expected to convert lost revenues to new profits, to replace inefficiencies with productive operations, to modify, and in some cases to eliminate existing outdated infrastructure. In effect, leaders are expected to initiate and bring about profound and sustainable change. The transformational leader is adept at delivering in this regard. This perspective is shared by Crant and Bateman (2000), as cited by Belschak, Deanne and Hartog in the following comment: "Transformational leaders are more change oriented and proactive themselves and thus may act as role models" (2012, 195).

In the quest for credibility, perhaps the most assumed quality that a leader possesses is the intellectual wherewithal to stimulate the thoughts and creativity of others. Indeed, positioned correctly, learning is fun, and employees do well to know that they can be taught new strategies, approaches, and ways of thinking. Transformational leaders thrive on intellectual stimulation as supported by the following comment offered by Bass (1985); Avolio and Bass (1988, 1990a, 1990b); and Howell and Avolio (1993), as cited by Atwater, Avolio, and Bass: "transformational leadership has been shown to include inspirational [and] intellectual stimulation" (1996, 9).

Finally, leadership credibility is also about caring for and supporting those whom the leader is entrusted to lead. You should not assume that listening (discussed earlier) is necessarily synonymous with caring as listening alone could, in some instances, represent a purely perfunctory event aimed solely at advancing the leader's agenda. Transformational leaders gain credibility through sincere actions and caring. According to Bass (1985, 1998), as cited by Liu, Siu, and Shi, "transformational leaders … show their concern for their employees' individual needs for growth and development" (2010, 457). Leadership style, whether it be TL, XL, or otherwise, is not achieved without cognition.

In the next section, we discuss the psychological implications of leadership.

1.7 The Role of Psychology in Leadership

Let's begin by recalling the definition of psychology, which may be summed up as the characterization of human behavior. Perhaps leadership can be viewed as an attempt to positively influence follower cognition and emotion such that the followers feel good about themselves, and what they can accomplish, and are thus motivated to execute their jobs with quality.

We have discussed several approaches to leadership. We have visited theoretical leadership models and have discussed available leadership tools. What remains an open area for discussion is how the cognitive process functions while interpreting the various leadership approaches. Why is it important to understand the role of the cognitive process in leadership? Or said differently, why is leadership motivation necessary at all? One response is that "it has been estimated that organizations suffer up to $370 billion in lost productivity every year in the United States alone due to workers not feeling engaged" (Lawrence 2011, 15). Thus, an understanding of the cognitive process, coupled with the appropriate leadership motivation, offers the potential for tremendous returns.

While intellect is a prerequisite for good leadership, intellect "alone will not make a leader; leaders execute a vision by motivating, guiding, inspiring, listening, persuading—and, most crucially, through creating resonance" (Boyatzis et al. 2002, 27). The section of the brain that controls and provides intellect is separate from the section that guides emotion. Yet, under the appropriate circumstances, the two are integrated such that emotion takes over and, in effect, rules (Boyatzis et al. 2002, 29). It should not be surprising that the brain succumbs to emotion because emotion serves as the off/on switch for responding to stressful situations—such as to the performance review I discussed in section 1.4 of this chapter. Indeed, the "thinking brain evolved from the limbic brain and continues to take orders from it when we perceive a threat or are under stress" (Boyatzis et al. 2002, 28).

The problem with the brain is that it originally developed to protect us from physical environmental threats. The brain is not innately structured to handle the stresses associated with a bad performance review or to respond to office politics. Importantly, though, one's ability to circumvent sudden and perhaps unwanted reactions in such situations is attributed to the brain's executive center or, neurologically speaking, the prefrontal area of the brain. The circuitry responsible for actions executed by the executive center also controls drives and impulses. Unlike the process required for technical learning and skill development, EI oriented skills are "best learned through motivation, extended practice and feedback."

The emotional, or limbic, side of the brain is far less developed than the thinking brain (the side that aids in technical learning). As a consequence, a great deal of limbic learning results from repeated exposure and early behavior introductions. This early information is accessed through maturity and in a manner, "as if it were factual." Thus, decision making is predicated on our cultural preferences and biases, which could very easily result in disconnects with contemporary environments.

As leaders, the same bias carries forward in the direction that we provide to others, and as followers, our cultural biases serve as the basis for how we interpret information received from leaders. These comments, however, are not at all intended to suggest that the brain cannot be taught to act in an emotionally responsible manner because "human brains can create new neural tissue as well as pathways throughout adulthood" (Boyatzis et al. 2002, 28–29, 102–3; Bailey 2007, 130).

When a new idea is presented, say a new sales goal or mission, the prefrontal area of the brain is asked to consider this new information and compare and contrast it to prior similar information, such as the old sales goals or mission. Another part of the brain, "the basal ganglia" is engaged for routine activities, like driving a car, and represents the part of the brain that stores habits and routines. Under change conditions, however, such as driving a car on the left side of the road, the prefrontal cortex becomes active.

This same cognitive dynamic occurs when employees are exposed to organizational stresses and change. The norm is for our brains to gravitate toward things with which we are both familiar and comfortable. Thus, under change conditions, especially conditions that deviate from expectations, the brain emits strong signals that reflect acknowledgement of the deviation. The part of the brain in which these deviation signal emissions occur is the orbital frontal cortex, as part of the brain's fear circuitry. The occurrence of such signal emissions can precipitate emotional or impulsive responses, propelling us to fight or flight behaviors.

Some have posited that changed behavior can be accomplished via *behaviorism* oriented approaches. One example would be to associate a desired behavior with a reward, as in the so-called carrot-and-stick approach, which, despite its convincing appeal, has been proven by clinical research to be ineffective (Rock & Schwartz 2007, 11–12; Bailey 2007, 130).

Given the complexities of the human brain, it is imperative that effective leaders make appropriate connections with those whom they lead toward change. (Recall discussions regarding resonance.) Often, communication serves as the enabler for such connections. It must therefore be executed with the utmost care and scrutiny.

This perspective is shared by Kussrow, who writes, "since it is people's brains that leaders try to influence … it follows that it is critical that the individual being [led] accurately interprets what the leader intended to communicate" (2001, 10). Within this communication should be options and choices for followers—a sort of participative versus dictatorial style of leadership. The reason for this is that "humans have a social brain that loves to anticipate, to be given choices" (Kussrow 2001, 10).

Despite the brain's desire for expectation and variation, humans bring to the table old habits that are often difficult to change, including pessimistic views about planning and executing their daily responsibilities, about meeting project deadlines, about solving old problems, and about proactively identifying and resolving latent problems. These attitudes are the norm. Indeed, "changing behavior is hard, even for individuals and even when new habits can mean the difference between life and death" (Rock & Schwartz 2007, 10).

Every organization comprises individuals with disparate habits and varying levels of organizational commitment. Thus, it is not at all surprising that any attempt to change an organization's mindset may be extremely difficult. "Organizational transformation that takes into account the physiological nature of the brain, and the ways in which it predisposes people to resist some forms of leadership and accept others [may offer the best chance for success]" (Rock & Schwartz 2007, 10, 11).

In my previous discussion regarding an annual performance review, the focus was on the disappointed recipient (the subordinate). It suggested that the opportunity for the application of EI rested with the follower. However, given the foregoing discussion regarding the limbic system and its relationship to EI, an alternative perspective would be to view the responsibility for a successful discussion to rest with the deliverer (the superior). Said differently, the superior's awareness of how the limbic system functions, coupled with his maturity in EI, affords him the opportunity to change the conversation at the outset so that the subordinate needn't encounter the fight, flight, freeze syndrome.

Leaders should also be cognizant of the four basic drives of leadership. According to Lawrence, these include the drive to acquire, defend, bond, and comprehend. While the drives to acquire and defend are principally concerned with survival and self-preservation, the drives to bond and comprehend focus more on relationship building and individual perception respectively (2011, 13).

If something does not progress according to plans or expectations, such as sales results not meeting forecast levels, the "drive to defend" may move a leader to overlook key information that explains why sales fell short. Recognition of your position as a leader in such a situation will allow you to engage your executive center to respond appropriately.

Building on this point, according to Lawrence, "to be effective, leaders must take into account how the four drives affect the following group characteristics: purpose, competencies, trust building [and] motivation" (2011, 14). Returning to the performance review discussion: An employee could perceive the absence of a "good review" as a threat to the right to acquire. This could give rise to the development of barriers to trust building with the leader.

Another perspective on human requirements is seen in Maslow's hierarchy of needs (mentioned previously). According to Ivancevich and Matteson, Maslow's five-stage model includes the following five human needs, listed hierarchically: 1) physiological; 2) safety and security; 3) belongingness, social, and love; 4) esteem; and 5) self-actualization. Returning to the performance review discussion, the threat to an employee's right to acquire (in this case, a good performance rating) could also represent a threat to physical needs, including food and shelter (Ivancevich & Matteson 1993, 143).

Food and shelter, of course, represent components that are essential for meeting human physiological needs. You might question the relevance of physical or biological needs to psychology. The bearing of such is actually quite simple and can be explained by recalling a natural disaster—Hurricane Katrina. Coverage of the hurricane aftermath showed the victims as missing the most fundamental of human needs: "food, drink, shelter and relief from pain" (Ivancevich & Matteson 1993, 143). Yet the degree to which these needs no longer exist is somewhat psychological and relative. For example, some of the victims, despite having lost homes, were provided shelter and food by philanthropic organizations such as the Red Cross. So the reality is that while the victims no doubt suffered hardship, in the purest sense of Maslow's hierarchy of needs, the first level in the needs hierarchy might have been met, albeit with the assistance of others.

This disconnected observation (failure to recognize fulfillment of Maslow's first order need) may be attributed to perception based on the victim's pre-hurricane frame of reference. Psychological factors may certainly give rise to feelings of pessimism. Indeed, many third world cultures would find great solace in the levels of post hurricane provisions (also addressing Maslow's first hierarchical need of food, water, and shelter), as were afforded to some people impacted by Hurricane Katrina. Psychology affects perception, and perception in turn, is linked to motivation. Effective leadership, therefore, must also address the notion of perceptions and instill feelings of optimism.

I certainly do not aim to downplay the disruption caused by Hurricane Katrina. Without a doubt, enduring it was a tremendous psychological and biological injustice to everyone who was impacted by it. Rather, my objective was to illustrate the power of perception and how important it is for leaders to be cognizant of psychological influences and motivations. Having established the link between perceptions, psychology and effective leadership, the next section discusses construct-based methods for the identification of certain leader attributes which may also be predictors of effective leadership.

1.8 Predicting Leadership Behavior

Although advancement has been made in predicting leadership behavior based on psychometric modeling, the fundamental concept is not new. According to Lynam and Miller, "since its inception, the field of personality research has been concerned with identifying the basic traits that serve as the building blocks of personality" (2001, 767). Among some of the most researched behavioral models are: Five-Factor Model (FFM), (McCrae & Costa 1990); Three Factor Model (PEN), (Eysenck 1977); Three-Factor Model, (Tellegen 1985); Temperament and Character Model, (Cloninger et al. 1993), (Lynam & Miller 2001, 767).

Lynam and Miller also suggest that the basis for these models ranges from "lexical hypothesis" associated with the FFM to "factor analysis and mood scales," used by Tellegen, to "biological/pharmacological," associated with the Cloninger and Eysenck models (2001 767–68). There is also the Myers-Briggs Type Indicator (MBTI) designed by Briggs and Myers which, according to Carlson, "is a test designed to implement … theory type … therefore, like the projective techniques, the MBTI is closely allied with psychodynamic thought, at least in its original conception" (1985, 365).

Expanding discussions regarding the FFM, we find, according to Costa and McCrae (1992), as cited by Kornor and Nordvik, it is "a hierarchical model of personality traits with five big traits called domains on the top, that is, Neuroticism, Extraversion, Openness, Agreeableness, [and] Conscientiousness" (2004, 49). According to Levine and Raynor, each of these five domains is further defined as follows: "openness—refers to intelligent, imaginative, curious, flexible and broad minded; conscientiousness—refers to striving for competence and achievement, and being self-disciplined, orderly, reliable, and deliberative; extraversion—refers to enjoying the company of others, and being active, talkative, assertive and seeking stimulation; agreeableness—refers to being courteous, good natured, cooperative, tolerant, and compassionate rather than antagonistic; neuroticism—refers to easily experiencing unpleasant and negative emotions, such as fear, anxiousness, pessimism, sadness, and insecurity" (2006, 73).

There has been much discussion regarding the FFM and its ability to predict leadership or other behavior-based traits (such as conscientiousness). To this end, according to Srivastava, "my thesis is that we will never really understand the Five-Factor Model until we more fully come to grips with the scientific implication of lexical hypothesis" (2010, 69). However, as also pointed out by Srivastava, "the Five-Factor-Model is first and foremost a model of social perceptions" (2010, 69). Srivastava's position is somewhat supported by Saucier and Goldberg (1996) as they stated, "the big five [FFM] are dimensions of perceived personality." Also, D.W. Fiske wrote, as also cited by Srivastava (2010), that the FFM is useful for "the analysis of how people perceive people and what words they use in formulating such perceptions" (2010, 70).

Considering the breadth of the English language, it is perhaps unthinkable to consider that the lexical approach may be constrained in its capacity to fully describe personality traits. Yet words are just that, and how they are interpreted from one human being to the other is not as consistent or black and white as their use might suggest.

An analogy to this thinking is offered by Palmer (1999) and Adelson (1990), as cited by Srivastava (2010), in the following statement: "But color perceptions have unique qualities and special relationships that do not purely reflect the extra human physical world, and the perceptual processes that ordinarily help us perceive color can lead to errors under some conditions" (2010, 70). Inconsistencies of interpretation notwithstanding, the comments offered by Srivastava, as well as his cited sources in this area, precipitate recollection of an adage that we have all heard: "perception is reality." Thus, valid as arguments may be on both sides, the FFM construct is quite relevant to the core of leadership style measuring instruments as it evidences the capacity to offer individual behavior validity through observation.

Having laid a comprehensive foundation for leadership, leadership styles, and measurement constructs, the subsequent chapters in this book provide opportunities for application of the preceding review. They also seek to broaden the leadership repertoire via practical corporate simulated scenarios.

CHAPTER 2

The Performance Appraisal

MY FIRST EXPOSURE to the performance appraisal occurred many years ago, after having transferred from the blue-collar (paid by the hour—also known as "hourly") workforce to the white-collar (salaried) ranks. Needless to say, I had no idea what it meant to receive an appraisal of my performance. After all, as an hourly paid technician, my pay increases were the same as everyone else's in my work unit. Sure, we had goals and objectives, but we also had *negotiated* and *fixed* wage increases.

In sharp contrast, as a salaried employee, the performance appraisal and all that it represented served as my negotiator, and the respective rating, I also learned, seemed inextricably linked to my merit increases. For me, back then, the language characterizing the performance of a 3 rating (on a scale from 1 to 5), sounded so eloquent that I felt pretty good about my work and being part of the team. Of course, that was before I learned that I was rated two levels below the top rating.

Earlier, I wrote about Hurricane Katrina and how, when considering Maslow's hierarchy of needs, some might view the relief efforts, particularly the supply of food and water, as meeting fundamental needs at the time. (My point was not at all to undermine the significance of Hurricane Katrina's impact to the community and surrounding areas. Rather, it was to highlight the role of psychological influences and perceptions.) Viewed in this way, the 3 rating for my first performance appraisal may not have been such a bad deal after all. Initially, I was quite satisfied with the rating, given my path from blue-collar to the salaried ranks, where I was viewed as a valuable team member. With this 3 rating came a decent raise. But because I decided to move onto the salaried payroll, I was already receiving less compensation than my final year as an hourly paid technician, which included overtime wages—under $22,000 annually. (This was back in 1978, so don't chuckle too much.)

The reality of the rating, coupled with the link to my merit increase, began to refocus my attention. Compensation seemed so much simpler as a blue-collar worker. I didn't have to worry so much about *how* I got things done or whether I used a word out of context in a discussion or memorandum. (This was before the days of Microsoft Word with its spell checker and thesaurus.) Had I made the right decision to move to the salaried ranks? Would I ever catch up to my hourly paid pals, who, being generally aware of my compensation, tacitly questioned my intelligence in taking the salaried job? Unbeknownst to me at the time the answers to these questions were yes and yes.

As I began to fully understand the performance appraisal system, I thought the path to the top rating was clear: simply delivering according to the organization's goals and objectives would earn a better rating. The next performance cycle I learned that everyone else was vying for that same top rating, and there were mathematical constraints on the number of salaried employees who could receive the top rating.

What exactly is performance, and why is it so important to most corporations, particularly in its use as a metric? Focusing on the latter point first, Ivancevich and Matteson stated with regard to expectancy theory: "performance of individuals is a critical issue in making organizations work effectively" (1993, 175). This would suggest that reliance upon individual performances enables the organization to realize its commitment to its owners—the shareholders. And, according to Ayers, "a U.S. Government Accountability Office (GAO; 2008) report recently suggested a key to improving government through performance information is to create a clear line of sight linking individual performance with organizational results" (2015, 170).

The linkage between individual performance and organizational goals would seem intuitive. Yet, perhaps the most consternation in the area of performance management arises when individual performance results (as measured by actual ratings) are not simply linked to successful achievement of organizational goals but are also tied to consequences if and when such goals are not met. This perspective is also shared by Ayers, as she stated: "just as award expectancy is expected to motivate employees, employees must also see there are consequences for nonperformance and great performance alike" (2015, 175). Bateman and Zeithaml shared a similar perspective regarding setting performance standards and developing applicable measures, stating: "a standard is the level of expected performance for a given goal" (1993, 540).

As used here, "standard" can take the form of various measurable objectives. For example, a quality assurance manager may be measured against a zero defect quality standard while another manager may be measured based on deviation from a cost standard or the amount of labor that is used to produce a certain product.

Having established the link between performance and organizational goals, we now turn our attention to the link between performance and performance appraisal. Turning to an authority, *Merriam-Webster* defines performance as "the execution of an action … something accomplished … the fulfillment of a claim, promise, or request … … the ability to perform … efficiency" (2007). Summarizing might suggest that performance is about delivering results or, in contrast, the lack thereof.

Linking this perspective to organizational goals and objectives, we now have the building blocks for performance assessment, which is documented by the performance appraisal. Bateman and Zeithaml defined the performance appraisal as "the assessment of employees' job performance [which has three purposes.] First, it provides information for making salary, promotion, and layoff decisions … second, it contributes to employee growth and development by giving feedback on how to improve performance or identifying specific training needs … third, it provides documentation of HR activities that can justify the organization's HR decisions in court" (1993, 359).

Employee performance, as measured by organizational performance appraisal ratings, also serves as an enabler for incentives to include bonuses and stock awards. Likewise, poor performance results have served as the impetus for the reallocation, demotion, and ousting of CEOs and executives, the shuffling of boards, and the termination of employees, indiscriminant of level, throughout the organization.

Wielding the power to affect the careers and lives of individuals, the performance appraisal is a friend to some and a foe to those who question its true worth. The latter perspective is somewhat shared by Pichler and Teckchandani, who stated: "research shows that employee performance actually decreases after a performance review about 60 percent of the time" (2015, 17). In the same writing, it was pointed out that "a survey by Ed Lawler and colleagues at the Center of Effective

Organizations found that almost every organization uses performance appraisals, yet only 6 percent perceive appraisals as being effective" (2015, 17).

It is worth noting here that, in consideration of some of the more contemporary forms of employee performance assessment, the performance appraisal may be subsumed in the broader performance management system. Yet, when viewed as separate performance measurement approaches, clear differences exist. And while it is beyond the scope of this book to offer comprehensive insights as to the pros and cons of the two approaches, listed in figure 2-1 are the more salient differences.

Figure 2-1 (Armstrong 2009, 27)

Performance Appraisal	Performance Management
Individual objectives may be included	Focuses on organizational, and individual objectives
Some qualitative performance objectives may also be included	Covers both outputs (results) and inputs (competencies)
Annual appraisal	May not have ratings
Backward looking	Forward looking
Focus on levels of performance and merit	Focus on development as well as performance
Top-down system	Joint process
Monolithic	Flexible process
Usually tailor made	Tailor made
Complex paper work	Paperwork minimized
Often linked to performance pay	May not be linked to performance pay
Applied to all staff	Applied to all staff
Owned by HR department	Owned by managers

In situations where the performance appraisal serves only as a portion of a system designed to improve organizational performance, the resulting performance management system serves as a strategic and integrated approach to delivering successful results. The success in this area may be attributed to developing capabilities of teams and individuals (Armstrong & Baron 1998). Now that we have established a common understanding of the fundamental performance appraisal system, note that it may be but one tool in the much larger performance management system. The aim of the performance appraisal should be only to document what both the subordinate and superior already acknowledge. Very often, either during or subsequent to the performance appraisal delivery, a development plan is created. This plan serves two principal purposes. First, it identifies and documents employee weaknesses or capability building areas. Second, it identifies resources, timing and strategies for execution of the plan. There are also situations during which an out of cycle development plan is created resulting from the need for immediate performance improvement. At previously established intervals throughout the performance period, usually one calendar year, the subordinate and superior engage in constructive dialogue regarding expectations versus performance. They also recalibrate their perspectives regarding employee accomplishments. Ivancevich and Matteson concur with this viewpoint regarding performance evaluation and dialogue in the context of socialization, stating, "[it] provides important feedback about how well the individual is getting along in the organization." (1993, 689). The authors discuss the importance of accurate and objective feedback as well as the significance of face-to-face communications. Likewise, they highlight the value added by the allocation of challenging objectives and assignments.

Armstrong shows (in figure 2-1) that both the performance appraisal and performance management are "often linked to performance pay" and "may not be linked to performance pay" respectively (2009, 27). Regarding the performance appraisal, this leaves a bit of a gap in how pay for performance is actually determined and, in particular, how employee ratings stack up among peer employees. Not to worry—this gap is often resolved mathematically, using an employee ranking system.

I recently caught the tail end of an interview on CNBC during which the following was presented.

General Electric—Killing Annual Performance Reviews:

Our introduction of performance development represents a move away from a looking-backwards, event-oriented (once-a-year), and system-driven approach to performance management in GE.

Upon googling this topic, I retrieved an interesting article posted by *Harvard Business Review* that expounds upon the statement above, offering more detail as to the ostensible change in the performance management approach, which, at the time of this writing, was expected to be fully implemented within the year. While I will leave analysis and interpretation of the details of this apparent shift in performance management to you, it is in the spirit of author awareness that I referred to the article. It should also be noted that key portions of the performance distribution system used at GE in the past remains relevant and contemporary at other organizations. Thus, this system has significant touch points in this and subsequent chapters.

Perhaps one of the most renowned components, often linked to performance appraisal and management systems, is a *vitality curve.* This method for ranking employees, based on their organizational contributions, was introduced by Jack Welch during his tenure with GE and characterized in Jack's book, *Jack: Straight from the Gut*. Focusing for the moment on Jack Welch's rank-based construct, the area being assessed represents a form of a work group such as a department or work unit. Within these, each member's productivity is assessed. Many have termed this and similar distributive systems as *forced ranking*, *forced distribution*, *rank and yank*, *quota-based differentiation* and even *rack and stack* (Armstrong 2009; Welch 2001).

Implementation of the vitality system was initiated with the GE business owners' ranking of their top executives using the 20-70-10 model. The number 20 represents the percentage of top-performing employees (20 percent). Considering the remaining 80 percent, the overall split approaches an 80/20 split.

Drilling down a bit regarding the 80/20 split, quality expert Dr. J.M. Juran explained the *Pareto principle*, commonly called the *80/20 rule* resulting from his realization that, relatively few factors influence a final effect. Dr. Juran also referred to this relationship as "the vital few and the useful many" (1995, 47). Said differently, the 80 might represent 80 percent of salaries paid to employees of a corporation received by only 20 percent of the employees—these of course being the company executives.

Or, consider a consumer products company that sells multiple products (twenty of them) which, in aggregate, generate $1 billion in revenues. Of those twenty products, however, only four of them might be responsible for generating $800 million in revenues.

As mentioned, Jack's view of the vitality model was characterized as a *20-70-10* system. He believed that the top 20 percent of the workforce was the most productive, and 70 percent, which he also referred to as the "vital 70," met job or position requirements, and the remaining 10 percent comprised the less productive or bottom employees. These were subsequently segregated into A, B, and C players, with the A players being the most productive. In Jack's view, the A players were those who exemplified passion and could make things happen. They were receptive to new ideas from elsewhere in the organization. (Jack defined this as *boundaryless* behavior—also discussed in his book.) They were believed to be charismatic (a key component of TL); they also excited others (perhaps demonstrating inspirational leadership—another key component of TL); and they achieved productivity gains and executed consistently while also getting satisfaction from their work. He summed this up by the *four E's:* energy, energize others, edge, and execute. He viewed the B players as vital and necessary because they comprised the preponderance of the business leaders. The remaining group, the C players, was viewed as likely to enervate rather than energize an organization. Jack's view was that the C players ought to be terminated, in contrast to the A players, who he believed should be rewarded with promotions, bonuses, and stock options.

To Jack's credit, it is believed that the use of this performance management system made significant contributions to GE's overall earnings during his tenure there (Welch 2001). Despite the preponderance of negative press associated with forced distribution systems, the concept may have actually been founded on the ideal that, without such a system, managers might undermine the aim of performance management to the extent that they may be reluctant to make the tough calls because "no one likes to be the bearer of bad news." This view is somewhat supported by Armstrong as he stated, regarding the forced distribution, "the aim is to get what is believed to be a 'proper' distribution of ratings and overcome the central rating tendency of managers who do not like committing themselves to very low ratings, or even high ones" (2009, 151).

Research, studies, and results from polling of human resource personnel point to the lack of support for the forced distribution approach. Indeed O'Malley (2003), as cited by Armstrong, "described [the forced distribution] as a 'gross' method of categorizing employees into a few evaluative buckets" (2009, 152).

A variant of the 20-70-10 performance distribution is 10-20-60-10, whereby the first 10 represents the highest performing individuals, the 20 the next highest, and so on. The manner in which the performance distribution is disseminated to the corporation's employees may take several different forms. For example, the employees may receive a rating in the form of 1, 2, 3, 4, or 5, where 1 represents the lowest level of performance and 5 the highest. Conversely, these numbers could represent the highest performance in descending order. Assuming the highest performance is represented by the 5, the 20-70-10 distribution might be allocated as follows: top 20 percent (represented by the 5 rating), the next 70 percent (represented by the 4 and 3 ratings), and the final 10 percent (represented by the 2 and 1 ratings).

To this point, we have discussed only numeric performance ratings. Sachs identified descriptive criteria for association with numeric values as follows: "1—needs much improvement, 2—needs some improvement, 3—satisfactory, 4—very good [and] 5—excellent" (1992, 22). Although not directly used to represent final performance appraisal ratings, their application in this regard does offer insight as to how such descriptive language might be linked to final employee performance ratings.

The above distribution and descriptor examples reflect only the corresponding and respective numerical relationships but do not include any verbiage for each of the categories. Normally, working in concert with the human resources department, corporate leaders attach certain criteria to each of the categories. For instance, the 3 rating might include the following:

- Meets critical deadlines for assignments
- Achieves business results and objectives with some assistance
- Demonstrates competence in key skills required for the position
- Requires some guidance in formulating plans

Similarly, criteria supporting the 5 rating might include the following:

- Consistently exceeds critical deadlines for assignments
- Consistently achieves business results and objectives autonomously
- Consistently demonstrates competence above current graded level
- Is viewed as a leader and assists others in formulating plans

While the foregoing discussion was centered around evaluation of the subordinates' current role, the significance of the role that performance evaluation plays in documenting the potential for employees to function above current levels (e.g., to be promoted vertically) or to function in a horizontal position (at the same level but with different responsibilities), should not be understated.

Finally, there is the allocation of salary increases based upon employee performance appraisal ratings. As I expected, literature searches failed to identify specific percentages or dollar values linked to the respective performance ratings. However, one approach to determining the level of pay increase might be to consider the cost of living or inflation rate of the company's geographic location and to allocate increases accordingly.

To ensure reader calibration, I'd like to explain some key terms: *inflation, cost of living adjustment* (COLA), *current dollar wages*, and *constant or real dollars.*

According to Nordhaus and Samuelson, "inflation denotes a rise in the general level of prices … the rate of inflation is the rate of change of the general price level and is measured as follows: rate of inflation (year t) = (((price level year t) – (price level year t - 1))/(price level year t - 1)) × 100." In simpler terms, the rate of inflation for a given year (t) equals the price level in that same year minus the price level of the prior year (t-1) divided by the price level of year t-1. This, of course, multiplied by 100 to get percent. (1992, 587).

To illustrate this equation, consider the price that the consumer pays for items such as fuel, food, and transportation. As these prices rise, the buying power of the dollar decreases proportionately. According to Nordhaus and Samuelson, COLA "adjusts wages upward when consumer prices rise rapidly" (1992, 252).

The COLA is most often associated with collective bargaining agreements and is therefore a negotiated item, typically invoked in response to sharp rises in consumer prices (Nordhaus & Samuelson, 1992). As posted by the United States Census Bureau (USCB), "Current dollars is a term describing income in the year in which a person, household, or family receives it … for example, the income someone received in 1989 unadjusted for inflation is in current dollars" (census.gov). The terms constant or real dollars are, according to the USCB, "terms describing income after adjustment for inflation" (census.gov).

As an example of the effect of inflation on wages, McMenamin (2014), in an article published regarding wages of hospital staff registered nurses, noted that although an increasing trend of 1.29 percent in annual current dollar wages existed (from 2008 to 2014), the effect of inflation more than offset this increase, resulting in a 0.71 percent annual decrease during that same time period. Thus, "in 2008 dollars, the estimated June 2014 annual salary was $64,268 rather than the constant dollar amount of $72,862" (McMenamin 2014, 321). Buttressing McMenamin's findings regarding the impact of inflation on wages, Chan, Jalbert and Jalbert (2012), regarding a study of community college faculty salaries, cited Williams, stating, "on an inflation adjusted basis, faculty salaries have declined in recent years" (2012, 25). The key point here is that any pay raise that does not at a minimum cover the cost of inflation does little to grow the real income of a company's employees.

Given the impact that inflation can have on employee income, we are positioned to consider the potential linkage between actual performance ratings and employee pay raises. Recognizing that "a large majority of employees feel that they are underpaid (by an average of 19 percent (Heneman & Judge, 2000)), and average pay raise levels fall short of or barely exceed inflation" (Gupta, Jenkins, Mitra & Shaw 2015, 150), we will assume for our example a hypothetical inflation rate of 1.0 percent. And we will further assume that the rating system considered is graduated in five levels, with a 5 being the highest possible rating, and that the company in question endeavors to provide a fair and equitable salary increase to its employees. This approach is adequately modeled by the data listed in figure 2-2.

Figure 2-2: Merit Increases as a Function of Performance Ratings

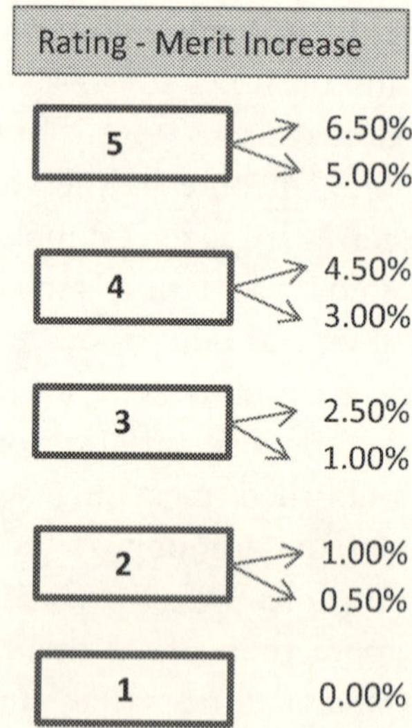

From this table, it should be apparent that an employee who receives a 5 (top) rating should expect to also receive a merit (pay) increase ranging from 5.0 percent to 6.5 percent. Likewise, an employee who receives a 1 rating, assuming that person is not terminated, should not expect to receive any merit increase.

You may question the range associated with each rating. Consider the scenario in which an employee receives the 4 rating but was just shy of the next level up, a 5 rating. In this case, the company wants to send a message: the employee was not far from the top rating and received the maximum allowable for that category.

Conversely, receiving the lower end of the available pay increase level might suggest that while the employee achieved a 4 rating, it's time to up the game or the rating might change during the next period. Regarding the employee who receives a 1 or even a 2 rating, while termination is indeed an option, perhaps consistent with Welch's vitality curve approach, another course of action might entail implementation of a personal development plan, coupled with intense manager coaching. As previously discussed, employee coaching is recognized as a viable method for correcting employee performance issues. Armstrong also recognized the benefits of coaching, stating, "in a coaching culture managers believe that people can succeed, that they can contribute to their success and that they can identify what people need to be able to do to improve their performance [Armstrong also cited Hamlin, Ellinger and Beattie (2006) who commented], 'truly effective managers and managerial leaders are those who embed effective coaching into the heart of their management practice'" (2009, 172).

Finally, I'd like to point out how the performance appraisal might be viewed in a leadership context. Because the performance appraisal system is linked to employee contingency rewards, it clearly demonstrates XL type attributes. Consequently, you may view this as less than optimal leadership—particularly given the positive view of TL. This should not be the case, however, when considering a couple of key mitigating factors.

First, it is incumbent upon leaders to make clear the expectations for subordinates, such as goals and objectives. This obligation may also be viewed in the context of providing what to do. How and why subordinates achieve goals and objectives may be linked to, among other things, motivation and inspiration provided by the leader. According to Avolio and Bass, some of the qualities associated with XL include: "provides assistance in exchange for efforts, discusses who is responsible for what, makes clear [the] rewards for efforts, focuses attention on mistakes and attention [is] directed to failure" (2004, 102). The same for TL include: "inspire, instill pride, sense of purpose, displays confidence, talks optimistically, articulates a vision [and] questions assumptions" (2004, 101).

From these comments, it should be apparent that effective leaders must both provide what is to be done and, concurrently, offer vision and strategies regarding how such may be accomplished. Supporting this point, Avolio and Bass stated that "the transactional process, [contingent reward] in which the leader clarifies what the associates need to do for a reward, is nevertheless viewed … as an essential component of … effective leadership" (2004, 21). Second, contingent reward (see appendix D) is only one of two XL constituents, thereby accounting for 50 percent of the total perceived style rating. The other constituent for XL is *management by exception active* (MBEA). Bennett cited works of multiple authors who argued that contingent reward is, in itself, related to TL (2009, 6).

Despite its linkage to XL, the performance evaluation process remains an entrenched piece of organizational infrastructure that, in some instances, transcends or undermines even the best friendships. Buttressing this view are the following comments provided by former president of NBC Andy Lake regarding Jack Welch's focus on performance management, taken from *Jack: Straight From the Gut*.

"Jack and I have been friends for eight years, and our wives see each other all the time … if I started down a path where I made four incredibly bad decisions, I know he would fire me … he'd hug me, say he's sorry and maybe you won't want to go to dinner with me anymore, but he wouldn't hesitate to get rid of me … it's all about performance" (Welch 2001, 168).

CHAPTER 3

The Corporation Speaks

BEFORE I DISCUSS the simulated corporation, Summit Consumables Incorporated, a bit of discussion regarding corporations is in order.

When most people think of corporations, they think of certain organizations, such as Apple, Proctor & Gamble, Alcoa, Verizon, Southwest Airlines, or Google. Few people think about the core purpose of any given corporation. Indeed, "the bulk of economic activity in an advanced market economy takes place in corporations" (Nordhaus & Samuelson 1992, 105). While initiation of a corporate charter today can be accomplished with the help of service organizations such as LegalZoom, such was not always the case. "Centuries ago, corporate charters were awarded by special acts of the monarch or legislature … the British East India Company was a privileged corporation and as such it practically ruled India for more than a century" (Nordhaus & Samuelson 1992, 105).

Contemporary corporations can be formed by just about anyone for a myriad of purposes and with various operational objectives. Once formed, "the corporation has a separate legal identity, and [by law] is a legal person that may on its own behalf, buy, sell, borrow money, produce goods and services, and enter into contracts" (Nordhaus & Samuelson 1992, 106).

One of the benefits afforded by law to a corporation is the limitations on liability. For example, damages awarded to plaintiffs resulting from legal action brought against a corporation are limited to the assets of a corporation. Personal assets of noncorporate officer employees are off limits to such actions. Another important point associated with corporations is that "the ownership of a corporation is determined by who holds the shares or common stock of the company" (Nordhaus & Samuelson 1992, 106). Years ago, I opened my first online stock account and became the proud owner of several companies—including Fortune

500 corporations—well not exactly 100 percent owner, but ownership as determined by the number of shares that I purchased.

Another way of viewing corporate ownership resulting from the purchase of common stock is "if you own 10 percent` of a corporation's shares, you have 10 percent of the ownership" (Nordhaus & Samuelson 1992, 106). Many corporations also offer stock dividends. At the time of this writing, for example, and as listed on etrade.com, Intel Corporation was paying a stock dividend of 2.98 percent. This means that based on an investment of $9663.00 (which at the then current stock price of $32.21 would purchase 300 common shares of stock) the annual dividend received by the new partial owner would be $9663.00 × 0.0298, or approximately $288, which would be paid in four quarterly payments of $72 each. In addition to collecting stock dividends, "in proportion to the fraction of shares that they own, [the shareholders also] elect directors and vote on many important issues" (Nordhaus & Samuelson 1992, 106). Corporations also pay taxes, like most everyone else. And, according to the Organization for Economic Cooperation and Development (OECD) as posted on the Tax Foundation website at taxfoundation.org, US corporations face the highest income tax rate in the world at 39.1 percent, which is a combination of a 35 percent federal rate and the average rate levied by US states.

Corporate stock is sold through an exchange such as the New York Stock Exchange (NYSE) or the NASDAQ. You may also be familiar with the Standard & Poors 500 (also known as the S&P 500), which is a stock market index made up of five hundred different stocks. When a company becomes a public company (owned by shareholders), the first issuance of common stock is referred to as an *initial public offering*, or IPO.

The *ticker symbol* is a series of letters that are used as a means for identifying a stock for purchase or for conducting company research. INTC, traded on the NASDAQ, is the ticker symbol for Intel Corporation, and AMZN is the ticker symbol for Amazon.com, Incorporated, also traded on the NASDAQ. PG is the ticker symbol for the Proctor & Gamble Company, which is traded on the NYSE.

There are a couple of metrics associated with stock of which you should be aware. First, there is the *price-earnings ratio*, or P/E ratio, the price of the stock divided by the company earnings, which "shows how much investors are willing to pay per dollar of reported profits [for the stock]" (Brigham & Gapenski 1991, 883).

The other financial metric is *earnings per share*, or EPS. To better understand this metric, consider the Intel Corporation. At the time of this writing, as posted on etrade.com, Intel Corporation had 4.8 billion common shares outstanding with an EPS of 2.36, meaning that earnings were approximately $4.8 billion × 2.36, or $11.3 billion. The corresponding P/E ratio is the stock price $32.21, as shown above, divided by the EPS (2.36) which yields a P/E of 13.65. Also, as posted on etrade.com's website, "Intel's P/E Ratio [at the time of this writing] was lower than 78% of other companies in the Semiconductors industry … this typically means that investors are willing to pay less for its level of earnings relative to future growth" (etrade.com).

The important characteristic of stock ownership is that "the shareholders control the companies they own" (Nordhaus & Samuelson 1992, 106). Many proponents of corporations believe that the sole purpose of a corporation is to return value to the shareholder. Indeed, Milton Friedman (one of the most notable free market advocates of the twentieth century), as cited by Martin and Schinzinger, "argued that the paramount, indeed the sole, responsibility of management is to satisfy the desires of stockholders who entrust corporations with their money to maximize return on their investment" (2010, 21).

OK, almost done—just a few more comments regarding a corporation.

Corporations don't run themselves. Many, if not all, corporate organizations include boards of directors to whom the president and chief executive officer (CEO) must answer, and possibly some corporate executives who may report to the president and CEO. In some instances, the president's and CEO's job responsibilities may be split into two separate roles, one being the president and the other the CEO. In some instances, the president may be focused on the internal workings of the organization while the CEO may, among other things, focus on external corporate activities as well as provide overall strategic direction for the organization. Often, perhaps in lieu of the president, there is a chief operating officer (COO) who, in addition to stepping in when needed to perform CEO duties, is often also responsible for internal organizational operations. Organizationally, the COO usually reports directly to the CEO. While there are any number of organizational structures or hierarchies to be found within a corporation, figure 3-1 shows an executive level structure for a consumer products company.

Figure 3-1: Consumer Products Organization Structure

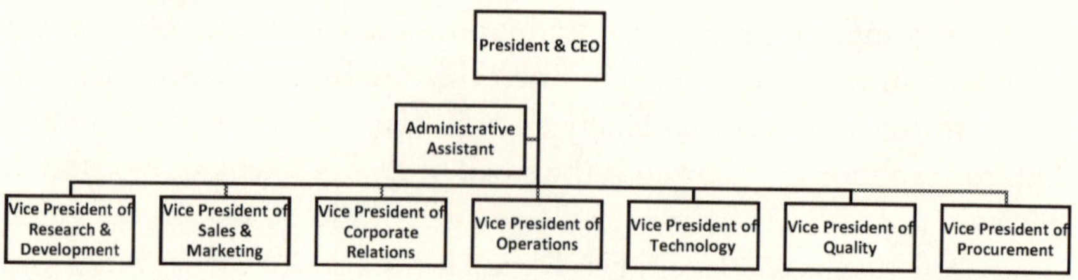

Not shown in the chart are those reporting to the executive levels, to include senior directors, directors, senior managers, and managers, all of whom may also have direct reports flowing down to the lowest salaried level and, particularly in the operations area, possibly including hourly employees, those paid by the hour rather than an annual salary (exempt or nonexempt). By the way, exempt salaried personnel may be required to work overtime without pay, whereas nonexempt salaried personnel are usually paid overtime, or given compensatory time off when they are required to work overtime.

Roles and responsibilities of the executive levels may vary, again depending on the organization's business intention. In general, however, the President and CEO has overall responsibility for the corporation, the VP of research and development is charged with developing new products, the VP of sales and marketing is charged with marketing and selling those products, the VP of operations is charged with delivering those products, the VP of quality is charged with assuring quality of the products, and the VP of procurement is charged with purchasing raw materials for the manufacture of those products. The VP of corporate relations is often charged with external representation of the company and solidifying community relationships, making clear and preserving the corporate stance in key corporate citizenship areas. The VP of technology is often charged with supplying, maintaining, and upgrading or replacing IT infrastructure.

Also not shown on the organization chart is one of the most important positions within a corporation—executive legal counsel. This internal law department is often charged with advising the executive and other levels regarding business issues falling into this area, such as external contract issues, environmental issues, policy issues, product liability issues, and intellectual property issues. Finally, some corporations also include departments focused specifically on *organic* growth (for example expanding through new product development) or *inorganic* growth (which includes mergers and acquisitions).

With that exposure to fundamentals associated with corporations and corporate structure (and noting that many corporations are much more complex than presented), my discussion shifts to consideration of a corporate context involving Summit Consumables Incorporated, which has been in the business of making and selling consumer products for decades. And like most large corporations, Summit Consumables has shifted its growth strategy many times, trying both organic and inorganic approaches. Over the last few years, Summit Consumables has been receiving pressure from its competition, especially from a relatively new and more efficient and agile competitor. The stock price has begun to take a hit, and based on revenue declines, the company is contemplating reducing its current dividend yield. Analysts are critiquing Summit Consumables' cost structure and are suggesting that the company could do a great deal more to get costs in line with decreasing revenues. Moreover, compared to the industry average, Summit Consumables' P/E ratio of 42.5 is excessive. Some of the changes discussed in the boardroom following the last earnings report (which missed analyst estimates yet again) include the following:

- Slashing the workforce by 10 percent
- Modifying the current executive compensation program
- Eliminating cash bonuses for employees reporting more than four levels from the regional president
- Expanding the managerial span of control to a minimum of ten direct reports
- Reducing operations costs by 10 percent
- Delaying all nonvital capital projects until year end

Despite the tough talk about performance and competition, the message from headquarters is that the company vows to fully reward employees who demonstrate leadership in all areas of their responsibility. Just before kickoff of the annual performance review cycle, Summit Consumables sent out an email to all salaried employees containing an article regarding TL that included the following excerpt and comment:

Avolio and Bass reported that "when all levels of managers, students, and project leaders around the world were asked to describe the characteristics and behaviors of the most effective leaders with whom they had worked in the past, the characterizations were more transformational than transactional. Among the specific descriptors used for these leaders were "inspirational, intellectually stimulating, challenging, visionary, development oriented, and determined to maximize performance" (2004, 3). We believe that these characterizations essentially mirror the five constituent elements of TL. Thus, the presence of these attributes in any one or more of the tested groups might also identify a leadership feeder pool for future effective leaders.

—Dave Sterling, Chairman

A snapshot of the corporate financial structure is reflected in figure 3-2.

Figure 3-2: Summit Consumables Financial Snapshot

The Corporation: Consumer Products	
Market Capitalization	$ 105 billion
Shares Outstanding	$ 1.4 billion
Current Stock Price	$ 75.09
Dividend Yield	0.035
P/E (Trailing 12 months):	42.5x

Headquartered in Wilmington, Delaware, Summit Consumables also has physical manufacturing and distribution locations in Texas, Georgia, Kentucky, and New Jersey. Leading the operations of each of these facilities is a regional president. Services such as product quality monitoring, environmental engineering, employee safety, legal support, human resources, and community relations are sourced from headquarters and are reflected in the organization charts only as applicable to the referenced Summit Consumables employees. There has been a great deal of buzz regarding the potential closure of one of the facilities located in the South, resulting in operations consolidation, and potentially resulting in incremental job loss beyond the 10 percent contemplated above. Summit Consumables continues to use the annual performance appraisal approach, and the word from the executive level is that "based on the current performance appraisal, all employees need to fully understand the gravity of the competitive landscape."

Jessica Wright, Johnny Goode, Kimberly Hours, Maria Summers, Earl Easy, Kenneth Bethone, and Josef Brilliant are all employed at the Georgia facility. All have just received their respective performance evaluations, and the pressure is on to turn the facility around in hopes that it will withstand the external competitive environment. Summit Consumables uses a 5-point rating system of the type I described previously, with a 5 representing the highest available performance rating and a 1 the lowest. Let's spend a bit of time reviewing the job assignments for each of the seven employees as well as their performance results.

As shown in figure 3-3, Jessica Wright is the director of manufacturing operations, with twenty-four-hour responsibility for receiving, processing, and packaging (there's that IPO again—inputs, processing, and outputs) of necessary raw and packaging materials required for close to thirty-five separate product SKUs. Jessica and the director of maintenance and engineering, in contrast to the job levels of their peers, who are vice presidents, are said to be in developmental positions. Summit Consumables has typically looked to these two positions as succession for the vice president level positions. Several months back, the vice president of finance (Mack) announced his retirement by the end of next year.

Jessica has been employed by Summit Consumables for six years and has an MBA, with an undergraduate degree in finance. She joined the company as a leadership development entrant and exited the program three years ago to accept her current assignment. Not shown on the organization chart in figure 3-3 is that she currently has eight direct reports. Jessica has received a 4 rating in four of her last five ratings, with the last of these five ratings being a 3. Due to R&D's aggressive efforts to respond to competitive pressures, Jessica's product mix has increased, resulting in frequent changeovers.

Let's now take a look at her feedback and performance rating.

As shown in figure 3-4, Jessica's current performance rating was well below her expectations, coming in at a 2. However, her boss (Art) did convey that it was a tough call, and he, too, was a bit surprised when it all shook out. And although she had indeed received performance feedback throughout the year that pointed out improvement opportunities, she was surprised and disappointed to receive a performance rating that was

Figure 3-3: Jessica's Organization Structure

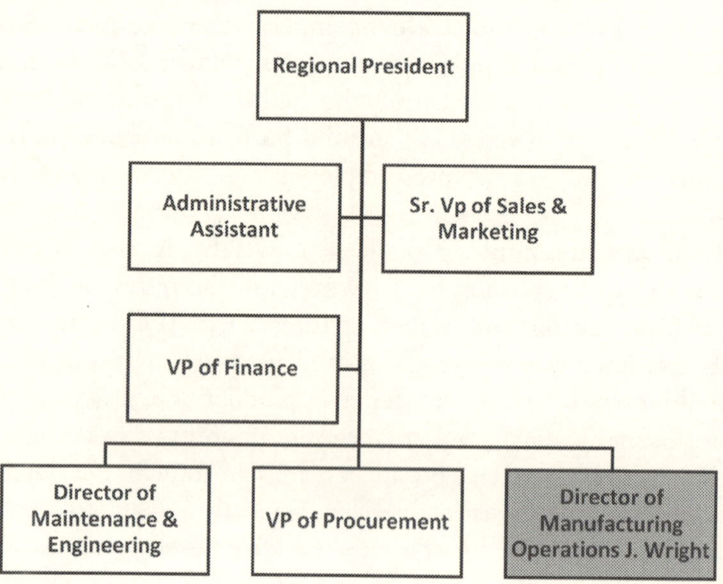

not only the lowest in five years, but in her view, well below what she deserved, particularly given the effort she expended last year to improve her department's performance. Likewise, she assumed that due to her rating falling to the low side, she must also be included in the employee population located on the wrong side of the ranking curve.

Figure 3-4: Excerpt from Jessica's Performance Evaluation

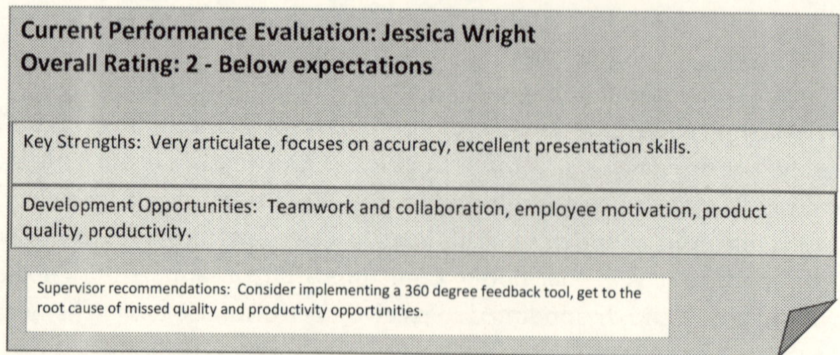

Current Performance Evaluation: Jessica Wright
Overall Rating: 2 - Below expectations

Key Strengths: Very articulate, focuses on accuracy, excellent presentation skills.

Development Opportunities: Teamwork and collaboration, employee motivation, product quality, productivity.

Supervisor recommendations: Consider implementing a 360 degree feedback tool, get to the root cause of missed quality and productivity opportunities.

Within moments of conveying the performance evaluation rating and also communicating that a 10 percent reduction in departmental budget was required, Art stepped away to take an ostensibly urgent phone call, leaving Jessica alone in his office. While adjusting her seated position, Jessica happened to glance at a document left face up on Art's desk. To her surprise, the document included her performance rating as well as that of her peers. In addition to her rating being the lowest, she also noticed that her best friend, Mack, received a performance rating of 5. This was even more discouraging because the talk around the water cooler was that Mack had checked out (exerting little to no effort in his current position). This was a topic that he and Jessica joked about during lunch breaks from time to time. And although Mack had not directly said so, he had hinted that Jessica was being considered as his successor and that her knowledge of manufacturing was sure to aid in her chances of getting there.

Let's talk next about Johnny Goode, who was hired by Summit Consumables as a buying analyst, where he worked for two years before being promoted to senior buying analyst, as shown in figure 3-5. Johnny has been employed at Summit Consumables for five years. He has a BS in operations research and has responsibility for the purchase of all product packaging materials, including finished product cases. Not shown on the organization chart is that he has five direct reports.

Figure 3-5: Johnny's Organization Structure

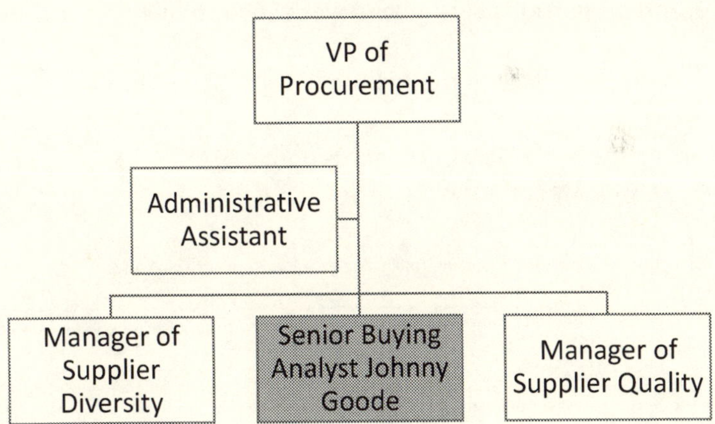

Johnny's initial performance rating in his current role was a 4, after having received a 5 before being promoted to his current level. Despite the significant contribution that Johnny made early in his career with Summit Consumables, during the last two years he was viewed as having coasted along, focusing only on problems that had reached the level of proverbial fires. Perhaps this view resulted from comparing the stellar year he enjoyed before being promoted, to his performance in his current position. Like most corporations, Summit Consumables believes strongly that employees (particularly those who have been promoted) are expected to make greater contributions in all measurable areas each year. In other words, you are judged not by what you accomplished in the past, but by what you accomplish in the current performance period.

Let's look at Johnny's feedback and current performance rating. As shown in figure 3-6, Johnny's performance rating, while not tremendously surprising to him, was below his expectations, coming in at a 3. Since he had previously shared his aspiration to move to the manager of supplier quality position, succeeding the relocating incumbent, Johnny's view was that he needed to get at least a 4 rating to have a chance at doing so. However, Johnny's boss Teresa did convey that she saw lots of potential in Johnny and that, in her words, it was up to him to make or break his next career move—assuming opportunities for growth were available. She reiterated the company's focus on TL as well as the need for a 10 percent cost reduction, and also pointed out that she had heard lots of noise regarding product shipment cases collapsing at retail and during shipping, resulting in damaged product, increased returns, and proportionately higher rework and product destruction costs.

Figure 3-6: Excerpt from Johnny's Performance Evaluation

Current Performance Evaluation: Johnny Goode
Overall Rating: 3- Satisfactory

Key Strengths: Reliable, consistent, approachable, excellent supplier knowledge.

Development Opportunities: Communication, being in touch with supplier progress versus goals and objectives.

Supervisor recommendations: Consider the development of effective planning and communication tools.

As a final note, Teresa pointed to a supplier cost chart that reflected price increases occurring three of the four quarters in the previous year at a time when the expectation was that costs should be decreasing or, at a minimum, match original budget levels.

We now shift to Kimberly Hours, who is the regional sales director for the southeastern region, as shown in figure 3-7. This is her fourth year with Summit Consumables after transferring from a competitor company, where she served as a territory sales manager (TSM). She has a bachelor of science in economics with a minor in psychology. Her responsibilities include all tasks associated with the nurturing of existing and identification of new retail contracts, resolving retailer customer complaints regarding sales and service, analyzing sales statistics, monitoring customer preferences to determine the focus of sales efforts, and directing fifteen TSMs in the execution of product promotions, sell-ins, product displays, inventory management, and product returns. Affected by R&D's efforts to push new products into retail, Kimberly is being asked to pressure the retail accounts to take on more products, resulting in increased store stock keeping units (SKUs), which, if successful, will require those stores to remove competitive or other products. Making this even more difficult to accomplish is that due to the sudden surplus in gasoline, convenience store owners are not able to take advantage of fuel pricing as in the past. Consequently, these retailers are interested in carrying only incremental products that are sure to generate significant revenue.

Figure 3-7: Kimberly's Organization Structure

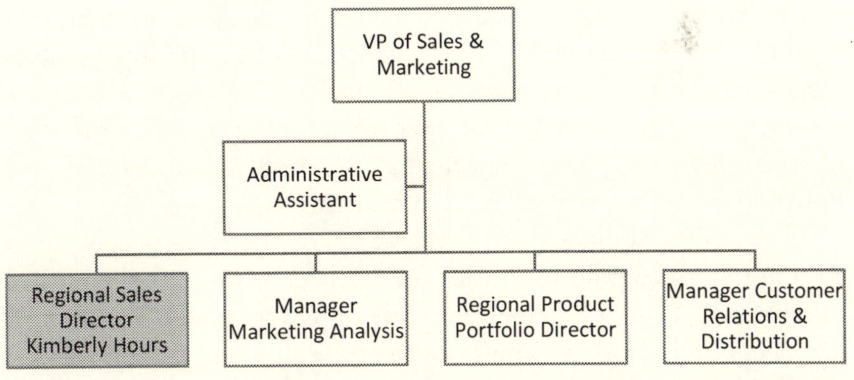

Kimberly has received a 4 rating on two of her last three annual performance reviews, with the last of these three ratings being a 3. Let's now take a look at her current feedback and performance rating.

As shown in figure 3-8, Kimberly's performance rating was below her expectations, coming in at a 3. It is her fear that if she receives two consecutive 3 ratings, she will be pushed aside and considered to be an average performer.

Figure 3-8: Excerpt from Kimberly's Performance Evaluation

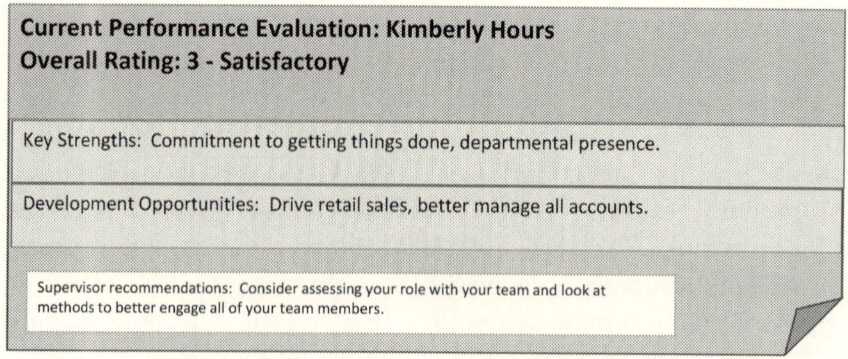
Current Performance Evaluation: Kimberly Hours
Overall Rating: 3 - Satisfactory

Key Strengths: Commitment to getting things done, departmental presence.

Development Opportunities: Drive retail sales, better manage all accounts.

Supervisor recommendations: Consider assessing your role with your team and look at methods to better engage all of your team members.

Kimberly's boss, Seth, was unable to spend a great deal of time with her for this review meeting since headquarters had scheduled an unexpected but mandatory emergency meeting. However, Seth did point out that Kimberly should review her feedback and consider what she plans to do to turn things around, particularly relative to sales revenues, if she wants to be viewed as above the pile next year. He also suggested that Kimberly speak with his administrative assistant to set up a follow-up meeting to discuss the review further. Just before his exit, he also conveyed that he had received feedback from multiple sources suggesting that Kimberly appears to play favorites with some of her team members and that she is viewed by some as taking credit for the work of others. Seth also pointed out that, although she spends a lot of time in the office, such is not reflected in her results.

The notion of playing favorites, while not good practice, is not at all unusual. According to Pichler and Teckchandani, "managers tend to form high-quality relationships with employees they like more and low-quality relationships with employees they like less" (2015, 18).

A review of Kimberly's feedback suggests that she was not asked to reduce her budget by 10 percent as was the case with Jessica and Johnny. The reason for this is that the obvious goal of the sales department is to increase revenue. Thus, as will also be the case with Maria, it is not at all uncommon for budgets in this area to increase despite required reductions in other areas. However, Kim was challenged to "drive retail sales and to better manage all accounts."

We now shift to Maria Summers, who is the regional product portfolio director for Summit Consumables' southeastern region, as shown in figure 3-9. This is her fourth year with Summit Consumables since transferring from a business-to-business (B2B) marketing company. She has a master of science in business management with a concentration in marketing. She has some central marketing responsibilities. And with help from a team of five section leaders, she is responsible for the overall regional product management plan development, including collaborative development, creation, positioning, price recommendations to corporate, promotion, and life cycle management. It is her job to ensure that the plan supports overall corporate objectives and expectations.

Figure 3-9: Maria's Organization Structure

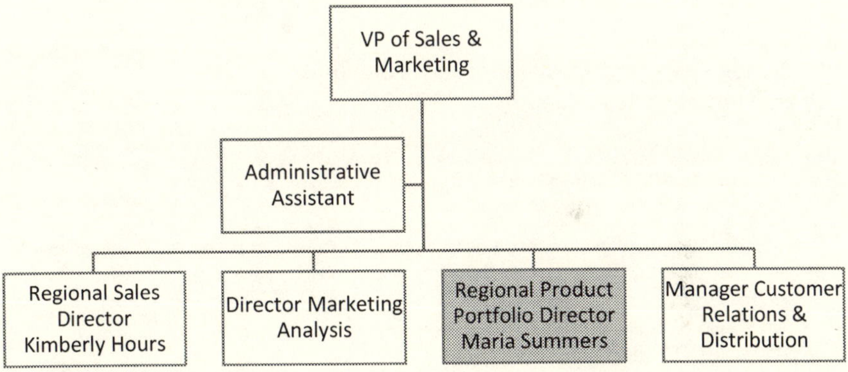

VP of Sales & Marketing

Administrative Assistant

Regional Sales Director Kimberly Hours

Director Marketing Analysis

Regional Product Portfolio Director Maria Summers

Manager Customer Relations & Distribution

As evidenced by data provided by the director of marketing analysis (as will be discussed in chapter 8), promotional campaigns appear to be floundering, and the competitive landscape is becoming quite challenging, particularly in the area of product pricing. Although not fully verified, organizational chatter suggests that feedback received from some retailers operating in the southern tier indicates that the recent promotional campaigns have not been received very well by consumers and require excessive retailer time to implement. Fully verified feedback from northern tier retailers suggests that promotions designed to revive products residing in the mature stage of their life cycle appear to be inconsistent at best in delivering predictable results. Likewise, based on recent Nielsen data, the related prepurchased TV advertising space has lost viewership and is no longer among the top rated programs.

Maria has received a 3 rating in two of her last three performance ratings. Her last rating, in the words of her departing boss, was "a 4 at the low end."

Let's take a look Maria's current feedback and performance rating.

As shown in figure 3-10, Maria's performance rating came in at a 3, which was quite surprising to her. While she recognized that some opportunities existed with some of her work, her departing boss also assured her that she was on the right track to earn a great rating for the current cycle. Given the pressure being felt by Summit Consumables to turn things around, Maria is somewhat anxious that receiving a 3 rating in three of the last four years might result in some questioning her contribution to the company.

Figure 3-10: Excerpt from Maria's Performance Evaluation

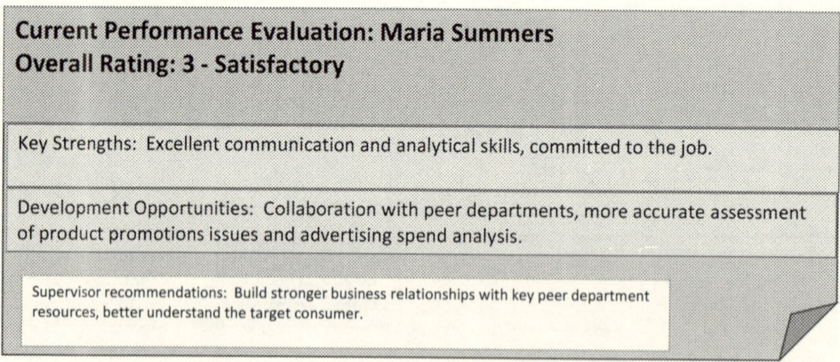

Current Performance Evaluation: Maria Summers
Overall Rating: 3 - Satisfactory

Key Strengths: Excellent communication and analytical skills, committed to the job.

Development Opportunities: Collaboration with peer departments, more accurate assessment of product promotions issues and advertising spend analysis.

Supervisor recommendations: Build stronger business relationships with key peer department resources, better understand the target consumer.

Maria's new vice president Seth, who is also Kimberly's boss and has a sales background, appears to spend a disproportionately high amount of time focusing on sales, doing so, in Maria's view, at the expense of marketing. Maria pointed this out during her performance review, but Seth didn't receive it very well. He stated that his expectation was that all his direct reports should, in essence, manage themselves, and that he viewed his role as one of "correcting things when they got out of hand."

Seth did point out, however, that Maria does not appear to be as collaborative with peer departments as he would like and that Maria's lack of understanding of consumer promotion preferences is "creating revenue issues and the lack of predictability for product promotions." He also pointed out that Maria is very talented, but in order to be truly effective, she needs to put on the business hat a bit more by returning to some of the basics of marketing.

A review of Maria's feedback suggests that, like Kimberly, she was not asked to reduce her budget by 10 percent. The reason for this, as was explained earlier, is that the obvious goal of the marketing department is to increase revenue. So it is not at all uncommon for budgets in this area to increase despite required reductions in other areas.

In January of last year, the corporate IT department decided to relocate some of its IT staff from the central location to the supported operating facilities. However, the responsibility for some central services, such as the company website, remained with the reallocated IT resources. In addition to reducing travel costs, there was an expectation that facility IT systems and infrastructure would be made more robust due to the increased on-site focus.

Earl Easy is the IT Manager. (See figure 3-11.) Not shown on the organization chart is the large number of retained contract resources managed by Earl's direct reports. This *buy* versus *make* cost reduction business structure was adopted in an effort to optimize the IT department.

Figure 3-11: Earl Easy's Organization Structure

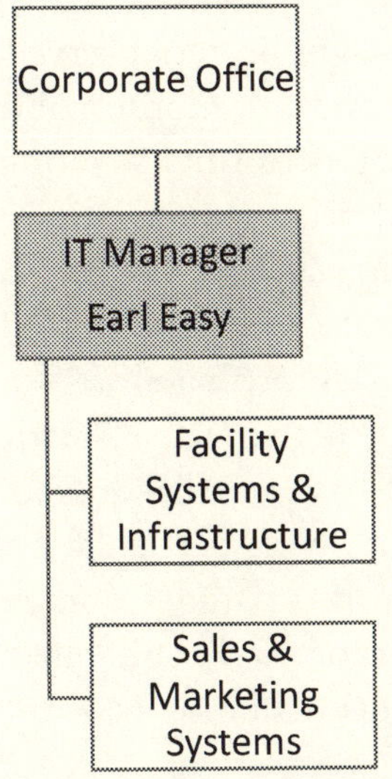

It is not at all uncommon for corporations to purchase contract resources, to *buy* rather than carry headcount on the corporate payroll (also referred to as *make*). This approach minimizes costs (for example through reduced benefits), particularly in situations where the services are temporary. Often the allowable duration for temporary employees is twelve to twenty-four months or so. Maintaining temporary employees longer than this may suggest that the employees are equivalent to permanent employees and should therefore receive full benefits such as health care and 401(k)s.

Earl has a bachelor's degree in information technology management with a minor in finance. He has the responsibility to deploy new hardware and software according to Summit Consumables standards and policies, to manage hardware and software updates, patches, and maintenance, to define backup policies for local applications, monitor and guarantee the success of the backup systems, and to handle upgrade and replacement of facility inventory infrastructure systems.

A major focus area for Earl and his team is getting the company website upgraded and running, and to accept one of several contractor proposals for replacing the current raw materials and finished product inventory management infrastructure. His team members have, on average, received higher performance ratings than most of their peer groups, and the buzz around the water cooler is that Earl awards ratings that are not really earned. Over the last several months, rumors have leaked from headquarters suggesting that the entire IT services at Summit Consumables might be better served if it were outsourced.

Earl has been with Summit Consumables for four years and has consistently received the 3 performance rating. Let's now take a look at his current feedback and performance rating. As shown in figure 3-12, Earl's performance rating was a 3.

Unlike the performance reviews discussed previously, Earl's review was conducted via web. Unfortunately, there appeared to be a glitch in the system, resulting in the lack of clarity of feedback provided. However, Earl was able to learn that his boss, Frank, was not at all pleased with his progress, with particular emphasis on the company website and infrastructure upgrades and replacements. Frank also expressed concern regarding Earl's suitability to continue leading the team and suggested that the 3 rating was very generous. If it were left

Figure 3-12: Excerpt from Earl's Performance Evaluation

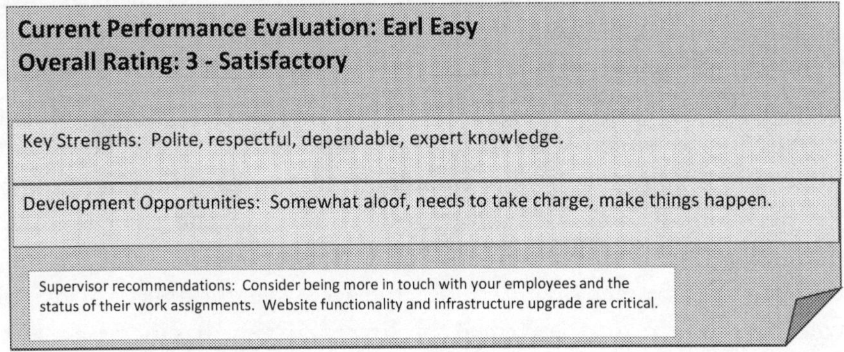
Current Performance Evaluation: Earl Easy
Overall Rating: 3 - Satisfactory

Key Strengths: Polite, respectful, dependable, expert knowledge.

Development Opportunities: Somewhat aloof, needs to take charge, make things happen.

Supervisor recommendations: Consider being more in touch with your employees and the status of their work assignments. Website functionality and infrastructure upgrade are critical.

solely to Frank, the rating would have been a 2 at best. Although Earl was disappointed with his rating, he was even more anxious at the thought that he must demand more from his team members. In his own words, he "didn't want to stir the pot."

Now we shift to Kenneth Bethone, the call center manager for the southeastern region, as shown in figure 3-13. This is his third year with Summit Consumables. He has a bachelor's degree in industrial engineering, and he is a Six Sigma Black Belt. (I'll discuss Six Sigma in chapter 10.)

Figure 3-13: Ken's Organization Structure

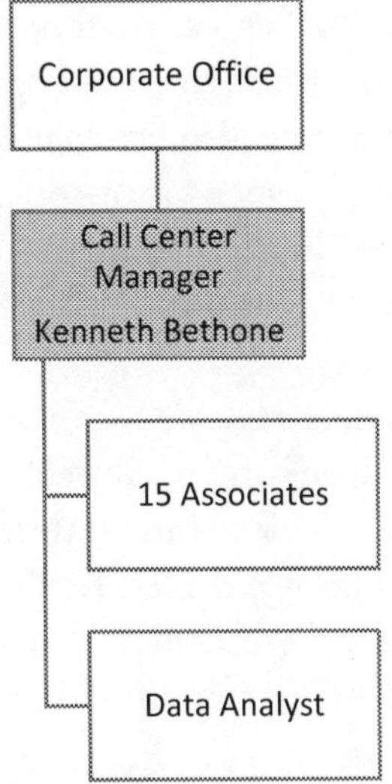

As shown on the organization chart, Ken, who reports to the corporate office, is responsible for fifteen associates who receive product-related calls from Summit Consumables consumers. He is also responsible for a data analyst, who is responsible for assisting Ken in identifying continuous improvement opportunities regarding call execution and remedial strategies. Depending upon the type of call (for example a product quality complaint, recommendation or product use question), Ken delivers information to his boss and the respective peer departments, usually in the form of a report. As evidenced by data provided by Ken's data analyst, the average call time per associate continues to increase, the average consumer wait time has increased, and the *call drop* level (the number of consumers who remove themselves from the cue after waiting to be engaged) have all moved in a direction that suggests significant customer focus opportunities exist within the call center. Secondhand feedback from some of the associates suggests that Ken spends too much time in meetings and trying to rub elbows with the bosses in lieu of allocating time to manage the department and, in particular, not enough time guiding them in efficiently engaging consumers using the relatively new call center system.

Ken has received a 3 rating for the last two years at Summit Consumables. He is interested in moving to the director level but, surprisingly, given his Six Sigma Black Belt status, appears to be struggling in the area of applying analytical tools to identify and resolve key business issues and opportunities.

As shown in figure 3-14, Ken's current performance rating of 2, was quite disappointing. And although he recognized that opportunities exist within the department, he also felt that such would be overlooked given the amount of time he spent in meetings with his boss and his boss's peers, coupled with the significant number of assignments that he volunteered to complete that had little if anything to do with his area of responsibility.

During the performance review, Ken shared his perspective with his boss, Victor, who became somewhat defensive, suggesting that had he known how poorly Ken's departmental deliverables to Ken's peers had been, he never would have accepted Ken's offers to complete, in the boss's words, "tangential assignments." Ken pushed back, raising the point that he thought his being a good soldier by sacrificing (reducing)

Figure 3-14: Excerpt from Ken's Performance Evaluation

Current Performance Evaluation: Kenneth Bethone
Overall Rating: 2 - Below expectations

Key Strengths: Highly collaborative.

Development Opportunities: Analytical focus, reduce call waiting time, reduce reporting error rate.

Supervisor recommendations: Exhibit leadership in identifying and bolstering the individual team member skills and focus.

the yearly performance ratings of his associates to allow his boss to meet forced distribution targets would have bolstered his performance rating since doing so reflected his unfettered willingness to be a company-focused leader. In his words, his team was performing as well as, if not better than, those operating in peer departments. Ken also reminded Victor of his exemplary progress and academic achievements in all business, management, and leadership courses taken in school. In fact, Ken was voted most likely to succeed in business leadership by his graduating class peers.

Victor replied that the 2 rating was not determined only by him, but that "the forced distribution" required that someone in his area of responsibility receive this rating and Ken just happened to meet the criteria this time. He also suggested that Ken do some soul searching and figure out if the Call Center Manager role is what he really wants to do and, if so, work on his ability to proactively identify and overcome departmental performance issues. Moreover, he suggested Ken may not be viewed by others as the great leader that he believes himself to be and that perhaps Ken should try to measure his overall effectiveness as a leader in his current capacity. Ken jumped to his feet and flippantly thanked his boss for the review as he exited the office.

A review of Ken's feedback suggests that, as was the case with Kimberly, Maria and Earl, he was not asked to reduce his budget by 10 percent. Because Ken reported to the central group, he did not have the same budgeting constraints as the operations areas. However, quantifiable opportunities were identified for Ken regarding a reduction of consumer call waiting time and report errors.

Josef Brilliant is a senior electrical engineer serving the entire facility. Although he does not have any solid line (direct) reports, he does serve as the team leader for all maintenance and engineering projects. One such project was the recent modernization effort to replace all equipment with newer, faster machines that were capable of responding to the increased changeovers required to accommodate R&D's recent influx of new product trials. Figure 3-15 reflects his location in the organization. This is his fourth year with Summit Consumables after joining the company as an entry level engineer. Having a bachelor of science in electrical engineering and a minor in engineering management, Josef has openly expressed his desire to progress into management, preferably in the production area.

Figure 3-15: Josef's Organization Structure

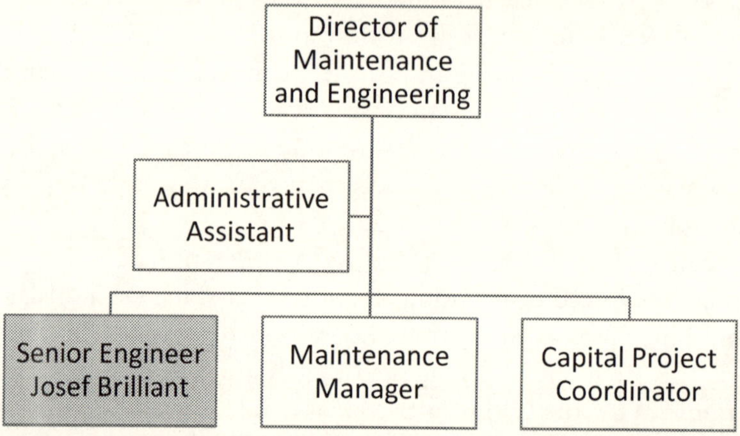

Josef received a 4 rating in two of his last three ratings, with the last of these three ratings being a 3. Let's now take a look at his current feedback and performance rating.

As shown in figure 3-16, Joseph's performance rating was a 3. This rating was also below his expectations as he had been told by a prior manager that he would need to get at least two 4 ratings out of the last three evaluations in order to be considered for another position, either promotional or developmental. Josef's current director, Daniela, thinks that he has a great deal of potential but in her words, he needs to "ease up" and not appear to be "on edge" all the time.

Figure 3-16: Excerpt from Joseph's Performance Evaluation

Current Performance Evaluation: Josef Brilliant
Overall Rating: 3 - Satisfactory

Key Strengths: Intelligence, commitment, customer focus.

Development Opportunities: Communications (written and oral), does not receive feedback well.

Supervisor recommendations: Consider being more in touch with your emotions and how your actions detract from your work.

The new equipment installation has begun to slip on the schedule, and there has been some talk of having an engineer from the central group in headquarters "look over Josef's shoulder" to get things back on track. Daniela further stated that her personal observations of Josef's communication skills, supported by feedback from multiple unsolicited sources, suggests that clarity and brevity would be extremely helpful in getting him a better rating in future performance periods. Daniela ended the meeting with Josef by saying that "even the most brilliant engineers can run into significant career headwinds if they are unable to articulate to the lay community."

It is an understatement to say that all these employees were disappointed with their performance evaluations—some more so than others. And while the discussion was hypothesized, it is sure to ring true to the most important input device currently in operation—you the reader. You may also recognize opportunities for leadership development among the bosses as reflected in their communication of performance appraisal information. In particular, their lack of empathy for employees was demonstrated as was the ambiguity with which some of the feedback was communicated.

However, the aim of this book is not to focus on the conveyors of performance information. It is, instead, to identify leadership opportunities among those previously cited and to take advantage of key business processes and leadership theory to correct or mitigate the impact of those opportunities.

You may have also noticed the absence of any discussions regarding employee development plans. In practice, as mentioned in the previous chapter, such plans are typically developed in conjunction with the performance review discussion or completed shortly thereafter.

Digressing slightly for a moment, I would like to pass along an anecdote characterizing my interaction with someone several years ago during the early stages of my corporate career. I approached someone who I believed would provide excellent advice and mentoring to aide in my leadership development. When I asked him if he would be interested in providing such advice and mentoring, his response stuck with me for many years thereafter.

In essence, he said that while he would certainly enjoy acting in the requested capacity, much of what I would learn from him would be what not to do. And while I did not observe much from him that fell in the category of what not to do, I did learn a great deal about the importance of learning through observation. So while this book does not focus on the development opportunities of those delivering the performance appraisals, you as the reader can and certainly should recognize critical "what not to do lessons" from each of them.

OK, you have received the performance evaluation and the respective rating. And you understand the psychological affects (discussed in chapter 1) that may potentially result from the reception of such information. But so far I've offered no solution regarding how you should respond. Let's see what the next chapter has to offer in this regard.

CHAPTER 4

Now Comes Enabling Infrastructure

IN THE FOREGOING chapter, I introduced you to seven people employed at Summit Consumables Incorporated and described their respective performance evaluations, reflecting the prior year's results. In this chapter, I introduce you to two distinct models that, when integrated and put into action, provide a clear path to performance improvement through the exhibition of leadership.

We begin with the acronym IPO—no, not initial public offering as was discussed in chapter 3 regarding a company going public. Here IPO refers to inputs, processing, and outputs, as we briefly discussed in section 1.1. Almost every response or action is preceded by some input that is subsequently processed before drawing a conclusion or acting on the input. It may occur on either the macro or micro level (explained later). Even while you are reading this paragraph, you are taking in (inputting) information, processing that information, and no doubt will subsequently formulate an opinion or output based on that information.

I hedge here with the word *almost* to recognize the will and capacity of pundits to find some esoteric exception to this model and also to recognize that, despite your ontological position, very little in this world can be assumed to be 100 percent applicable in every situation.

Be that as it may, I now invite you to think of a situation to which this model is *not* directly applicable. Keep in mind, however, that as you contemplate a scenario for which this model is not applicable, you are searching your brain's database (as simulated in figure 4-1) for an IPO scenario that may not align with this model. Your act of thinking about it (input) and effectively "processing" that input will no doubt result in your determining the relevance of this model to that situation (output). And in doing so, you will implement all stages of the IPO model.

As I said, the IPO model may operate at the micro or macro level. Said differently, inasmuch as the effect of the output stage of the model extends beyond the person who has received the input—to include others or society at large—the IPO is said to be operating at the macro level. Likewise, in cases where only the person receiving the information (input) is affected, particularly when the output takes the form of a thought without action, the model is operating at the micro level.

So here is a quiz question for you: How would you apply the IPO model to the presidential election, whereby the population votes for their candidate of choice? Perhaps the simplest way to do this would be to consider the votes as inputs to the voting machines in aggregate. The counting of votes, whether completed by humans or machines, means processing the votes to yield an output, which is, of course, the next elected president. The significance of this model is discussed later.

Figure 4-1: IPO Model—In Search of a Contrary Activity

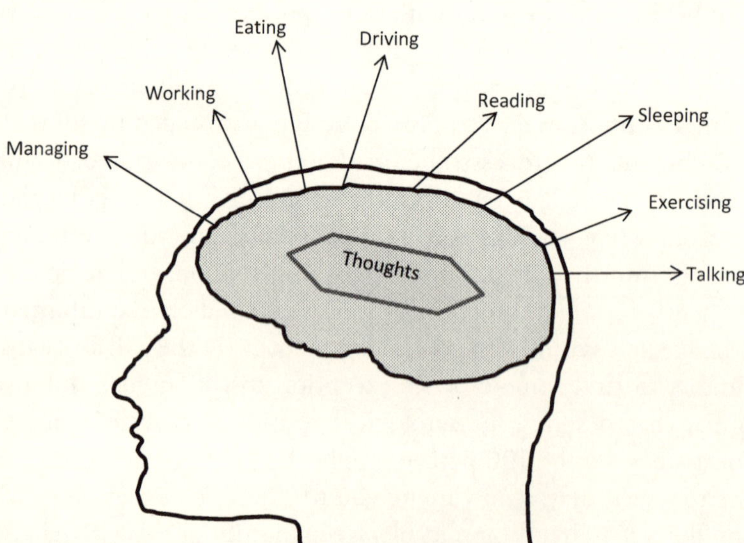

Here I introduce you to the 5C (conversation, calculation, collaboration, communication and cognizance), leadership improvement model (LIM) discussing the 5C LIM first at a high level.

In figure 4-2, the model is initiated with a conversation aimed at issue or opportunity identification. The next step is to implement some sort of situation driven calculation (such as math or logic) aimed at satisfying the issue or opportunity previously identified in the conversation stage. With the calculation in hand, it is time to collaborate or engage with others, during which time key calculated communication takes place to assist in the planning phase of a broader communication. And yes, communication is just as it implies—getting the message out regarding what needs to be done in support of the first three stages.

Notice that the cognizance stage acts as a sort of "umbrella," with tentacles touching all the remaining model stages, which are referred to as the *core stages* or *components*. Why is this the case? Because not only does use of the model require a keen awareness of the efficacy of the communication to address the issues and opportunities identified in the conversation stage, it is also required throughout process implementation to ensure IPO calibration.

Figure 4-2: 5C LIM

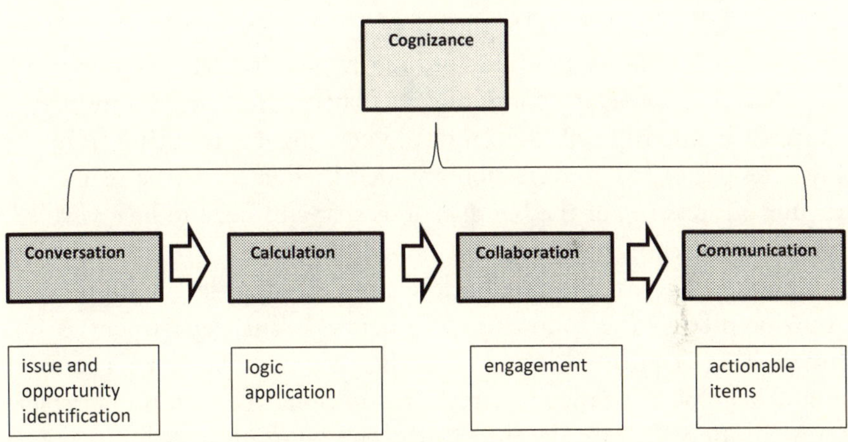

Merriam-Webster defines conversation as: "an informal talking together" (2007). We know that the IPO model begins with some sort of oral or written input followed by processing of that input before issuing the output. Just as the front end of the IPO model requires initiation from some form of interaction, so does the *conversation* stage of the 5C LIM. For example, when you receive feedback, say during a performance evaluation discussion, it initiates the conversation stage of the model. However, keep in mind that this level of conversation does not complete this stage of the model. Most often it serves only as the impetus for additional conversation, such as seeking clarification, alignment, or calibration regarding the received input.

This stage of the model can also serve to determine what can or should be done, resulting from the conversation. Figure 4-3 reflects this approach. Inasmuch as the IPO model is involved, this stage may take on macro or micro attributes.

Figure 4-3: The Conversation Stage

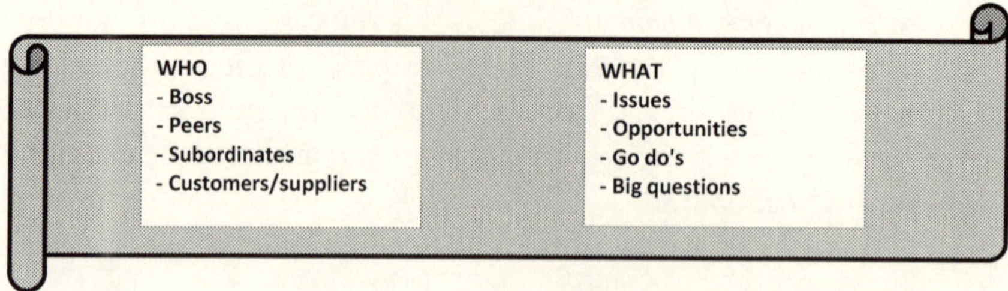

WHO
- Boss
- Peers
- Subordinates
- Customers/suppliers
WHAT
- Issues
- Opportunities
- Go do's
- Big questions

Notice the word *WHO* to the left of the scroll, which speaks to those with whom a conversation may ordinarily be initiated. Keep in mind, however, that core stage conversations may originate from a myriad of sources. To the right of the scroll, the key nuggets resulting from the initial stages of the conversation are identified, such as the issues that require addressing, or the big questions that still need to be answered, or simply the things that must be done (the *Go-d*os).

Expanding on the feedback example, suppose an employee's superior offered the following comments: "Your department is not functioning at optimal levels, resulting in a negative impact to your end-of-year performance." Certainly additional conversation, replete with questions, is in order here as the employee must drill down to a level that is actionable—in order to identify issues and opportunities. Circumstances could even dictate the need for multiple conversations before moving to the calculation stage.

Continuing with this example, let us suppose further conversation revealed that one of the opportunities identified was something easily quantified such as high error rates on reports completed in the employee's department.

Moving to the calculation stage of the model, the employee now has identified a clearly measurable opportunity on which to apply the appropriate logic aimed at some level of improvement. For example, the employee might calculate that a 10 percent reduction in error rates will result in a 20 percent reduction in time required to reprocess the reports. Figure 4-4, though not all-inclusive, conveys key characteristics contributing to the completeness of this stage. Note also that the WHAT outputs from the first stage, conversation, serve as the inputs to this stage. This output-feeds-input sequence is repeated for all the remaining core stages of the model.

Figure 4-4: The Calculation Stage

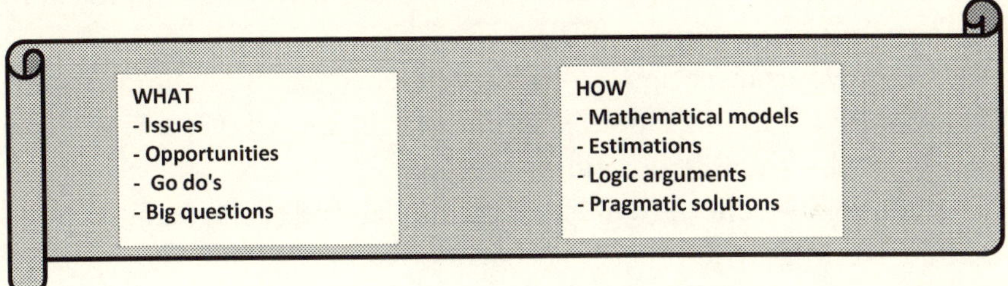

WHAT
- Issues
- Opportunities
- Go do's
- Big questions
HOW
- Mathematical models
- Estimations
- Logic arguments
- Pragmatic solutions

Merriam-Webster defines calculation as "the process or an act of calculating." *Calculate* is defined as "to determine by mathematical processes … to reckon by exercise of practical judgment … to design or adapt for a purpose by forethought or careful plan …" (2007). While mathematical approaches are most often associated with any form of calculation, as supported by the definition, we also see the significant role that judgment plays in this stage. For example, while the employee can easily calculate the effect of reduced reporting errors on rework time, it was the employee's judgment that the target of 10 percent be set. Notice also the word *Logic* in the descriptor set under the calculation block in figure 4-4. The intent here is to recognize the vital role that logical arguments play in this stage. This is not argument in the emotional sense, but in the structured sense of one of more premises followed by a logical conclusion. And while in the technical sense a premise does not have to be true for the construction of a valid argument, to achieve maximum effectiveness, the assumption in the calculation stage is that the user of the model has indeed verified, validated, or otherwise confirmed the IPO components, meaning the one doing the calculating has confirmed the premises for calculations, which are integral. The outputs from the calculation stage, indicating how issues and opportunities may be quantifiably or otherwise logically resolved, are then passed to the next core stage: collaboration.

In the chapter about performance appraisals, I mentioned the planned changes in performance management at GE. Also of note here are comments from the *Harvard Business Review.*

As managers in a large, complex organization at GE, we face a daily challenge: ensure that our employees collaborate, make quick and effective business decisions, and provide our customers with superior products and services … to cultivate empowered, collaborative, cross-functional teams, we have been experimenting with a new approach to performance development. (HBR)

I call your attention to GE's reference to "collaborate" and "collaborative," as this represents a nice transition to the next stage of the 5C LIM—the collaboration stage.

Collaboration, in the context of the model, and as the name implies, is about working with others as needed, possibly on a 360-degree basis, to develop the plan of action that may be later communicated to those responsible for its implementation. (The term 360-degree basis, used here, simply refers to one's subordinates, peers and superior.)

So why is collaboration the next stage in the model? Once the calculation stage is complete, why not forego the collaboration stage and simply demand improvement via the communication stage? Despite the unhealthy transactional nature of that approach, "collaboration offers the best chance of reaching mutually satisfactory solutions based on the ideas and interests of all parties and of maintaining and even strengthening work relationships" (Bateman & Zeithaml 1993, 489). Figure 4-5 reflects key characteristics of a complete collaboration stage.

Figure 4-5: The Collaboration Stage

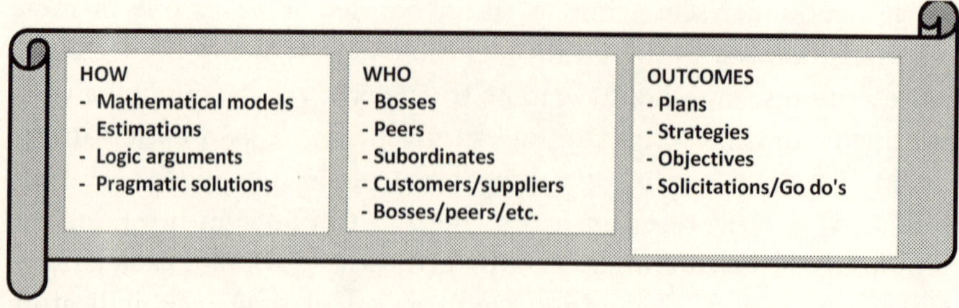

Upon receipt of the outputs from the calculation stage, key stakeholders listed under *WHO* collaborate to develop plans, strategies, objectives, solicitations, and other desired outcomes that will be shared in the next core stage.

The word *Go-dos* in the chart is a placeholder for outcomes that may not require quantification. For example, if a manager were to communicate the addition of a weekly staff meeting, as contrasted with, for instance, a reduction in headcount, this action is a go-do. The go-do items may originate during any or all the core stages.

It could be argued that collaboration is nothing more than an extension of conversation. However, while conversation may certainly serve as a first step in collaboration, it is not in itself representative of the entire collaboration stage. What is expected in the collaboration stage is a true sharing of ideas and perspectives, a sort of give and take while considering the views and interests of others rather than one's own self-interest.

Wait a minute! Regarding self-interest, you might recall that Adam Smith (renowned economist and author of *Wealth of Nations*) paved the way for self-interest and the "I" versus the "we." Does not his advancement of the "invisible hand" metaphor obviate the need for anything less than self-interest? Let us address this point by first restating that which is in question. Adam Smith stated:

It is not from the benevolence of the butcher, the brewer, or the baker, that we expect our dinner, but from their regard to their own interest … he intends his own security … he intends only his own gain, and he is in this, as in many other cases, led by an invisible hand to promote an end which was no part of his intention … by pursuing his own interest, he frequently promotes that of society more effectually than when he really intends to promote it (Smith 1776, 12–300).

Let's translate this into more contemporary jargon. The key point being made here is that, as an example, a new supermarket is not constructed close to a housing community simply to reduce the travel time of the residents there. The intent for locating the supermarket in this location is for the owner to make a profit. But in doing so, the housing community benefits, too, because its residents now spend less travel time, consume less fuel, and can spend more quality time with their families.

In business, particularly when the person directing the efforts of others must rely on others to meet critical metrics and objectives, failure to engage the team through collaborative efforts could yield disastrous results. Adept as the leader may be, having different sets of eyes and ears assist in problem resolution will always result in a better solution than going solo. Yes, this is the case despite the teeth provided by transactional methods afforded the leader aimed at forcing optimization. (Recall that XL refers to contingent rewards such as performance evaluation ratings, reduction in incentives, and bonuses.)

To illustrate this stage further, read the following statements and consider the common thread being conveyed:

- The president signed a landmark bill that will attract new businesses to the United States, resulting in tremendous positive impact to GDP.
- Peyton Manning broke the single-season passing touchdown record.
- The Tesla Motors Corporation's CEO announced the introduction of hybrid vehicles.
- Amelia Earhart was the first female aviator to fly solo across the Atlantic Ocean.
- Jack Welch increased General Electric's market capitalization by $450 billion.
- Taylor Swift released a new album that is expected to climb the charts.

On the surface, each of these statements attests to the individualism exhibited while the one doing it accomplished the unthinkable. And each of the people named should be commended. However, although each made significant contributions to history, athletics, economics, or entertainment, none of the accomplishments were actually achieved without contributions of countless others not mentioned in the statements.

Consider, for example, the president's endorsement of the business bill. Were it not for Congress and, yes, perhaps some degree of lobbying, the bill would not have made it to the signature stage. Likewise, were it not for the receivers, the offensive line, the play calling, and the team practices, it is unlikely that Peyton Manning would have set the single-season passing touchdown record. And the tremendous success realized during Jack Welch's tenure at GE could not have resulted without the support and efforts of his team. Indeed, as Jack stated in his book, "nearly everything I have done in my life has been accomplished with other people" (Welch 2001). Without teamwork and collaboration, none of the statements above would be true, and none of those achievements would have happened.

According to *Merriam-Webster* (2007), *collaboration* is defined as "the act of collaborating or a situation marked by collaborating." *Collaborate defined is:* "to jointly work with others"(146). Thus, collaboration may be viewed as the "enabler," or in more vogue terms, developing the strategy for accomplishing that which has been identified and calculated. Typically, some sort of planning (short- or long-range) comprises the output for this stage of the model. Insomuch as this stage dictates interactions beyond the person directly involved, its IPO is almost always operating at the macro level.

Communication, shown in figure 4-6, is the final core stage. Notice something familiar to the far right of the scroll. Those for whom the communication is intended may be the same people the initial conversations were held with – also serving as the impetus for implementing the model core stages. What's up with that? The answer is quite simple, actually. As an example, it is not at all uncommon to identify an issue or opportunity in the course of conversation with a boss or a subordinate, and upon identifying a solution, to return to the originator for buy-in or recommended modifications. (Recall figure 1-1: Leadership Systemization.)

Notice also in figure 4-6 the term "Quantifiable Conversion (Measures of Effectiveness)" The job is not completed with the development of plans. There also needs to be an established method for measuring the success or effectiveness of those plans, such as by time or percent improvements. For example, if the plan required development of a new product, lots of questions would remain, such as when is it to be developed, how much market share is expected, and … well, you get the point.

Figure 4-6: The Communication Stage

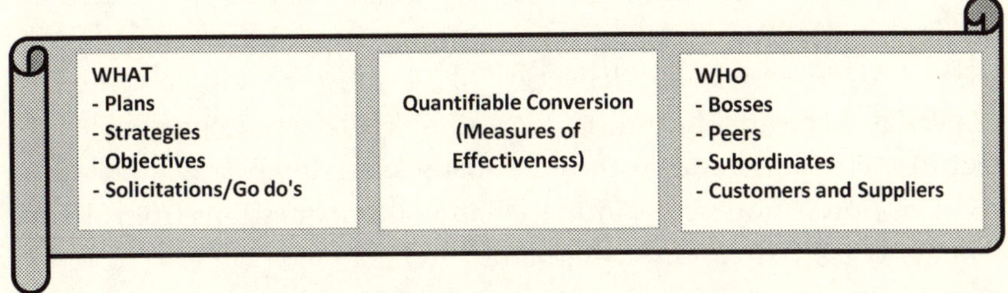

WHAT
- Plans
- Strategies
- Objectives
- Solicitations/Go do's
Quantifiable Conversion
(Measures of
Effectiveness)
WHO
- Bosses
- Peers
- Subordinates
- Customers and Suppliers

Merriam-Webster defines communication as, "an act of transmitting … information communicated … a verbal or written message … exchange of information or opinions …" (2007).

Upon completion of the collaboration stage, which may involve only key team members, what often follows is a broader conveyance of the message, whether oral, paper, or electronic. As shown in figure 4-6, the *WHO* (distribution) may include, separately or in concert, peers, subordinates, and other people, potentially including the lowest-level employees in the department or organization.

Say for example that the person delivering the message is the director or senior manager of a sales department. To facilitate this communication, someone might call a mandatory departmental meeting in a neutral forum so as not to detract from the delivery. The information disseminated might include the new sales goals, the strategy for implementation, or the sell-in plan. While the inclusion of all subordinates who must share in the message's execution in such a meeting is quite logical, it is also important to ensure that bosses and peers receive the same message.

Therefore, communication should occur on a 360-degree basis when possible. Why is this so important? The need for alignment is of the utmost importance, particularly in instances where the effect of the information shared might result in significant shifts in organizational performance. Once a communication has been delivered, it is not at all uncommon for its receivers to initiate discussions with their superiors' superiors, if for no other reason than to seek discrepancies in objectives. Likewise, it is typical for the communicator's superior to initiate discussions with those levels down in the organization in hopes of validating the success of message delivery.

Message delivery in this stage of the model is extremely important. The communicator must understand that in the purest sense, "communication is the transmission of information and meaning from one party to another through the use of shared symbols" (Bateman, & Zeithaml 1993, 503). So it's not enough to exercise verbal skills (clear and crisp message delivery). These must be supplemented by nonverbal behavior, including the use of visual restatements such as pictures, face and hand gestures, … pauses, eye focus, and concluding the communication with summaries and taking questions from anyone willing to ask (Bateman & Zeithaml 1993).

At this point, conversations to determine or confirm forward direction have been implemented, presumably with subordinates and possibly peers; necessary calculations, such as percent improvements in productivity, have been determined; and rational arguments have been constructed and delivered in a crisp, clear, and receiver centric manner. The best method for conveying a message regarding plans, objectives, or strategies remains face-to-face delivery, even in this age of technological advances in communications.

Earlier I referenced various definitions of leadership. It's time to add another, this one by Ivancevich and Matteson: "Leadership is an attempt at influencing the activities of followers through the communication process and toward attainment of some goal or goals" (1993, 438). Although communication is only one component of the 5C LIM, it is the most effective tool available to a leader.

This discussion regarding communication concludes a general discussion of the core stages of the 5C LIM. We have discussed its components assuming a sequential and standard "left to right" flow. Practically speaking, the application of these core stages is more iterative. Figure 4-7 captures this point.

Figure 4-7: Iterative Process for Core Stages

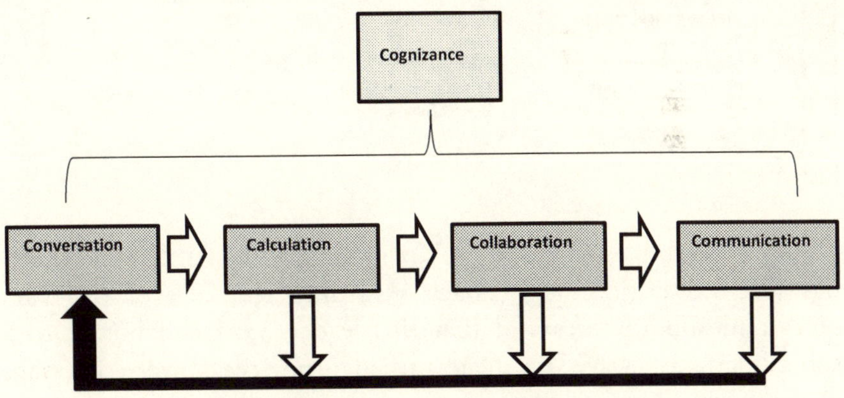

During an initial boss-subordinate conversation, certain order-of-magnitude assumptions might be made regarding operational metrics or associated opportunities. During the calculation stage, these assumptions could be refined, resulting in even greater opportunity. Likewise, execution of the calculation stage might reveal unintended consequences from prior discussions, resulting in the need for further conversation and potential adjustment, precipitating another pass through the cycle.

And if the calculation stage identifies new issues or opportunities that were not factored into the original conversation, the need for follow-up conversation becomes apparent, making it necessary to repeat the process. Likewise, when moving from calculation to collaboration, new information could surface resulting in the need to modify or rebalance the initial calculation outcomes. And once again the process will be repeated.

As a practical matter, there is also some degree of overlap in each of the core stages. For example, a leader may determine that a key message must be delivered to those engaged during the collaboration stage, as shown in figure 4-8. This key message could take the form of a tacit behavior demonstrated by the leader (such as effective listening) or more overt actions, including the leader's dissemination of a high-level plan, strategy, vision, or any other applicable message.

Figure 4-8: Collaboration Stage With Key Message Delivery

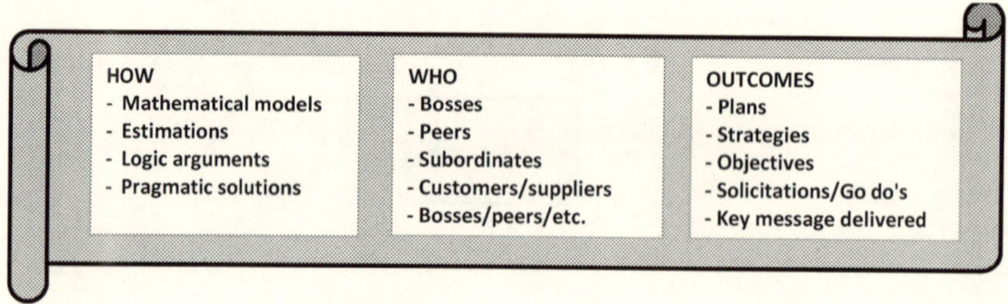

HOW
- Mathematical models
- Estimations
- Logic arguments
- Pragmatic solutions
WHO
- Bosses
- Peers
- Subordinates
- Customers/suppliers
- Bosses/peers/etc.
OUTCOMES
- Plans
- Strategies
- Objectives
- Solicitations/Go do's
- Key message delivered

As an example of offering a key message, assume that the leader has received critiquing feedback regarding the lack of inclusion of certain subordinates and that this leader must collaborate with subordinates to resolve an issue identified during the conversation stage of the model. The leader might approach the collaboration stage in a manner projecting inclusiveness, such as by prompting subordinates to volunteer suggestions and actively listening to them, or suggesting that subordinates take on new assignments. Thereby, through both verbal and nonverbal behaviors, the leader is delivering a message not simply of feedback acknowledgement, but also a desire to act on such feedback.

In the discussion of communication, the final core stage, I addressed how the message might be conveyed, how to communicate it to others, and also the overlap that may occur with collaboration. I didn't talk about effective communication in the conversation, calculation, and collaboration stages.

In order to achieve optimal execution of the conversation stage, particularly if such conversations are linked to performance, effective communication is imperative. This includes listening, reading verbal and nonverbal cues, seeking to understand, being open and honest, and finally, summarizing, thereby providing confirmation and understanding. This overlapping of communications, as well as the general overlap inherent in the model, is illustrated in figure 4-9.

Figure 4-9: Core Stage Overlap

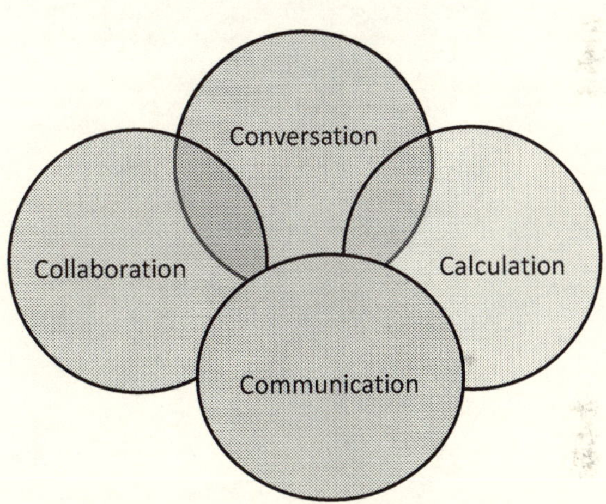

Inasmuch as it is imperative to have a keen awareness of how information is communicated, such also speaks to the more general topic, and final 5C LIM stage component: *cognizance.*

Merriam-Webster defines cognizance as "apprehension by the mind … awareness … notice, heed … particular knowledge … conscious recognition" (2007). Earlier in this chapter (in figure 4-2), we introduced cognizance under the guise of an umbrella. As we have continued to flesh out all aspects of the model, however, we have also further defined the role that cognizance plays as it interacts and cycles within the entire model. Figure 4-10 captures the enhanced 5C LIM.

Figure 4-10: Cognizance Integration

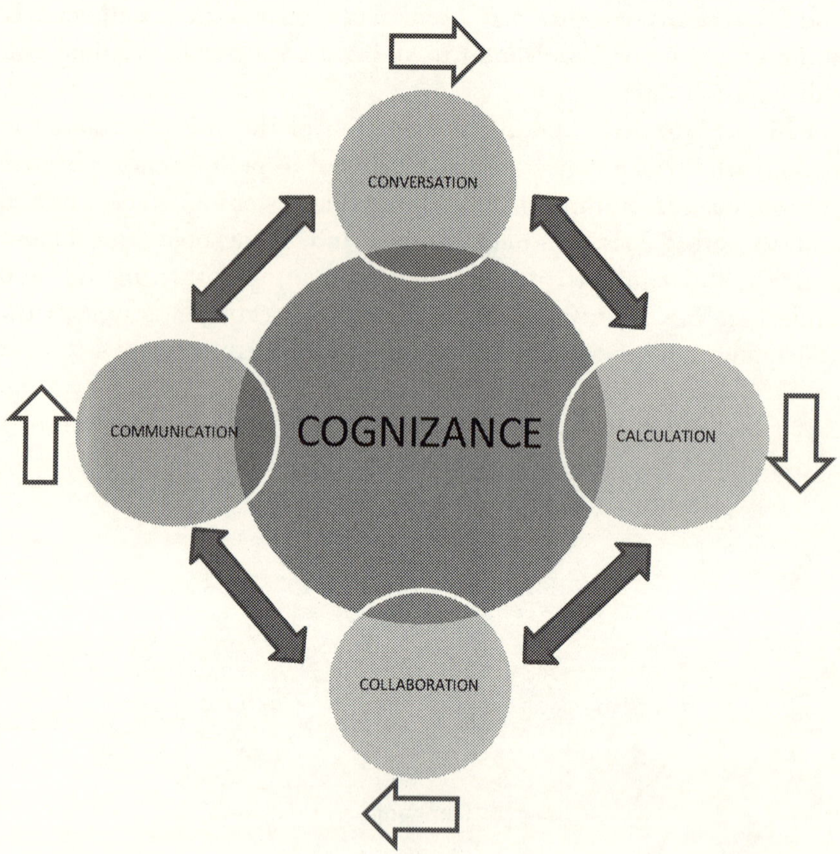

Despite the general clockwise progression of the model, and bi-directional stage-to-stage interactions, cognizance must be present in all stages of the model as reflected graphically in figure 4-10. Thus, its influence is not circumscribed by any particular stage. Being aware of communication style is imperative, and awareness is a key defining factor of cognizance. However, cognizance, in the context of the 5C LIM, also suggests a keen awareness of the efficacy of executing any of the core stages.

Let's say that the message output from the communication stage comprised the annual operations improvement plan. Let's further suppose that key goals, objectives, strategies, milestones, and metrics were included in that plan. Is it enough to simply assume that, despite the resonance of the connection made during the communication, all key milestones and metrics will be met and that no further inquiry is required on the part of the communicator?

The shrewd business leader recognizes the need for implementation of incremental awareness infrastructure in the form of monitoring and measures that enable the tracking of progress toward improvement. While there are many convenient mechanisms to accomplish this, one simple and efficient way of monitoring is a *dashboard review*. The best analogy for this approach is a vehicle dashboard. When you're driving, there is perhaps nothing more important than focusing on the road ahead. But many things vie for our time and attention during our time behind the wheel: our passengers, the vehicles in front of us, beside us, and behind us, and more. So as drivers, we need to know certain critical information about our vehicle, such as how much fuel we have, the speed we are traveling, and the engine temperature while concurrently maintaining focus on our surroundings.

This information is provided to us in a concise manner by our dashboard. Each time we glance at it, we implement a dashboard review. Compared to some earlier model vehicles, contemporary vehicle dashboards include much more information than simply fuel level or battery charge. Among contemporary automobiles, some include more information than others.

Similarly, in an organization, the dashboard review can take on as much or as little detail as necessary, which may also be a function of the audience for that dashboard. A CEO, for example, might be interested in the company sales, manufacturing costs, policy compliance, and public relations while a project manager may be interested in knowing the progress of multiple ongoing construction efforts.

As an example of the use of dashboard infrastructure for tracking, assume the following metrics were communicated in a department meeting focusing on the upcoming year:

1. Reduce overall operating supply orders by 10 percent by the end of the first quarter.
2. Reduce inventory reporting errors by 20 percent by the second quarter.
3. Improve sales in region Z by 15 percent by the third quarter.
4. Procure, install, and transition to new PCs for all employees by the fourth quarter.

Here we have two dimensions to be aware of as the year progresses. We have quantifiable requirements of "N percent," and we have time-driven milestones. What we want to do here is have some method to understand the progress or lack thereof at a glance and to provide any necessary information to the stakeholders for the deliverables that they believe to be of concern. Let's concentrate on creating a tracking mechanism for these items. We'll use a traffic light to represent progress like this:

- [R] (Red): Significant issues have surfaced that render this deliverable unachievable.
- [Y] (Yellow): Issues are on the horizon that, if not addressed, could impact the deliverable.
- [G] (Green): All aspects of the deliverable are on track, no issues identified.

The terminology used for each of the traffic light colors will vary from textbook to textbook, and it certainly isn't my aim here to reconcile the colored indicator descriptors. Likewise, those fluent in project management may recognize this approach to be similar to the standard monitoring infrastructure. The application of purest project management techniques would also include risk analysis and mitigation strategies and would focus on the relationship between scope, time, and cost. This is discussed a bit more in the next chapter, however, it is beyond the scope of this book to address project management components in detail. Additional inquiry into this area, if desired, is left to you.

Let us consider how the objectives presented above might be presented in a dashboard view using the traffic indicators. Please refer to figure 4-11 for this discussion.

Note that the dashboard has a heading labeled *Strategy*. So, what's up with that? "Although business strategy is fairly new, many of its concepts and theories have their antecedents in military strategy, which extends back to principles enunciated by Julius Caesar and Alexander the Great" (Grant 1995, 10). The strategy listed above—maximize revenues and employee effectiveness while minimizing costs—may be thought of as a means for channeling resources to execute broader business goals. Chandler, as cited by Grant, shared this perspective,

Figure 4-11: Dashboard Simulation

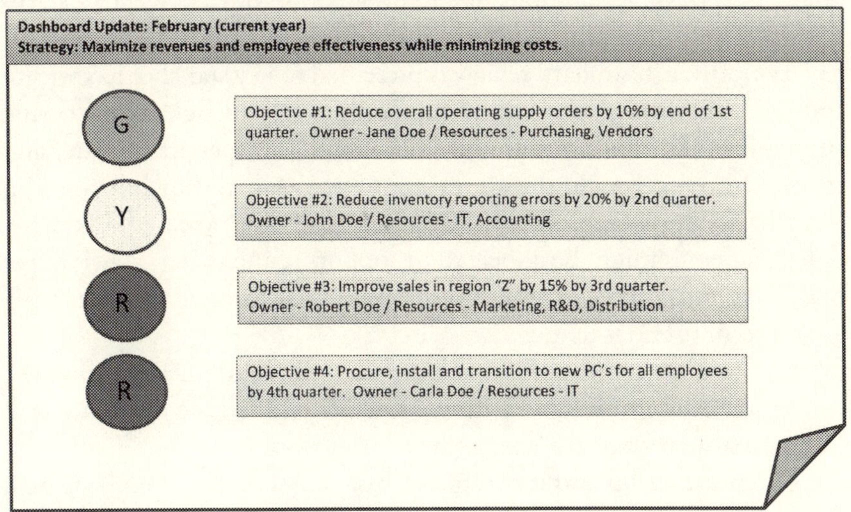

suggesting that a strategy is "the determination of the long run goals and objectives of an enterprise, and the adoption of courses of action and the allocation of resources necessary for carrying out these goals" (1995, 11).

Dashboard Update: February (current year)
Strategy: Maximize revenues and employee effectiveness while minimizing costs.
G
Objective #1: Reduce overall operating supply orders by 10% by end of 1st quarter. Owner - Jane Doe / Resources - Purchasing, Vendors
Y
Objective #2: Reduce inventory reporting errors by 20% by 2nd quarter. Owner - John Doe / Resources - IT, Accounting
R
Objective #3: Improve sales in region "Z" by 15% by 3rd quarter. Owner - Robert Doe / Resources - Marketing, R&D, Distribution
R
Objective #4: Procure, install and transition to new PC's for all employees by 4th quarter. Owner - Carla Doe / Resources - IT

Notice also the reference to resources included in the dashboard. These are the departments and areas that will be required to assist in the completion of the objective. Choosing the right resources is a critical step in the dashboard review because it allows the key stakeholders to recognize their roles in strategy execution. Focusing specifically on the internal aspects of the dashboard, we can quickly observe that all the objectives fall under a much broader strategy (maximize revenues and employee effectiveness while minimizing costs). Objective #1 is on track, with no issues identified. Objective #2 will require some intervention in order to avoid missing the target completion date. Regarding objectives #3 and #4, significant issues have surfaced that render these deliverables unachievable.

Also notice that in addition to the specific objective, an *owner* has been included. This is extremely important for several reasons. First, by allocating a name to the specific objective, the stakeholders are now able to engage with the owner in hopes of removing barriers or offering suggestions that may have otherwise been overlooked. Second, assuming that the owner was made aware of the dashboard review process, it ensures that before that review the owner had assessed all angles and possible solutions before designation of the objective status and now welcomes assistance and input from others.

Typically, a dashboard review is presented to key stakeholders within the organization with the intent of not only notifying but also garnering support for the allocation of additional resources (people, dollars, and time). On objective #3, the allocation of people could include interim increases to the sales force such that retailer calls are increased. Likewise, dollar increases might be allocated in support of increased "buy two get one" programs aimed at building product trial in hopes of increasing longer term product usage.

The reference to time is in the context of potentially extending the deliverable date, in this case, allowing Carla to shift the due date back to the first quarter of the next year.

Often the dashboard is completed by a resource designated within a department or by a central departmental resource within an organization, based on inputs received from the deliverable's owner—the owner being the person responsible for the line item. All updates are supplied by the owner and are issued to the compiling person or area, along with some sort of explanation (not shown in this example) of what factors are driving any deviation from green. It is also common for the owner of any deliverables or objectives whose status is not green, to comment in the review forum about the specifics listed in the status area (if included) and to offer suggestions on how to mitigate the deviation. It is also likely, and strongly encouraged, that the owner of any objectives that are not green will forewarn key stakeholders, informing them of the issues before the dashboard review meeting, so they won't be surprised during the meeting.

The dashboard is a powerful and robust tool for initiating post communication of key strategies, objectives, and milestones. Although it is presented here in the context of a much larger stakeholder environment, someone operating in the role of an individual contributor will also find the dashboard useful, particularly when the responsibility for multiple projects or priorities rests with a single person.

Consider, for instance, a procurement analyst who is collaborating with several vendors in an attempt to lower supply costs. Each of the objectives in the example dashboard could be supplanted by supplier targets for raw materials cost reductions. A quick analysis of the completed dashboard would facilitate necessary conversations, potentially resulting in new calculations, thereby driving the need for collaboration.

The frequency with which a dashboard review should occur is dependent on several factors, including the mean time between objective deliverable dates, the specific milestones associated with a certain objective, and the availability of key stakeholders to review the data. As an example, if a deliverable due date is one year from the current time, depending on the severity or magnitude of the deliverable, reviews occurring less than a monthly frequency may not allow sufficient time for key milestones to come to fruition. Likewise, if key stakeholders are available only quarterly, then the dashboard review frequency may be protracted accordingly, particularly in the case with long-term deliverables.

It should be obvious that the output of the 5C LIM predecessor stage in core components of the model generally serves as the input to the next. Likewise, although intended to progress in a clockwise manner, the model does not function solely in a sequential fashion. An iterative and overlapping functionality also exists. Also recall that cognizance should not simply influence the actions of each of the core stage components. Such awareness may also require implementation of applicable monitoring infrastructure such as the simulated dashboard (see figure 4-11).

Key here is that although the principal focus for the application of the 5C LIM resulted from a performance evaluation, such was intended only to offer a fundamental understanding of how each stage operates in concert with each other stage. Sources of "conversation" may include professional interactions on a 360-degree basis (between superiors, peers and subordinates).

It is important that in each instance an earnest effort be made to apply the model as designed. At a high level, the 5C LIM may be viewed as an expanded IPO model operating at the macro level whereby conversation is analogous to the input; calculation and collaboration represent the processing; and the resulting communication is considered the output. The cognizance (umbrella) stage represents an overarching component linked to, for the purpose of monitoring, each of the remaining four model stages. It seeks incessantly to adjust the output if and when required.

Earlier we discussed the 360-degree feedback form, another excellent example of the cognizance component of the 5C LIM. Through unbiased feedback, leaders become aware of how they are perceived. This knowledge may then serve as the basis for initiating the conversation stage. Being aware of their own and their subordinates' strengths and weaknesses can only make it easier for them to succeed. Therefore, cognizance serves as an enabler for acting on shortcomings (the leader's or the leader's subordinates) and for making continuous improvement of organizational infrastructure in the form of processes, people, and programs.

But wait a minute! you exclaim. What about all the leadership theory that we were forced to absorb in the earlier chapters? Where does that fit into this 5C LIM? Great question. This is a good time to bring it all together and to set the stage for the next chapter.

The role of the conversation and calculation stages, in the context of leadership, should be clear. Nothing—well almost nothing—gets done in business without a conversation, and very little else is accomplished without some sort of calculation. So let's begin by revisiting the final core stage of the model, communication. Then we'll circle back to collaboration and cognizance. Think back to an earlier reference in this chapter to leadership in the context of influence through communication. Before that, we saw that leadership was characterized as influencing others on matters of organizational relevance, which would imply that one of the principle responsibilities of a leader is to move the organization forward in a manner consistent with the best interests of the business. Also recall the Burns comments that define leadership as "leaders inducing followers to act for certain goals that represent the values and the motivations of both leaders and followers" (1979, 115).

With these comments in mind, I ask you: What better way is there to demonstrate leadership than through effective communications? Such is reflective of the common thread in these statements, and communication is certainly a critical component of the 5C LIM core stages. Regarding collaboration, Chemers (2001), as cited by Kark and Yaffe, defines leadership as "a process of social influence through which an individual enlists and mobilizes the aid of others in the attainment of a collective goal" (2011, 806). This perspective suggests that leadership involves not only the leader but also the stalwart participation of those to whom the leader is looked to for guidance and direction.

Said differently, when you consider the words *enlists* and *mobilizes*, it becomes clear that collaboration serves as a key leadership tenet and is itself a critical component of the 5C LIM.

OK, almost there.

Regarding cognizance, we saw that "[similar to] other situational or contingency leadership approaches, the path-goal attempts to predict leadership effectiveness in different [leadership] situations" (Ivancevich & Matteson 1993, 451). House and Mitchell (1974), as cited by Northouse, describe four leadership behaviors that are applicable to the path-goal theory: "directive, supportive, participative, and achievement-oriented" (2013, 139). The directive style focuses more on providing direction; the supportive and participative approaches tend to enlist collaboration from subordinates; and achievement orientation seeks to build capability among subordinates.

The key takeaway from the path-goal approach is that the leader must be fully aware of the situation at hand as well as the capability of subordinate staff, their motivational needs and the overall work environment. Additionally, cognizance (which is synonymous with awareness), is also a fundamental precept of emotional intelligence. Having an awareness of emotions (self and others), and their potential situational effects, could allow the leader to circumvent any potentially regrettable actions that may have otherwise resulted. Whether acting in a sole contributor or leadership capacity, with such awareness you will understand the relationship between your feelings and your performance. It is only after you are in tune with your emotions, having self-awareness, that you will be able to self-manage and subsequently resonate with others. This perspective is shared by Boyatzis et al. in the following statement: "self-awareness also plays a crucial role in empathy or sensing how someone else sees a situation" (2002, 30). And, of course, cognizance permeates the entire 5C LIM.

So, there you have it, the link between the 5C LIM and leadership theory. The foregoing discussion provides an excellent means for transitioning to practical application. The next several chapters offer insights that show how the 5C LIM may be used to change employee narratives presented in chapter 3, "The Corporation Speaks." You will also be exposed to more detailed theoretical leadership methods for responding to performance feedback.

TL is widely recognized as being a highly effective leadership style. With this in mind, missed opportunities in leadership will be discussed relative to this style. Perhaps the best approach for processing the model application is for you to identify with the one or two scenarios that most closely relate to your current environment or circumstances and to consider how implementation of the 5C LIM might modify your own narrative.

CHAPTER 5

The Buck Stops Here—Jessica Wright

ALTHOUGH THE IMPETUS for initiating the 5C LIM discussed in this and subsequent chapters is the performance appraisal, it is only one of many situations in which the model may be used. Many persons may even find the model useful in circumstances having nothing at all to do with the corporate environment.

We begin this chapter with discussions regarding how Jessica Wright uses the 5C LIM to get her edge back. Recall the extreme disappointment Jessica felt, driven not only by her performance rating, but also the shortened review and the unexpected observation of her peer's performance ratings. Despite the primal nature of emotions precipitated by the conversation with her boss, to Jessica's credit, while processing the inputs, she remained very much cognizant of such emotions (self-awareness). This, in turn, allowed her to manage (self-regulate) her output response. Thus, she was able to remain focused and objective throughout the conversation stage of the model. (The theory behind Jessica's emotionally intelligent behavior is explained in section 1.4.)

Before I discuss Jessica's application of the 5C LIM infrastructure, it may be helpful to review and disaggregate manufacturing and warehousing operations. While the manner in which consumer product organizations execute various processes required to bring a product to finished form may differ, this discussion focuses on some of the key process fundamentals.

Let us assume that you would like to sell your consumer food product in a retail grocery store such as Kroger or a convenience store such as 7-Eleven or a fueling station such as Wawa or BP. The process begins with identifying suppliers from which you purchase your raw ingredients. If your finished product is a candy bar, you might purchase some form of chocolate or other flavoring from a flavor supplier, you might purchase sugar from another supplier, you might purchase wrapping and packaging materials from another supplier, and the cases for shipping the finished product might be purchased from another supplier. Likewise, the equipment required to combine the raw materials to form a consumable good (the candy bar with peanuts in this scenario) as well as the same to subsequently wrap and package the finished goods in cases (finished product) would also be purchased. (Not all corporations manufacture their products; some purchase the contract manufacturing of such products.) The finished and cased product would then be moved to warehousing (inventory storage) for distribution to the desired retailer (in this scenario Kroger or Wawa). The sequence of operations by which the raw materials are converted to a product ready for shipment may also be termed the *production*. Figure 5-1 pictures the process of converting raw materials using the inputs, processing, and outputs analogy.

Figure 5-1: Product Conversion Analogy for Candy Bar

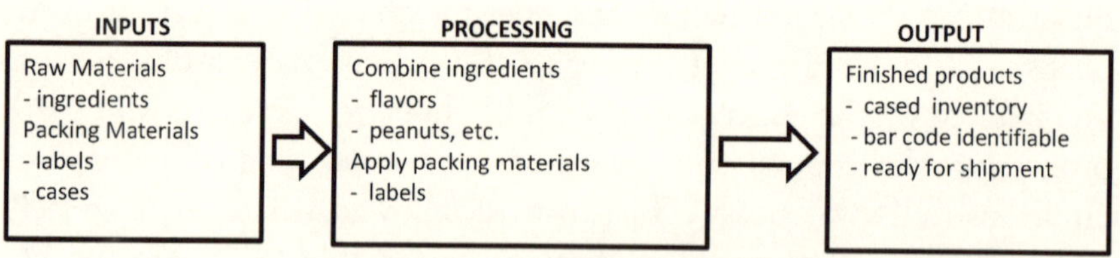

Typically, departments required to accomplish the steps as presented in figure 5-1 include a materials receiving and storage department, a processing and manufacturing department (often the raw materials require some level of processing before being routed to manufacturing for packaging), and an inventory storage department.

The scheduling department is usually responsible for determining the most efficient manner in which to run (manufacture) multiple products, also referred to as stock keeping units (SKUs). Schedule optimization may include allocating the production of certain SKUs to certain types of machines. For example, if one machine can produce one hundred candy bars per hour and another can produce only fifty per hour, it would be most efficient to produce the highest volume (driven by consumer demand for the product) on the machine that produces the greatest number of candy bars in a given amount of time. Thus, the equipment utilization is maximized.

Aimed at assuring the quality of the product manufacture, a quality assurance (QA) department is also usually present throughout the process from materials receiving to final product storage. The QA department may implement certain quality and process checks in each of the process stages and may also provide compliance protocols that must be adhered to by all departments and process stages. The end goal of the QA contribution is to assure the final product quality (as measured by the end user or consumer).

The research and development (R&D) department often develops new products and manufacturing specifications. Adhering to these assures that what is made meets consumer preferences. In most manufacturing companies, the engineering and technical departments are responsible for designing new, more efficient equipment and processes; maintenance of the existing processes; and, when necessary, resolving processing and manufacturing equipment issues.

In some organizations, certain engineering services are provided by means of procured (outsourced) resources that are managed by internal project leaders or coordinators. Departments such as finance and safety provide reporting and analysis in support of manufacturing operations. The information technology department (IT), which is similar to the engineering department, provides and maintains necessary technology-based infrastructure such as inventory management, production data, and internal communications media, also in support of manufacturing operations.

Throughout manufacturing, various salaried employees, including supervisors, engineers, and analysts, both exempt and nonexempt, and also hourly employees—operators, skilled craftsmen, and miscellaneous workers—all work in concert to deliver the finished product.

Now that you are an expert in the manufacturing operations process, we can turn our attention to figure 5-2. This shows how Jessica began to update the first stage of the 5C LIM (the conversation stage) that resulted from her meeting with her boss, Art. Recall that several action items were supplied by Art, including leadership opportunities, the 10 percent reduction in budgeted costs, operations productivity improvements and a reduction in consumer complaints.

Just as the front end of the IPO model requires initiation from some form of interaction, so does the conversation stage of the 5C LIM. For example, Jessica's receipt of feedback from her performance discussion with her boss initiated the conversation stage of the model. However, keep in mind that this level of conversation may not complete this stage of the model. It most often only serves as the impetus for additional conversation, such as seeking clarification, alignment, or calibration regarding the received input. This stage of the model can also serve in determining what can or should be done as a result of the conversation.

Figure 5-2: Jessica's Conversation Stage Scroll

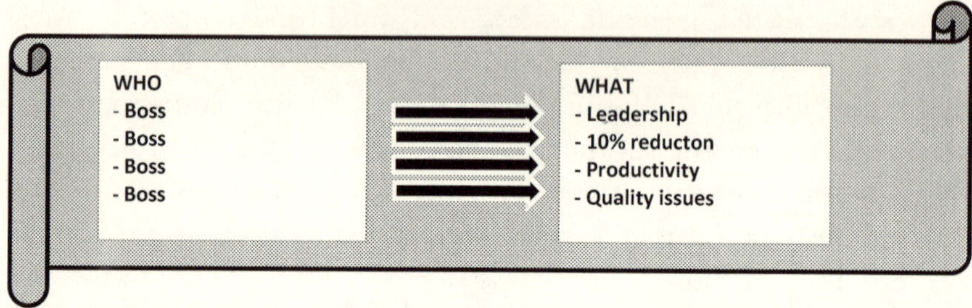

During the initial presentation of the conversation stage scroll (see figure 4-3 of the previous chapter), various *whos* and *whats* were discussed in an effort to reflect the types of items that may be allocated to each of the respective sections, with no direct column-to-column or row-to-row relationship suggested. In application, however, indeed such a relationship exists as shown in figure 5-2.

The significance of the four right-pointing arrows is that each of the items on the left (input) section of the scroll maps (corresponds) to the section and respective item listed on the right (output) side of the scroll. For example, Leadership listed in the WHAT section of the scroll was identified by the Boss, as shown in the WHO section of the scroll. In this case, all the items listed in the WHAT section were identified by Jessica's boss. However, if the quality issues had been identified by someone else, such as the QA manager, then QA Manager, the source of the issue, would replace Boss in the fourth position under the WHO section. In the spirit of simplicity, the mapping arrows are not shown in subsequent scrolls.

Notice the terseness of the opportunities and issues listed under the WHAT section of the scroll. This is by design, as these will be fleshed out by the work to be done in the calculation stage. Recall also that the functionality of the model is that the outputs from one stage become the inputs for the subsequent stage. So Jessica has enough information to move to the calculation stage, seen in figure 5-3.

Figure 5-3: Jessica's Calculation Stage Scroll

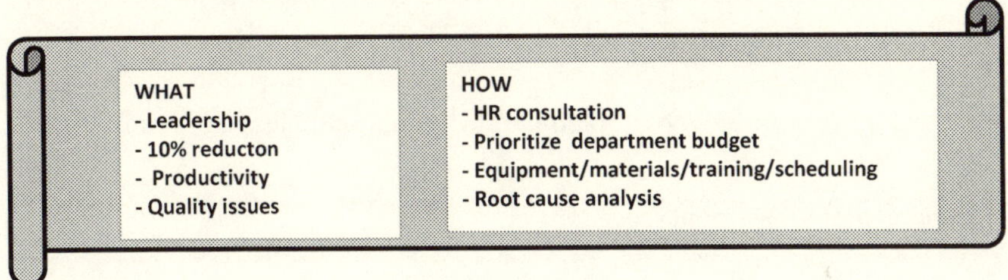

WHAT
- Leadership
- 10% reducton
- Productivity
- Quality issues
HOW
- HR consultation
- Prioritize department budget
- Equipment/materials/training/scheduling
- Root cause analysis

Recall that, the output from this stage may be several actions to be taken to the collaboration stage that, when implemented, are expected to resolve the current stage inputs. Additionally, the collaboration stage often serves as an extension of the calculation stage inasmuch as logical, mathematical, or other calculative approaches are implemented that are aimed at resolving items identified in the HOW section of the calculation stage. Regarding the WHAT item Leadership, recall that not all issues that move into the calculation stage will be as quantifiable as say a 10 percent budget reduction, and that the intent of this stage is not to simply apply mathematical or other deductive logic, but to consider pro and con arguments and possible approaches aimed at addressing any item identified in the conversation stage.

Although the 360-degree feedback was suggested by her boss, Jessica, recalling the memo issued by the company regarding TL, wanted to bring about profound and lasting change to her area of responsibility and, in particular, with her direct reports. Consequently, she collaborated with her Human Resources (HR) support representative (Sylvia) in an effort to identify a plan of attack. Based on Jessica's discussions with Sylvia, the recommended assessment tool for leadership assessment is the MLQ as was referenced in chapter 1. Sylvia issued the MLQ on Jessica's behalf to all subordinates. (See appendices A–D for details regarding the validity, use, and reliability of this tool.)

Jessica calculated carefully the timing for issuance of the MLQ. She set up a staff meeting for the following week that included her direct reports and support team members where they would discuss operations performance. She said that, where applicable, a consensus-driven approach would be taken during the discussion.

5.1 Leadership Reflection

To complement the MLQ rater feedback, Jessica also received the supplemental leadership feedback shown in figure 5-4.

Figure 5-4: MLQ Supplemental Feedback for Jessica Wright

Supplemental Assessment Questions:

1. What are two or three things that would help this person be more efficient?

Share the vision.

Encourage us based on things that are working

Take time to listen to our ideas

2. One thing that gets in the way of this person's effectiveness is:

Too much delegation with no direction

Lack of engagement of team members

3. What I admire most about this person's leadership:

Extremely bright

Excellent communicator

A review here suggests that Jessica might do well to not only interact with her team more but also to encourage and act as a visionary. The feedback also reveals some key strengths for Jessica that she might use to shore up some of the identified opportunities. Regarding the MLQ rater feedback, Jessica was rated the lowest in the area of *inspirational motivation* (IM). (This is detailed in appendix D.) However, leaders who exhibit this attribute "behave in ways that motivate those around them by providing meaning and challenge" (Avolio & Bass 2004, 103).

On a scale from 1–4, where 1 is the lowest and 4 is the highest, Jessica received an average rating of 1.5 in the area of IM. A look at the norm table in appendix C ("percentiles for individual scores based on lower level ratings") reveals that a score of 1.5 for IM is at the fifth percentile, meaning 5 percent of the normed population scored lower, and 95 percent scored higher than 1.5. This result along with the supplemental feedback suggests that in the upcoming meeting, Jessica has the opportunity to respond to the feedback, not in a retaliatory sense, but in a way that demonstrates the leadership desired by her direct reports.

Another area of concern was reflected in Jessica's score of 2.0 in the area of *management-by-exception passive* (MBEP), which corresponded to the ninetieth percentile. Leaders exhibiting this attribute "[are] more passive and 'reactive' [and they] do not respond to situations and problems systematically" (Avolio & Bass 2004, 103). A score in the ninetieth percentile means that 90 percent of the normed population scored lower than her, and 10 percent scored higher. In this instance, a lower percentile rating score is better, pointing to another significant leadership opportunity for Jessica. This MBEP perspective was supported by some of the comments provided in the supplemental feedback offered by Jessica's direct reports.

Turning now to Jessica's calculative approach for the upcoming meeting, as for the quantifiable opportunities to be addressed, she believes that the best approach for resolution is to revisit the department budget on a line-item basis in hopes of identifying cost elimination opportunities. She prefers not to resort to headcount reduction as a means for achieving the 10 percent goal. As for productivity, she feels strongly that some of the recently installed high-speed manufacturing equipment is not meeting its budgeted objectives, resulting in reduced output per shift, increased waste, and longer-than-anticipated changeover times. Further, she believes that the current production schedule can be optimized to reduce the product changeover frequency and waste.

Going into the collaboration stage, Jessica prepared the scroll as shown in figure 5-5. Because the collaboration with HR occurred ahead of meeting with the remaining individuals, sharing assessment results is included as an OUTCOME. This is perfectly acceptable given the calculative nature of the timing for issuing the MLQ rater forms. This sequence is also consistent with the designed sequence of the 5C LIM.

Figure 5-5: Jessica's Collaboration Stage Scroll

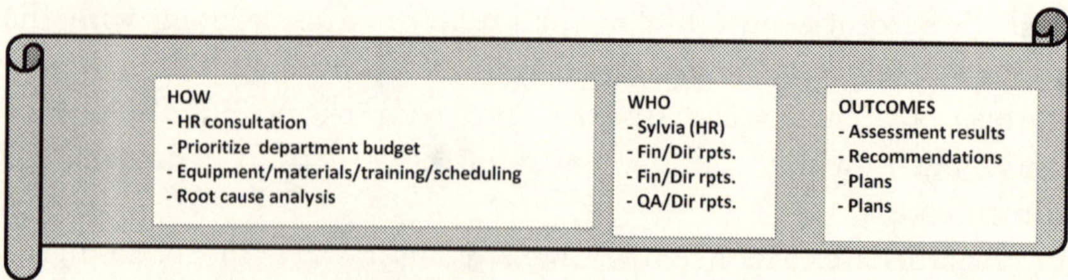

HOW
- HR consultation
- Prioritize department budget
- Equipment/materials/training/scheduling
- Root cause analysis
WHO
- Sylvia (HR)
- Fin/Dir rpts.
- Fin/Dir rpts.
- QA/Dir rpts.
OUTCOMES
- Assessment results
- Recommendations
- Plans
- Plans

It is always better to write resource names (or titles) next to incoming action items. This is better for two reasons: First, it encourages the stage owner to fully consider available resources; second, it's more efficient because you should not include unnecessary resources as you move into the collaboration stage. The outcomes from this stage are simply the desired deliverables based on the stage inputs. Further interpreting the scroll, Sylvia (representing the HR department) is listed specifically to assist in compiling the MLQ assessment results. Support resources from the finance department (Fin) as well as Jessica's direct reports (Dir rpts) and the QA representative, will assist in providing the remaining OUTCOMES as indicated.

It is a common practice to enter the collaboration stage intending to develop a plan of attack for one or more of the outcomes that includes input from all key sources. According to Avolio and Bass: "the need to promote change and to deal with resistance to it has, in turn, led to an emphasis on democratic, participative, relations-oriented, and considerate leadership" (2004, 19). Collaborating with others, including subordinates and peers, to develop a plan aimed at changing and improving operational efficiencies is not optional.

5.2 The Meeting

We now turn our attention to the meeting regarding prioritization of the department budget. Present in this meeting are Jessica, her direct reports, the on-site finance manager, and the QA manager. At the beginning of the meeting, Jessica summarized the MLQ and supplemental question feedback, focusing on themes instead of specifics.

Receiving feedback in itself can be difficult to endure, particularly when it's provided by those whom the leader is appointed to guide, coach, and otherwise mentor. The reactions to such feedback might include denial and extreme disappointment. Yet, as we learned earlier in this book, EI suggests that as leaders we must recognize our feelings (being self-aware) and regulate our responses—in this case, focus on the message instead of the messenger. Self-awareness enables the leader to empathize with the sender of feedback. It is in this context that transformational leaders are able to look past the superficial nature of feedback, recognize its constructive value, and make use of it, not only for personal development, but for the growth and development of those providing the feedback as well.

Upon completion of the feedback summary, Jessica circumvented what might have been an unpleasant environment resulting from her review of the results by saying: "Well, team, the good news is that I scored higher in the key TL attribute of inspirational motivation than 5 percent of those tested." The team all laughed at that, Jessica thanked them for the feedback, and the meeting moved forward beginning with a review of the operations budget.

While it is beyond the scope of this writing to offer a comprehensive explanation of budget construction, aimed at ensuring appropriate understanding of Jessica's work in this example, we begin with some general budget related definitions—Accounting 101.

All organizations use some form of budgeting. Indeed, if you are an employee, your annual salary and that of your peers, bosses, and any subordinates are *rolled up* to someone's budget. In fact, every asset that is used to operate a company is included in a budget. Kell, Kieso, and Weygandt define a budget as "a formal written summary (or statement) of management's plans for a specific future time period expressed in financial terms" (1990, 1031).

Of particular note here is that budgets typically reflect an annual period, but, as the period proceeds, changes to the budget may be necessary, resulting in budget revisions. For example, if your company decides to increase its salaried workforce after the original budget has been prepared, the increases would be reflected in the budget revision. Depending on your company's practice, several budget revisions, or at minimum solicitations for these revisions, might be required. There are also various budget components (or costs) that may fall into *fixed, variable, capital*, or other categories.

Defined specifically: "fixed costs are costs that remain the same in total regardless of changes in activity level [while] variable costs are costs that vary in total directly and proportionately with changes in the activity level" (Kell et al. 1990, 877–78). Examples of fixed costs include property taxes, insurance, rent, and depreciation. Depending upon the operation, they may also include management salaries. Examples of variable costs include the materials required to make a product (such as the materials that Jessica's department uses to manufacture Summit's Products) as well as the costs for labor required by the manufacturing workers to convert raw materials to finished products.

The general idea and the purpose for going into business is that profits will be made and continue to increase over time. Therefore, it may be necessary to expand to accommodate increased customer or consumer demand. When such growth requires the addition of incremental capacity, or when other operating efficiency improvements are required, these costs are typically categorized as capital costs (Kells et al., 1990).

There are also fixed and variable costs and how they relate to *cost per unit.* Assume that the total fixed cost for Jessica's area of responsibility is $125 million and that the total annual output from manufacturing operations was 100 million units. The fixed cost per unit would actually be $125 million per 100 million units, which equals $1.25 per unit. This key metric is often used to determine how much of the fixed costs is spread across the product mix. The goal, of course, is to increase the units produced (and presumably sold) such that the fixed cost per unit decreases. It should be apparent that any increase in fixed costs, such as increasing salaried employees, also increases the fixed cost per unit, assuming that the output remains constant.

Regarding variable cost per unit, let us assume that the manufacturing operations requires $0.50 for purchase of direct materials (packaging materials) and $0.90 for purchase of manufacturing labor for every unit produced, totaling $1.40 per unit. In this example, $140 million would be expended to produce 100 million units. Another way of looking at this is that for every unit produced, the cost is $1.40. As was the case with fixed cost per unit, the goal would be to produce (and presumably sell) as many units as possible while minimizing the costs of doing so.

So if the per-unit cost for direct materials could be reduced by say 20 percent (from $0.50 to $0.40), the new cost would be $1.30 per unit, and at 100 million units, total expenditures would equal $130 million, for a savings of $10 million.

Regardless of the products involved—human consumable products, such as those manufactured by Summit Consumables, or inconsumable products, such as cars produced by Tesla motors—the principles of calculating cost per unit are the same.

While it is beyond the scope of this writing to provide a comprehensive review of production processes and the respective costs therein, I would be remiss if I did not refer to the *economic production function*. According to Baye and Beil, "the production function is an engineering relation that defines the maximum amount of output that can be produced with a given set of inputs [and] mathematically, the production function is denoted as Q = F(K, L) that is, the maximum amount of output that can be produced with K units of capital and L units of labor" (1994, 155). I encourage you to review this or similar economic data at your leisure for a better understanding of the relationship between inputs (e.g., raw materials) and outputs (e.g., finished products).

Now that we have covered the fundamental aspects of budgeting, let us return to Jessica's scenario. One input to the collaboration stage is the need for a recommendation for prioritizing the operating budget in search for cost reduction opportunities of 10 percent. Prior to conducting a meeting with her direct reports, and during the calculation stage, Jessica printed off a copy of the department's fixed cost operating budget for the last three years, shown in figure 5-6. One of the things that stood out in her mind was from year 1 to year 3, the purchased services costs had doubled from $4 million to over $8 million.

Purchased services are those that a company gets from outside rather than using internal resources, such as janitorial and consulting services.

During the collaboration stage with her direct reports (in this case a meeting), Jessica pointed to the significant deviation in the budget and inquired regarding the respective driver. Upon completion of the discussion, it was determined that the purchased services cost resulted from headquarters' engagement of a consultant who committed to reduce total cost by 10 percent within one year. The cost for the consultant was transferred to Jessica's budget, but no additional money was transferred to cover this incremental cost. In addition, upon further

Figure 5-6: Three-Year Operating Budget

OPERATING BUDGET ($'s - millions)			
	Year 1	Year 2	Year 3
SALARIES	40	42	43
BENEFITS	60	63	64.5
PURCHASED SERVICES	4	8	8.25
OPERATING SUPPLIES	0.38	0.4	0.42
TRAVEL & SEMINARS	0.2	0.1	0.05
DEPRECIATION	10	12	13

inquiry, Jessica learned that the employees working for the consultant were not actually working on cost reduction activities because they were being used by Jessica's department to assist with the sudden increase in administrative and other duties, some of which resulted from R&D's efforts to get new products into the market, poor documentation to support the modernization project, and mandated process changes associated with records retention.

You may have already recognized that in the purest sense of the 5C LIM, Jessica should have been aware of the budget increase resulting from the consultant cost transfer. This lack of awareness mirrored some of the feedback received as per the MLQ supplemental questions.

Aware now of a key budget opportunity, Jessica proceeded to discuss equipment, scheduling, training, and materials. Summarizing the discussions in these areas, Jessica's production managers pointed out that, resulting from the complex mix of product that had to be run, the machines were difficult to set up. And once the production operators figured out how to set up the machines, the schedule changed again, requiring them to change the machine over for a different product. So there was little opportunity to optimize the running machines. Because the machines were not set up correctly, wrapping materials were being wasted at astronomical levels.

One supervisor reported that on her shift alone, over $10,000 worth of materials had to be disposed of due to poor machine setup during the first hour of the shift. It was also pointed out that none of the installed equipment was meeting its forecasted start-up production level. Moreover, the machines that had been placed into ongoing production were not meeting plan goals either.

Figures 5-7 and 5-8 appear to support the perspective of Jessica's direct reports regarding equipment output and material waste versus the budget. In figure 5-7, it is clear that the production output (actual) versus the planned output (budgeted) was much less. Whereas the budgeted output after four shifts was expected to be 4,000 units, the actual output was less than 2,000 units. Recalling the previous discussion regarding variable costs, based on Jessica's departmental budget, for every unit miss in output, the cost impact is $100, which is substantial.

Figure 5-7: Production Output

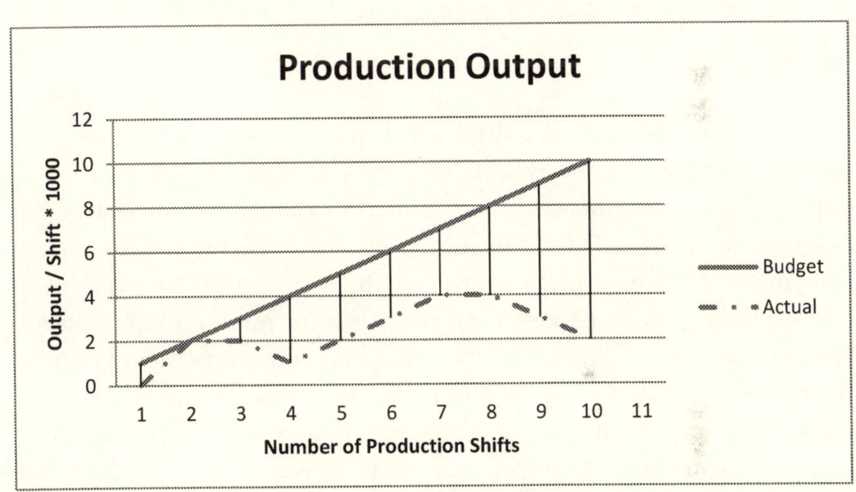

In figure 5-8, actual material waste levels exceed the amount budgeted by a significant margin. We see that while the budgeted waste level at seven shifts of operating is three trucks, the actual level was closer to nine trucks. For each truck of waste deviation from the budgeted amount, the resulting cost impact is $100,000. As shown, the deviation is close to 6 trucks, which equates to approximately $600,000.

Jessica's next objective was to get a better understanding of quality complaint issues, which had increased precipitously over the last few months.

Some discussion about consumer complaints and product quality is warranted.

Figure 5-8: Material Waste

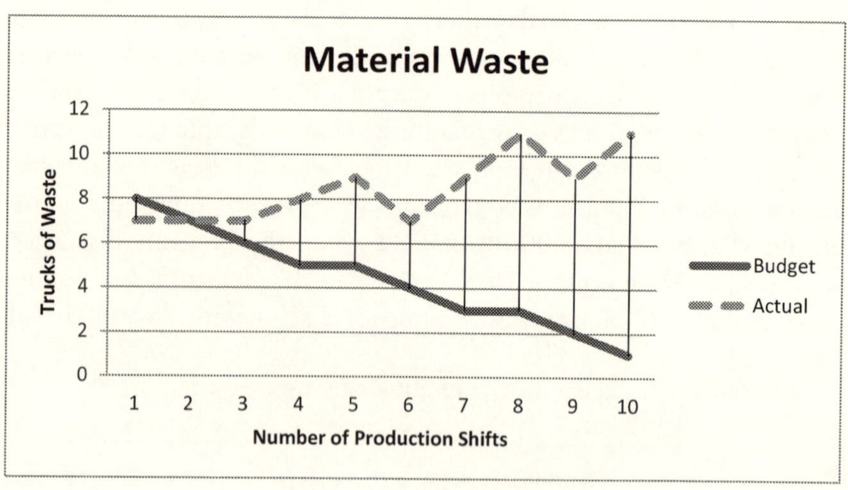

First, finished product complaints typically originate from the *end user*, also known as the *consumer*. On purchased products, an 800 number is typically included on the label to enable you to contact the manufacturer. Often a mailing address is also included for consumers who prefer to mail a complaint, and there may also be a company website listing. Perhaps you have made use of one or more of these contact avenues to file a complaint with some product's manufacturer. By the way, the technical difference between a *consumer* and a *customer* is that a consumer is someone who buys a product that may be consumed (e.g., chocolate bars); a customer is someone who buys a product that cannot be consumed, such as an iPhone (unless you are an electronic-instrument-eating robot). I use the word *technical* here because often the two words *consumer* and *customer* are used interchangeably.

So what's the big deal with product quality complaints? Well, since you asked, poor quality equates to lost consumers or customers, which in turn translates to lost revenues—something that Summit Consumables can hardly stand to experience at this point.

In addition to consumer-to-manufacturer contact, there is also *word-of-mouth* contact that occurs on a consumer-to-consumer or customer-to-customer basis. And even though this sort of contact may not find its way to the product manufacturer, its impact is quite relevant and cannot be overstated. In fact, "market research done by Ford showed that a happy customer tells on average eight people the good news about the product, but a dissatisfied customer tells on average more than twenty people of the ordeal with the product" (Aguayo 1990, 14). Bottom line: finished product quality is the voice of the manufacturer and for most consumers or customers the only voice that is ever heard.

OK, enough with the tirade. Let's return to Jessica's approach to fleshing out the quality issue. Having worked closely with the QA manager before the meeting and doing root cause analysis, which is "a problem solving process for conducting an investigation into an identified, incident concern or nonconformity" (Bhattacharya 2014, 12), Jessica identified the complaint sources shown in figure 5-9.

Figure 5-9: Consumer Complaints as a Function of Machines

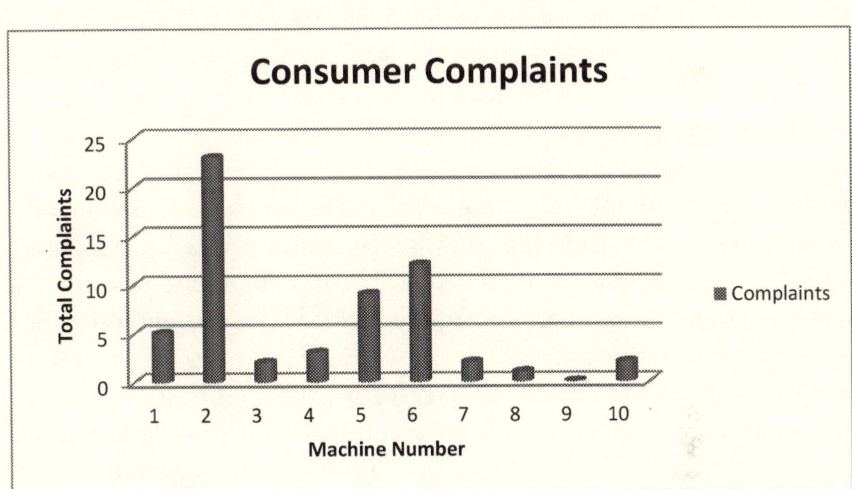

It is clear from figure 5-9 that the machines contributing the most to consumer complaints received are #2, #5, and #6. While the others made some minor contribution, the ones cited here represent by far the greatest opportunity. You may recognize this sort of bar chart as a form of Pareto analysis, which is somewhat correct, though I have more to say on this later.

During the meeting, Jessica did not direct her team to resolve the issues serving as collaboration outcomes. Instead, she sought to understand the source of the issues. This worked well for all items except the budget prioritization exercise. Here, her subordinates were not at all interested in pursuing headcount reductions to achieve the 10 percent reduction. At the same time, they did not want to eliminate the use of the consultant employees to assist with administrative duties.

Upon returning to her office and considering the rich discussion that took place in the meeting, Jessica contemplated the development of objectives that would be shared with her entire department later, during execution of the communication stage of the 5C LIM.

The first item to be addressed was the plan for the 10 percent budget reduction. Based on Jessica's conversation with the consultant, she felt confident that the targeted operations budget cost reduction of 10 percent (which the consultant had been contracted to figure out) was doable. She also believed this to be in addition to any productivity improvements achieved by her team. So although no team consensus was agreed on budget reduction, Jessica believed that the best approach was to refocus the consultant on the deliverable he was getting paid to bring about. Jessica recognized the merit of comments received regarding the increased administrative load placed on her team and recalled that her MLQ results suggested opportunities in the areas of listening to her direct reports and sharing the vision. So she desired to have a visible role in solving this budget reduction problem. Consequently, in addition to refocusing the consultants, Jessica decided to assign her special projects coordinator to determine the magnitude of increased workload due to administrative requirements. Having recently attended a seminar detailing aspects of the GE Work-Out process, she contacted a consultant versed in the area to assist her special projects coordinator in identifying and recommending the elimination of unnecessary work.

What is the GE Work-Out process? Great question! To summarize: It began with Jack Welch, then the CEO of General Electric, having meetings with some of the frontline workers in a town hall setting that excluded the employees' managers. During the meetings, employees pointed out that they had answers aimed at resolving quality and performance issues, but their suggestions were falling on deaf ears. When Jack asked the management team about this problem, they responded that due to reduced management staff, their concentration was on getting the same amount of work done that was present when the management staff was double its current size. They also said that when time allowed them to follow up on an improvement idea or suggestion, the chain of approval for resources (people, money, and so on) and the amount of paperwork that had to be completed were too onerous to take on.

A specific work-out opportunity, documented by Ashkenas, Kerr & Ulrich, was as follows:

> The product development teams were spending half of each month preparing for or conducting review meetings [with] different functions [manufacturing, marketing, product management, engineering and more], instead of working on new products … and each one required separate preparation and follow-up (2002, 17).

By combing these reviews (eliminating unnecessary work), valuable time was recovered that could be used to develop products. The work-out process was not limited to eliminating bureaucracy. Indeed, Jack "challenged everyone to use work-out to address more fundamental business processes such as order entry, product development, customer service, and collections" (Ashkenas et al. 2002).

So how exactly does this process work? It all begins with getting those closest to and most knowledgeable about a process in the same room to discuss what can and should be done differently. But the team's role does not end by simply raising an idea or concern. The development of a solution, often a more efficient way of doing business, is also brought forward.

The format for a typical express work-out process execution includes 1) identification of the problem to be addressed; 2) the impact of the problem; 3) the desired improvement; 4) the new plan for execution; 5) responsibility—who must modify their current activity; 6) participation—who must participate in plan execution; and 7) owner—who will own the plan's execution (Ashkenas et al., 2002).

Albeit brief and at the risk of oversimplifying, the preceding comments provide key components of the work-out process implementation. For a more comprehensive explanation, I encourage you to read *GE Work-Out*. (See the citation in the *References* section of this book.)

Let's return to Jessica as she continues to construct her departmental objectives. She believed it would be a good idea to personally champion the effort to consolidate R&D new product requirements and specifications, thereby resulting in a more predictable production run schedule. As reflected by the monitoring (dashboard) infrastructure shown in figure 5-10, Jessica included owners for each of the key operational objectives, which were aimed at resolving the quantifiable outcomes that she discussed during the collaboration stage meeting.

The key to developing an efficient objectives-based dashboard is the manner in which objectives are set. To this end, according to Armstrong, "many organizations use the SMART mnemonic to summarize the desirable characteristics of an objective [where the acronym is delineated]

- S = Specific/stretching—clear, unambiguous, straight forward, understandable and challenging
- M = Measurable—quantity, quality, time, money
- A = Achievable—challenging but within the reach of a competent and committed person
- R = Relevant—relevant to the objectives of the organization so that the goal of the individual is aligned to corporate goals
- T = Time-framed—to be completed within an agreed upon timescale" (2009, 100).

Having selected an approach for budget reduction of 10 percent (by means of the consultant), next on the list was to quantify the impact of the increased administrative load as indicated. Turning to material waste, Jessica reasoned that this issue should be addressed by working closely with both the engineering team and the scheduling department. She also believed that any attempt to fully resolve the issues should include those closest to and most knowledgeable about the issue, so she assigned her first shift production manager to work with the scheduling and engineering groups. In addition, she identified resources from the hourly workforce (production operators and maintenance support) to participate on the team, as reflected in the dashboard seen in figure 5-10.

The next area of opportunity was in consumer complaints. Although the QA manager did not report directly to Jessica, she recognized the value added by having him in the loop and therefore included him as a key resource in the dashboard. The overall owner for this objective was her second shift production manager, assisted by members of the production workforce.

In addition to the dashboard constructed to monitor certain critical objectives with defined timelines, Jessica also recognized the need to implement a dashboard she could refer to on an ongoing basis. She referred to this as her personal operations-wide dashboard. The key question that she had to address before its implementation was: What were the critical manufacturing operations metrics that may or may not have been addressed in her objectives-based dashboard?

Figure 5-10: Jessica's Objectives-Oriented Dashboard

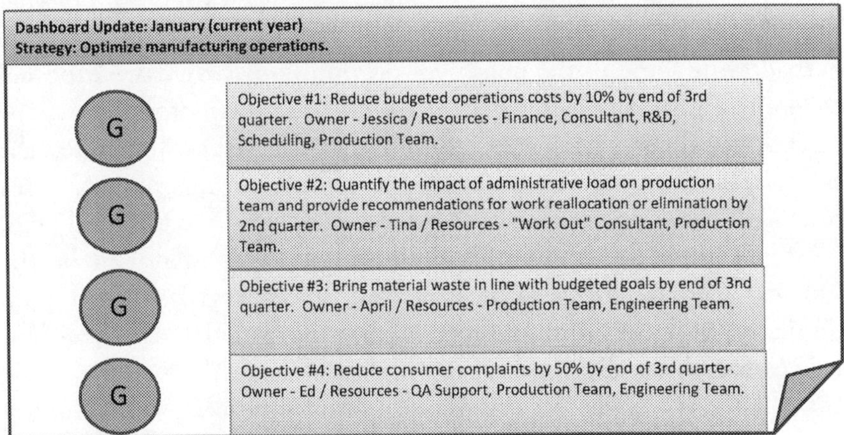

Dashboard Update: January (current year)
Strategy: Optimize manufacturing operations.
G
Objective #1: Reduce budgeted operations costs by 10% by end of 3rd quarter. Owner - Jessica / Resources - Finance, Consultant, R&D, Scheduling, Production Team.
G
Objective #2: Quantify the impact of administrative load on production team and provide recommendations for work reallocation or elimination by 2nd quarter. Owner - Tina / Resources - "Work Out" Consultant, Production Team.
G
Objective #3: Bring material waste in line with budgeted goals by end of 3nd quarter. Owner - April / Resources - Production Team, Engineering Team.
G
Objective #4: Reduce consumer complaints by 50% by end of 3rd quarter. Owner - Ed / Resources - QA Support, Production Team, Engineering Team.

Considering all the data and processes for which she was responsible as the director of manufacturing operations, Jessica landed on the dashboard shown in figure 5-11.

Figure 5-11: Jessica's Personal Operations Dashboard

Dashboard: January (current year)
Strategy: Optimize manufacturing operations.

G — **Employee Safety** - toggled by lack of compliance in OSHA training, major and minor accidents, and time between accidents.

G — **Product Quality** - toggled by consumer complaint levels (measured on a complaint / million unit basis), rising above predetermined levels.

G — **Departmental Compliance** - toggled by the lack of process compliance as measured by internal compliance department audits.

G — **Cost (fixed and variable)** - toggled by cost increases above budgeted levels.

Although the same strategy is listed as was the case with the objectives-based dashboard, in contrast, here Jessica focuses on what she believes are the critical ongoing operations metrics. Of note here is that while some of the objectives previously discussed are expected to positively impact her personal dashboard, their progress will be tracked separately. Jessica recognized that the responsibility for the safety of every employee working in the manufacturing operations area rests with her. Consequently, she listed this as her top dashboard item. Next, recalling the issues with product quality as identified by the QA manager, she included product quality as a key dashboard item. Similarly, because Summit Consumables is regulated by the FDA, it is extremely important that all employees correctly follow existing compliance protocols. So this was a critical metric as well. The last one listed is in the area of cost incurred in operations, both fixed and variable.

Jessica also contemplated the criteria she should use to switch (toggle) the status of those metrics from green to yellow to red. Recall that toggling criteria for a dashboard may vary widely depending on the application. Despite the criteria chosen, those affected by the status changes (for example direct reports) must also have a good understanding of the toggling criteria.

Beginning with employee safety, Jessica recalled that the Occupational Health and Safety Organization (OSHA) mandates that certain aspects of the workplace conform to federal standards. In particular, she recognized that OSHA's mission, based on the Occupational Safety and Health Act of 1970, is "to assure safe and healthful working conditions for working men and women by setting and enforcing standards and by providing training, outreach, education and assistance" (osha.gov).

With this in mind, she decided that any failure to complete OSHA-required training as per schedules would switch the metric from green to red, as would any major injury, such as on-the-job dismemberment. Likewise, if the average time between minor accidents (such as minor strains) decreased to a certain level, that too would switch the metric from green to red. Toggling from green to yellow would result from the number of minor accidents occurring regardless of the average time between occurrences.

Concentrating on quality for the moment, assume the historical product complaint rate is 320 complaints per million units. That is, for every one million units produced, a consumer complains about 320 of those units, meaning the complaint rate is 0.032 percent. If the current complaint rate were, say, 1.2 percent, this level would far exceed the historical rate, thereby forcing the metric to red. Jessica believes that switching to yellow would occur as long as the complaint rate is less than historical but greater than the rate that is believed to be achievable.

Jessica believes that the compliance metric is slightly different, that its switching mechanism would be driven by employee performance as measured by process audits. The processes that are to be audited by the internal compliance audit team are those aimed at ensuring product quality and integrity. In the event that all process audits identify no lack of compliance with process execution, then the metric would remain green. Otherwise it will switch to red or yellow based on the level of noncompliance. (Less than 100 percent but greater than 95 percent would switch from green to yellow, and less than 95 percent would switch to red.)

Jessica listed cost as the final metric on her personal dashboard. And despite the importance of fixed and variable cost, she listed it last to send the message that reduced costs must begin with stellar performance in employee safety, product quality, and process compliance. For consistency, however, she set a threshold of a 2.5 percent aggregate fixed and variable deviation from target to switch from green to yellow and greater than 2.5 percent aggregate deviation to switch to red.

An alternative construction of Jessica's personal dashboard is shown in figure 5-12. While the same critical metrics are listed, the manner in which the data suggests opportunities (the need for improvement) is shown graphically. In this case, Jessica must take a moment to read the specific data points in the charts to determine metric status. The traffic light indicators are a more efficient mechanism by which status may be determined, but the data shown in figure 5-12 offers a more comprehensive representation of that same information.

It is always a good idea to know how you are being measured. What is your boss focusing on as a means to judge and reward your accomplishments? For example, if you are the manager of an accounting department, you may be measured on how well the organization's books balance, the accuracy of reports that your team provides (measured by

Figure 5-12: Jessica's Alternative Personal Dashboard

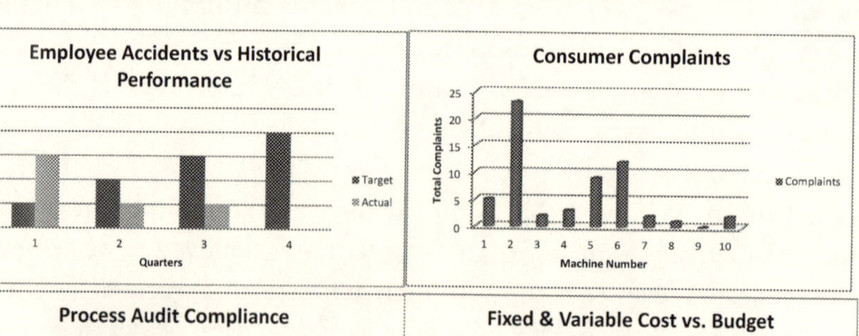

error rate), or the success of your internal reviews. Once you know how you are being measured, which might begin with a conversation, you should develop your own personal dashboard. It is best that you know when an item for which you are responsible is going to switch from green to yellow or red before your boss brings it to your attention.

Returning to Jessica, the final stage of the 5C LIM is communication. As shown in figure 5-13, her plan is to communicate the finished objectives-oriented and personal dashboards to her boss, her subordinates, support resources (quality and finance), and to all her departmental employees, including the lowest level hourly paid workers within manufacturing operations. This 360-degree communication approach offers the best chance for success. The communication to Jessica's boss was to occur one-on-one and was to be executed before the broader communication to allow for integration of and calibration with her boss's input.

Leadership Insights: Quantifiable leadership opportunities identified for Jessica included productivity (operating cost reductions) and quality (reducing consumer complaints). Nonquantifiable opportunities included not motivating the team, ineffective listening, passive and reactive behavior, the lack of engagement, the lack of setting expectations, and goal setting.

Figure 5-13: Jessica's Communication Stage Scroll

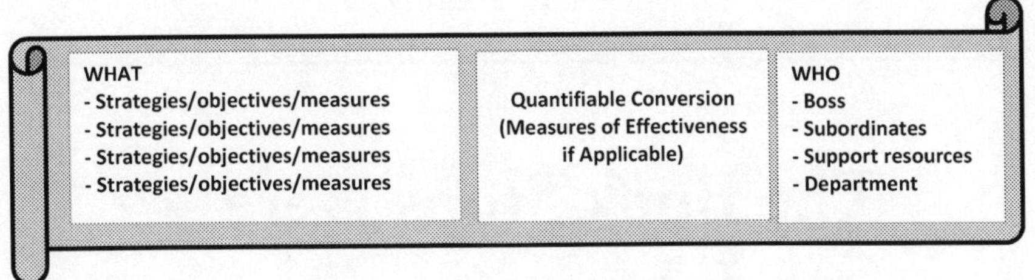

WHAT
- Strategies/objectives/measures
- Strategies/objectives/measures
- Strategies/objectives/measures
- Strategies/objectives/measures
Quantifiable Conversion
(Measures of Effectiveness
if Applicable)
WHO
- Boss
- Subordinates
- Support resources
- Department

In response to the quantifiable opportunities noted, Jessica enlisted her team's assistance in developing remedial plans and strategies. Facilitating the development of such plans was her use of key business tools, including fixed cost budgeting processes (year-over-year fixed operations costs comparisons), fundamental Pareto chart analysis (identifying material waste and consumer complaint sources), dashboard cognizance, and monitoring infrastructure.

Regarding the nonquantifiable opportunities, Jessica demonstrated excellent listening (TL) skills as she committed to implementing a work-out process aimed at eliminating unnecessary work for her team and incorporating the team's input in setting goals and objectives. As reflected by assignments listed in her objectives-oriented dashboard, Jessica also appropriately responded to her team's concerns about over-delegation and passive and reactive behavior by rolling up her sleeves and personally championing the objective to reduce operating costs.

CHAPTER 6

The Buck Stops Here—Johnny Goode

LET'S SHIFT THE discussion to Johnny Goode, senior buying analyst for Summit Consumables Inc. Figure 6-1 shows how Johnny began to update the conversation stage scroll, precipitated by the discussion with his boss. As was the case with Jessica, several action items were supplied by Johnny's boss, including leadership opportunities, the 10 percent reduction in budgeted costs as well as supplier pricing and quality issues. Consistent with Jessica's approach, Johnny, working with the HR department, elected to issue the MLQ. (See appendices A–D for details about the MLQ). And as was the case with Jessica, the timing for issuing the MLQ was calculated: Johnny set up a meeting for the following week with his direct reports to discuss the departmental budget and overall supplier quality and pricing issues.

Figure 6-1: Johnny's Conversation Stage Scroll

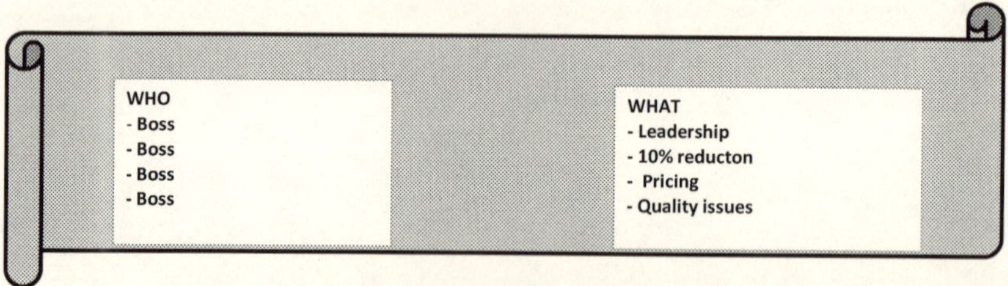

WHO
- Boss
- Boss
- Boss
- Boss
WHAT
- Leadership
- 10% reducton
- Pricing
- Quality issues

Moving to the calculation stage, figure 6-2 presents Johnny's plan to move forward.

Figure 6-2: Johnny's Calculation Stage Scroll

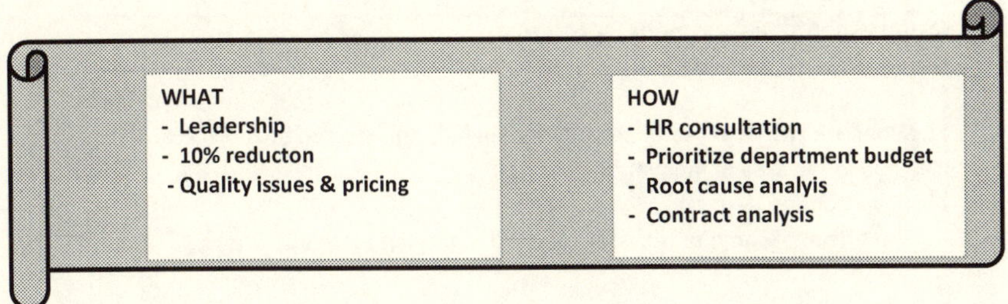

WHAT
- Leadership
- 10% reducton
- Quality issues & pricing
HOW
- HR consultation
- Prioritize department budget
- Root cause analyis
- Contract analysis

The output from this stage may be several actions to be taken to the collaboration stage. These actions, when implemented or otherwise addressed, are expected to resolve the current stage inputs. Notice that while there are three areas listed in the WHAT section of the calculation stage, there are four line items listed in the HOW section, resulting in an imbalance. The correct interpretation here is that the final WHAT item (Quality issues & pricing) is intended to be addressed in multiple areas (root cause analysis and contract analysis), as listed in the HOW section. It should be apparent at this point that this situation (imbalance relationships), can occur relative to one or more areas in the WHAT and HOW sections.

Regarding the item Leadership, as also mentioned previously, recall that not all issues that move into the calculation stage will be as quantifiable as, say, a 10 percent budget reduction, and that the intent of this stage is not to simply apply mathematical or other deductive logic, but to consider arguments (pros and cons) aimed at addressing any item identified in the conversation stage.

6.1 Leadership Reflection

Complementing the MLQ rater feedback, Johnny also received the supplemental leadership feedback listed in figure 6-3.

A review here suggests that Johnny might do well to not only lead in areas of innovation, perhaps during problem solving, but also paying attention to details. Another key bit of feedback suggests that Johnny may be perceived unprofessional in his interactions with his employees because he openly criticizes them. The feedback also revealed key strengths for Johnny, such as being well liked and having good insights regarding supplier processes.

Figure 6-3: MLQ Supplemental Feedback for Johnny

Supplemental Assessment Questions:

1. What are two or three things that would help this person be more efficient?
Lead in the area of innovation
Pay attention to details
Get ahead of some of the issues instead of playing catch up

2. One thing that gets in the way of this person's effectiveness is:
Does not try new approaches to resolve issues
Public critique of people

3. What I admire most about this person's leadership:
Is well liked by most everyone
Has good insights regarding supplier processes

The apparent conflicting feedback (public critique of employees versus being well liked by most everyone) should not be surprising. Indeed, it is quite possible, and perhaps typical, for those rating an individual to have varying emotions and perspectives. More important is that those offering the feedback feel comfortable doing so.

Having received the MLQ feedback, as evidenced by the issues to be discussed, Johnny was rated lowest in the area of intellectual stimulation (IS). (This TL attribute is discussed in detail in appendix D.) On a scale from 1–4, where 1 is the lowest and 4 is the highest, and substantiated by the supplemental feedback, Johnny received an average rating of 1.75 in the area of IS. The norm table in appendix C ("percentiles for individual scores based on lower level ratings") reveals that a score of 1.75 for IS occurs at the tenth percentile, meaning 10 percent of the normed population scored lower, and 90 percent scored higher than 1.75.

In the upcoming meeting, Johnny has the opportunity to respond to the feedback he received, not in a retaliatory manner, but in such a way as to demonstrate the stimulating leadership desired by his direct reports. Indeed, according to Avolio and Bass, leaders who demonstrate IS "stimulate their followers' effort to be innovative and creative by questioning assumptions, reframing problems, and approaching old situations in new ways" (2004, 102).

Another area of concern seen in Johnny's feedback and reflected by a score of 1.75, was in the area of passive avoidant behavior, laissez-faire (LF), which corresponded to the ninetieth percentile. Leaders exhibiting this attribute are considered to be missing in action (MIA), particularly when needed by subordinates. Perhaps this is what Johnny's boss, Teresa, intended with her comments regarding his lack of "being in touch with supplier progress versus goals," which is also consistent with supplemental feedback received. Because Johnny scored in the ninetieth percentile, 90 percent of the normed population scored lower, and 10 percent scored higher. In this instance, a lower percentile rating score is better. Johnny's score pointed to another significant leadership opportunity in this area.

Regarding objectively quantifiable opportunities (prioritize department budget, root cause analysis, and pricing), Johnny's plan was to first engage his team for budget review and root cause analysis for case issues and supplier price increases. Subsequently, Johnny planned to meet with suppliers to discuss the outcomes in these areas. Going into the collaboration stage, Johnny prepared the scroll as shown in figure 6-4. Recall that during the collaboration stage, the leader may choose to send a key message, particularly as such relates to feedback, to all those attending the meeting or other such collaboration forum.

Figure 6-4: Johnny's Collaboration Stage Scroll

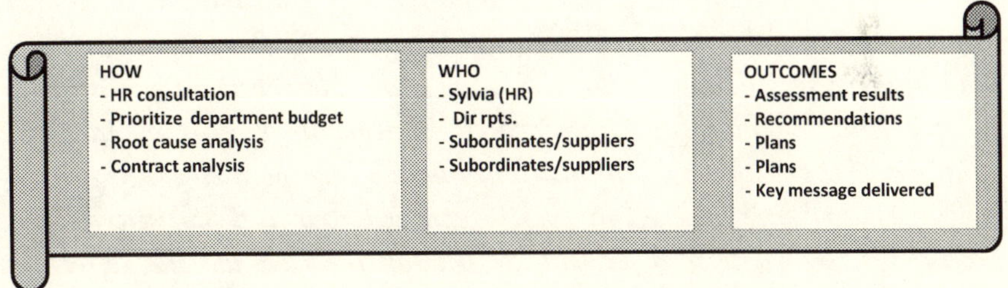

HOW
- HR consultation
- Prioritize department budget
- Root cause analysis
- Contract analysis
WHO
- Sylvia (HR)
- Dir rpts.
- Subordinates/suppliers
- Subordinates/suppliers
OUTCOMES
- Assessment results
- Recommendations
- Plans
- Plans
- Key message delivered

The outcome linked to the HR consultation has been modified to reflect assessment results. The significance here is that Johnny plans to discuss the results of this assessment with HR before meeting with his team. Johnny's goal is to first understand how he is perceived by his team and then make use of the upcoming meeting as an opportunity to send a key message (also included in the outcomes field) to his team and to the suppliers based on such feedback. (Recall that the imbalance listed in the OUTCOMES section, relative to the WHO section, results from the key message being delivered to the same group assisting in the plan development.)

6.2 The Meeting

At the beginning of the meeting, Johnny summarized the received MLQ and supplemental question feedback, focusing on themes in lieu of specifics. As happened with Jessica, he circumvented what might have otherwise been an unpleasant environment resulting from his review of the results by saying, "Well, team, thank you for the feedback. Let the record state that I scored higher in the key TL attribute of intellectual stimulation than ten percent of those tested." The team all laughed, Johnny again thanked them for the feedback, and the meeting moved forward.

Resulting from the meeting with his team, Johnny was able to find the required ten percent cost reduction in his operating budget using the same line item review approach that Jessica implemented. However, in an attempt to make use of the feedback from the MLQ survey, Johnny asked his team to offer suggestions regarding how they might resolve the supplier pricing and quality issues. Anthony, a member of Johnny's team, provided an excerpt from a contract with Atlantic Case Company, a supplier of Summit Consumables' cases, entered into for the current year. It read as follows:

The supplier (Atlantic Case Company) will endeavor to maintain constant pricing for the twelve months beginning January of current year, and ending December of the same year. However, in the absence of quantifiable and sustainable process improvement recommendations initiated by the customer (Summit Consumables Incorporated), such pricing will revert to being indexed by the Bureau of Labor and Statistics' (BLS) posting of the Producer Price Index (PPI) on the BLS website reflecting pricing for the previous quarter.

The Bureau of Labor and Statistics' website (bls.gov) provides all sorts of data and information, ranging from jobless rates, to import and export price indexes, to earnings by demographics, to wage estimates for management occupations, and … well, I think you get the picture. It may be beneficial to at least visit the site in your leisure, as I am sure there will be something there that you will find of interest.

We return now to Johnny's meeting.

Johnny appeared stunned by what he was hearing, particularly given that he believed he was hearing it for the first time. Atlantic Case Company, a relatively new player in the area of case manufacturing, had been identified by Anthony several months ahead of the contract endorsement. And before granting the contract, several product trials had been run using cases supplied by Atlantic with only minimal issues. Indeed, the few issues occurring with Atlantic cases were attributed to carrier handling, not the quality of the cases. Atlantic's bid for the supply of cases came in well under its competitors, one of whom was the previous case supplier for Summit Consumables, and Anthony received accolades from Teresa (vice president of procurement and Johnny's boss) for closing the deal with the new supplier.

When Johnny probed regarding the pricing clause, Anthony dug up copies of email messages that he had sent to Johnny, advising him of the pricing clause. He also produced the hard copy he had sent by way of company mail to Johnny for signature. Anthony also pointed out that he had reminded Johnny of the pricing clause during one of the very few instances that he saw Johnny in the cafeteria, but Johnny seemed to shy away from engaging in discussions regarding the details.

Johnny now recalled endorsing the contract, and he also began to recognize the impact of his aloof behavior. Anthony further noted that he had issued, via email, several process improvement recommendations for submission to Atlantic Case that required Johnny's approval but had not received a response and therefore assumed that Johnny didn't view the recommendations as viable.

At this point, there was no need for recriminations. An issue existed, and a solution needed to be identified, so the conversation shifted to the problem of case quality. Johnny thought there might be a connection between the lack of process improvement suggestions routed to Atlantic and the case quality issues.

Recalling Anthony's expertise in the area of statistics and statistical process control and the team's eagerness to solve problems, Johnny suggested that they take a break and, upon returning to the conference room, engage in a form of root cause analysis known as the *5 Whys*.

Several years ago, I visited a quality seminar (IMPRO 92) hosted in Chicago, Illinois. During that seminar, a gentleman shared an anecdote regarding root cause analysis and the value of asking *why* at least five times. My memory prevents me from sharing the story verbatim, but the method should be quite apparent. With this caveat in mind, the story goes like this:

The Jefferson Memorial had begun to deteriorate, and those servicing the park were asked to determine the cause. Upon asking those closest to the issue why *it was deteriorating, the first response was that it was due to the frequent cleaning of the structures with certain harsh chemicals. When asked* why *it needed to be cleaned so frequently, the response was that the cleaning was needed to remove pigeon droppings. When asked* why *there were so many pigeon droppings, the answer was that the pigeons were feeding on an increased spider population. When asked* why *there was an increased spider population, the answer was that the spiders were feeding on the increased gnat and other flying insect population. When asked* why *the insect population had increased, the answer was that a new lighting system had been installed to illuminate the memorial that was not being properly time regulated.*

Therefore the illumination time for the lights was changed, which in turn reduced the number of gnats and insects, which in turn reduced the number of spiders, which in turn reduced the number of pigeons, which in turn reduced the amount of droppings, which in turn reduced the amount of cleaning required, thereby resolving the issue.

The word *why* was asked five times in this anecdote en route to determining the root cause.

Upon returning from break, Johnny began by asking why some of the product at retail was being destroyed or returned. The team answered that such was due to cases collapsing. Johnny then asked why the cases were collapsing, and Anthony responded, somewhat flippantly, that this was due to the cases not being strong enough. Johnny then asked why the cases were not strong enough, to which the team responded: That's what we accept. Finally, Johnny asked why cases that are not strong enough were accepted, and following a moment of silence, Anthony pointed out that the case acceptance criteria required only that the supplier meet an average crush strength test for cases and that no specifications were issued that might eliminate weak cases. Johnny then asked why no specifications were issued. Anthony responded that he had developed a specification recommendation and emailed it to Johnny but had received no feedback and therefore assumed that the specifications were not required.

At this point, it might be helpful to review a few key statistical terms before discussing how Johnny and his team proceeded. Making no assumptions regarding your knowledge level, we begin with a review of *average*, also referred to as the *mean*.

According to Berk and Carey, "the average or mean is equal to the sum of the values [observations] divided by the number of observations" (2010, 154). To help solidify your understanding, assume that a manufacturing engineer working for a potato chip company wishes to determine how consistently a potato chip machine operates at placing the same number of potato chips in a chip bag. The engineer begins by taking samples of potato chips at different times from the same machine. The number of potato chips from each of ten bags is counted, as shown in figure 6-5. Calculating the mean would be the sum of all the observations (in this case 140 chips) divided by the total number of observations (in this case 10). Thus, the mean is 140 / 10 = 14, as shown.

Figure 6-5: Potato Chip Observations and Mean Calculation

Observation	No. of Potato Chips
1	16
2	18
3	15
4	12
5	9
6	14
7	15
8	13
9	12
10	16
Mean	14

Another useful statistical measure is referred to as the *median*. It differs from the mean in that it "represents the middle of the distribution [in other words] half of the values are less than the median, and half are greater than the median" (Berk & Carey 2010, 154). Referring once more to the potato chip example, the median is (14 + 15) / 2 = 14.5, which is the average of these two numbers. The reason for the addition of 14 and 15 is that they represent the two center values among an even number of values. Had there been an odd number of values, the median would have been the value in the middle once all values have been arranged in order from least to greatest.

Notice the significant *variability* in the values. What is variability you ask? Good question. Variability is "a measure of how much data values differ from one another, or equivalently, how widely the data values are spread out around the center" (Berk & Carey 2010, 159). In figure 6-6, although the means are the same for the two sample sets for the potato chip example, the values for group #2 have a much greater *range*. Oops—another new term. Not to worry. Range is "the difference between the maximum value in the distribution (sample values) and the minimum value" (Berk & Carey 2010, 159). In the potato chip example shown in figure 6-6, the greatest value in group #1 is 18, and the least value is 9, resulting in a range of 9. In contrast, in group #2, the greatest value is 21 and the least value is 5, resulting in a range of 16.

OK, almost done with this statistical review.

How do we measure this variability? The answer is *standard deviation*, which is calculated "by taking the square root of the variance [the variance considers squaring each of the differences between the individual values from the mean]" (Berk & Carey 2010, 161). Also shown in figure 6-6 are the respective standard deviations for each group which, considering the variability, also reflect a higher value for group #2 despite each group having equal means.

Another point to contemplate regarding the potato chip example is that the consumers may become disgruntled with the variation in chip numbers. While some consumers would be happy with 21 chips as reported by observation 10 in group #2, others would be happy with a consistent number of chips per bag, such as 15, as long as they could rely on there being 15 chips in each bag purchased.

Focusing on the latter consumer perspective (a consistent number of chips per bag), the key desire is to reduce and, to the degree possible, eliminate bag-to-bag variability (varying numbers of chips in bags purchased). And as we have seen from the statistical review, one way to accomplish that would be to reduce the standard deviation in the chip bag filling process.

Figure 6-6: Two Potato Chip Sample Sets

Observations	Group #1	Group #2
1	9	5
2	12	10
3	12	12
4	13	13
5	14	13
6	15	15
7	15	15
8	16	16
9	16	20
10	18	21
Mean	14	14
Std Dev	2.58	4.64

Aimed at further solidifying the concept of variation, shown in figure 6-7 are two histograms that graphically reflect the impact of variability. An analysis of these two histograms reveals that the one on the left (group 1) is not as wide (from left to right) as the one on the right (group 2). Also note that on the vertical or y-axis, the group 1 histogram appears to be higher in the center than the group 2 histogram. Generally speaking, it may be inferred from these two histograms that the wider the distribution, the greater the variability. And because we saw that standard deviation is also a measure of variability, it may also be inferred that the wider the distribution, the higher the standard deviation.

With this in mind, referring back to figure 6-6 above, and specifically focusing on the respective standard deviation values, which of the two potato chip sample sets, group #1 or group #2, do you believe would yield the histogram with the greatest variability? If you answered group #2, you were correct.

Finally, a *histogram*, according to Berk and Carey, is "a bar chart in which each bar represents a particular bin and the height of the bar is proportional to the number of counts in that bin" (2010, 139). So what does that mean? The histogram captures and positions in a bar chart the number of times a certain value appears in a data or sample set. With this in mind, referring to group #1, there are 9 values of the same level or magnitude in positions 7 and 8. Likewise, there are 5 values with the same level of magnitude in positions 6 and 9, and so on. Similarly, the same position-to-value relationship exists for group #2.

Figure 6-7: Histograms Reflecting Variability

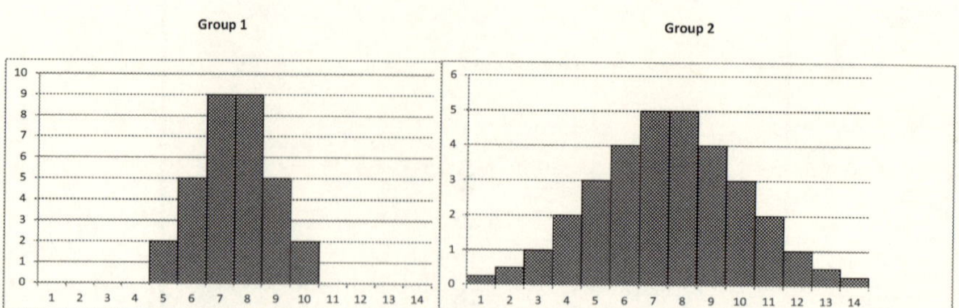

Whew! In summary, even though two sample sets may have the same mean, one could be highly variable, as measured by standard deviation. While the other is not. Additionally, by reducing process variation, fewer nonconforming (defective) process components will be produced, thereby reducing costs associated with rework, waste, and in some cases, reduced ingredient use.

Having covered some of the fundamental statistical measures, we now return to the issue involving Atlantic Case Company.

Take a closer look at the specification recommendation that Anthony issued to Johnny, shown in figure 6-8. We see three of four key pieces of information are included: the target (assumed to be the process mean), and the upper and lower specification points. In the example, the target refers to the desired case crush strength, and the upper and lower specifications refer to the highest and lowest values respectively for case crush testing that Summit Consumables would be willing to accept. There was no value included for process standard deviation.

Case crush testing, of course, refers to the amount of force required to cause the case to collapse. This testing may also be referred to as edge crush testing.

Upon seeing the specification sheet, Johnny inquired as to why the target was so high—20 kg (44 lbs.) when the desired standard case crush weight was set at 10 kg (22 lbs.). Anthony replied that due to Atlantic Case Company's process variation, the target crush weight had to be set at a much higher level to ensure that a sufficient number of good cases were produced. He further explained that because there was no consistency in process variability, no value was included for process standard deviation.

Figure 6-8: Recommended Specification for Atlantic

Specification Recommendation for Atlantic Case Company*

Process Target:	**20 kg (44 lbs.)**
Upper Specification:	**60 kg (132 lbs.)**
Lower Specification:	**10 kg (22 lbs.)**
Process Standard Deviation:	**TBD****

***Contingent upon review and approval of Johnny Goode.**
****Not listed due to lack of process consistency.**

Upon hearing this, although Johnny felt confident that he knew the appropriate path forward, recalling some of the feedback that he had received, he solicited the team for suggestions regarding what had just transpired. Margie, another of Johnny's direct reports who seldom spoke up, suggested that if Atlantic's process variation could be improved and measurably reduced, higher quality cases would be produced, and the case crush target could be shifted closer to 10 kg, potentially resulting in less consumption of a key processing ingredient and less waste.

Anthony interrupted, saying: "And that could reduce the cost of manufacturing ..."

Johnny finished Anthony's sentence: "and reduce supplier prices."

The team began exchanging high fives as they now had a solid plan to communicate to the supplier. Before adjourning the meeting, Johnny asked that the team work together to develop an updated specification sheet that could be used in communication with Atlantic Case Company.

Just as Johnny began to wrap up, Anthony asked if he could have a moment alone with Johnny. Johnny responded: "Anthony, if possible, I would prefer the team hear what you have to say. Go ahead; I'm a big boy and can take constructive criticism."

Anthony chuckled and said, "Well, I don't want to sound like I'm looking for brownie points or anything, but I just wanted to tell you that this was the best meeting that we have ever had, and I look forward to supporting you and the team in any way that I can in the future."

Before Johnny could respond, the remaining team members agreed and added that they thought they would like the "new Johnny."

Johnny, almost in disbelief, smiled and said, "OK all you flattering followers, if the next step is hugs and kisses, I'm out of here." Everyone laughed and the meeting was adjourned.

Later, upon receiving the requested specification sheet, Johnny had a few minor follow-up questions for Anthony and Margie. After implementing minor changes, he began preparing for a meeting with Atlantic.

Oops! There is one more statistical term you must be aware of before moving on—the *normal* (or Gaussian) *distribution*, also referred to as the *bell curve*. You may recall the vitality curve discussed in chapter 2 regarding the performance appraisal. The key thing to know about the bell curve is that 99.7 percent of all the data points comprising the bell curve fall within plus or minus three standard deviations of the mean, 95 percent will fall within plus or minus two standard deviations of the mean, and 68 percent will fall within plus or minus one standard deviation of the mean. And that 50 percent of the values that make up the bell curve are greater than the mean and 50 percent of these values are less than the mean. Don't worry if the bell curve explanation is not clear at this moment. It will be shortly.

One way to think of a bell curve is similar to a histogram as was previously discussed, with several values (or data points), an average, and a standard deviation. So if the mean of the histogram, or bell curve, is 40 lbs. and the standard deviation is 10 lbs., then 99.7 percent of all the values in the curve will fall between 10 lbs. and 70 lbs., (40 lbs. +/- three standard deviations of 10 lbs. each), 95 percent of all values are between 20 lbs. and 60 lbs. (40 lbs. +/- two standard deviations of 10 lbs. each), and 68 percent of all the values would fall between 30 lbs. and 50 lbs. (40 lbs. +/- one standard deviation of 10 lbs.). And each standard deviation from the mean in either direction is also expressed as one sigma. So saying "99.7 percent of the values" is synonymous with saying "the three sigma values," all of which occur within three standard deviations of the mean.

Let's assume that these values represent the weights of a certain component of a manufactured product that has a high end (upper limit) specification of 70 lbs. and a low end (lower limit) specification of 10 lbs. Therefore any weight either greater than 70 lbs. or less than 10 lbs.

is termed nonconforming or defective. If 1000 total units are involved in this process, then, according to our formula, 997 (99.7 percent) would be within the allowable specification and 3 (0.3 percent), would be defective.

If these values represent the crush test results of manufactured cases discussed in Johnny's staff meeting, and if the process from which the cases were taken resulted in an average crush result of 40 lbs. with a standard deviation of 10 lbs., then 68 percent of the cases would require between 30 lbs. and 50 lbs. (40 lbs. +/- one standard deviation of 10lbs.) of force for crushing. Now let us assume that the case manufacturing process approximated a normal distribution (or bell curve) and that the standard deviation (variation) has been reduced, resulting in the manufacture of cases that yield an average crush test of 40 lbs. but with a standard deviation of 4 lbs. We will refer to this new process as "process B" whereas the process having the higher standard deviation of 10lbs. is termed "process A." Applying the rules of the bell curve to process B, 68 percent of all crush test results will occur between 36 lbs. and 44 lbs., 95 percent between 32 lbs. and 48 lbs., and 99.7 percent between 28 lbs. and 52 lbs.

Contrasting these results with those above, the lowest three-sigma crush result from process B is 28 lbs., whereas the same for process A is 10 lbs. If Anthony's low-end specification for acceptance is set at greater than or equal to 20 lbs., then the percentage of cases that would be under this acceptance level with process A would be approximately 2.27 percent, whereas the same with process B would be 0.000028 percent. (Hold your questions for a moment!)

When you consider an annual production requirement of 10,000,000 cases, approximately 228,000 cases would be manufactured from process A (at or below the low acceptance level) and the same for process B would be approximately 3 cases. If the cost for each destroyed case is say $0.50, the cost of producing cases using process A would be $114,000.00, and the same for process B would be virtually $0.00. Clearly, process B would not only yield higher crush test cases, it would also result in less waste cost, less product damage due to collapsed cases, and greater case to case consistency.

I know you're wondering how the 2.27 percent and 0.000028 percent numbers were generated. It's all based on probability associated with the normal distribution, or bell curve. The question being addressed is:

What is the likelihood (probability) that manufactured cases will have a crush strength value of less than or equal to 20 lbs. given process A and process B?

The raw formula is z = (x - μ) / σ. In this formula, *z* is also referred to as the *z-score*, which is a value located in a probability table found in the appendix of most statistical textbooks. Lower case *x* is the value that you are looking to assess (20 in our scenario), μ, pronounced "mew," is the process mean, and σ, pronounced "sigma," is the process standard deviation. (Recall that 1σ is equivalent to one standard deviation from the mean, 2σ is equivalent to two standard deviations from the mean, and 3σ is equivalent to three standard deviations from the mean.)

Once the z-score is determined, a corresponding value is found in the probability table and is then multiplied by 100 to get the percent if you are looking for values less than or equal to x. If, on the other hand, the desire is to find the probability of values occurring that are greater than x, the z-score is subtracted from 1.0 and multiplied by 100 to convert to percent.

A more contemporary method for finding the desired percentage x is to use Excel and the NORM.DIST function, which can be selected from Excel's Formulas Insert function key. The resulting dialog box is shown in figure 6-9. (Details may vary depending on your computer platform.) The value entered for x is the probability of occurrence that you are seeking (20 in our scenario). The mean value entered is the process mean (40 in our scenario). The process standard deviation is entered in the Standard Deviation box (10 in our scenario).

Figure 6-9: Excel NORM.DIST Function Box

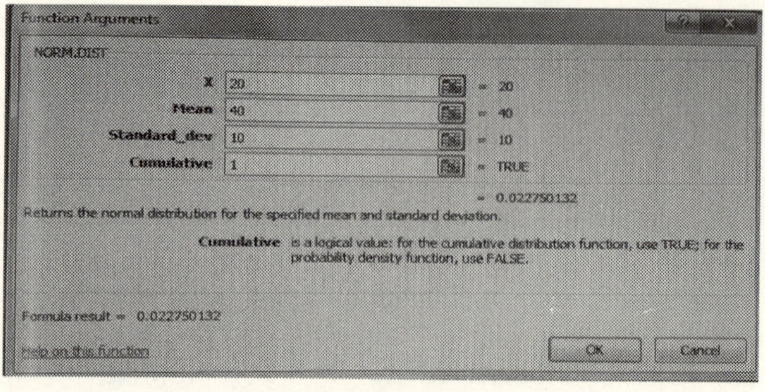

Function Arguments

NORM.DIST

X	20	= 20
Mean	40	= 40
Standard_dev	10	= 10
Cumulative	1	= TRUE

= 0.022750132

Returns the normal distribution for the specified mean and standard deviation.

Cumulative is a logical value: for the cumulative distribution function, use TRUE; for the probability density function, use FALSE.

Formula result = 0.022750132

Help on this function

OK Cancel

Note that a *1* is entered in the Cumulative data entry box. If it's not set to *1*, or *true*, it will calculate a value for probability density (a topic for another book). The probability that we are seeking is listed on the Excel dialogue box, and is also placed in the selected cell of the workbook when you select *OK*. Needless to say, while the Excel approach is much more efficient, it was not available during my early enrollment in statistics, so I was forced to use the z-score method.

For you statistical whizzes the above formula for the z-score can be modified to account for the standard error of the mean X. The updated formula is given by: $z = (x - \mu) / (\sigma/\sqrt{n})$. The $\sqrt{n}$ represents the square root of the actual number of samples taken from the process to be assessed. Another advantage of reducing the process variation is that with a tighter process (lower standard deviation), the mean target may be shifted closer to the lower acceptance level if doing so results in a cost savings while maintaining product integrity and consumer preference.

In the potato chip example, maybe the consumer is not as interested in the number of potato chips in each bag as in receiving bags of chips that from purchase to purchase have little variability in the number of chips contained inside. In this case, the target average of 14 chips per bag could be shifted down to say 12 chips per bag and, resulting from the lower process standard deviation, each bag would include a number of chips closer to the new target of 12 than would be received if the process average target remained at 14 but with a higher standard deviation.

A graphical representation of this scenario is shown in figure 6-10. As indicated in this figure, the distribution for the new process average target of 12 is much tighter, meaning that more bags contain a number of chips close to 12 when compared to the same for the old process target average of 14. Another advantage with this approach is that the percent of bags rejected due to the "low fill" specification is reduced, thereby reducing rework and waste costs. Likewise, and perhaps more important, the number of bags filled with chips approaching the "high fill" specification limit is reduced, thereby also reducing processing costs, which could be calculated using the approach discussed earlier.

Processing costs include the cost of raw materials required for chip processing. So how do I reduce process variation in my area, you ask? Great question! Because there is no process variation switch (that I'm aware of), that can be adjusted to reduce process variation. Pursuing this goal may be a formidable task—that is, if those "closest to and most knowledgeable about" are not engaged. Process and machine operators are an excellent source of information regarding how to reduce process variability. And making use of the 5C LIM in this regard, beginning with a conversation with operators, provides an excellent means for achieving the desired end—reduced process variability.

Figure 6-10: Reduced Process Variation

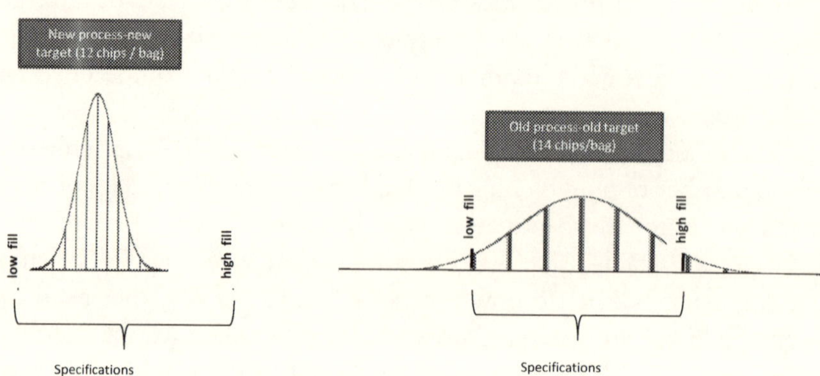

It's safe to say that we have "beat this one to death." We now move to the final core stage of the 5C LIM—communication.

As indicated by figure 6-11, Johnny's communication scroll focuses on communicating with suppliers and subordinates. Note also the reference to Go-dos located under the WHAT area of the scroll. Resulting from Johnny's leadership reflection, as well as his lack of cognizance (such as failure to implement detailed contract reviews and read critical emails), as pointed out during the meeting with his team, his current plan is to institute weekly staff meetings and one-on-one sessions with each of his direct reports. Implementation of the weekly staff meetings and one-on-one sessions is thus reflected as a go-do in the communication scroll. Of course, all communications are to be shared with his direct reports before he communicates to suppliers.

Figure 6-11: Johnny's Communication Stage Scroll

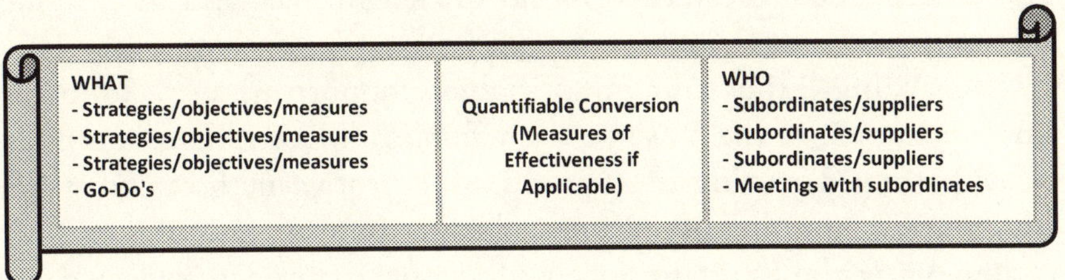

WHAT
- Strategies/objectives/measures
- Strategies/objectives/measures
- Strategies/objectives/measures
- Go-Do's
Quantifiable Conversion (Measures of Effectiveness if Applicable)
WHO
- Subordinates/suppliers
- Subordinates/suppliers
- Subordinates/suppliers
- Meetings with subordinates

As for the specific communications to the suppliers, Johnny plans to disseminate the strategies, objectives, and plans as indicated in the dashboard, figure 6-12.

Figure 6-12: Johnny's Dashboard

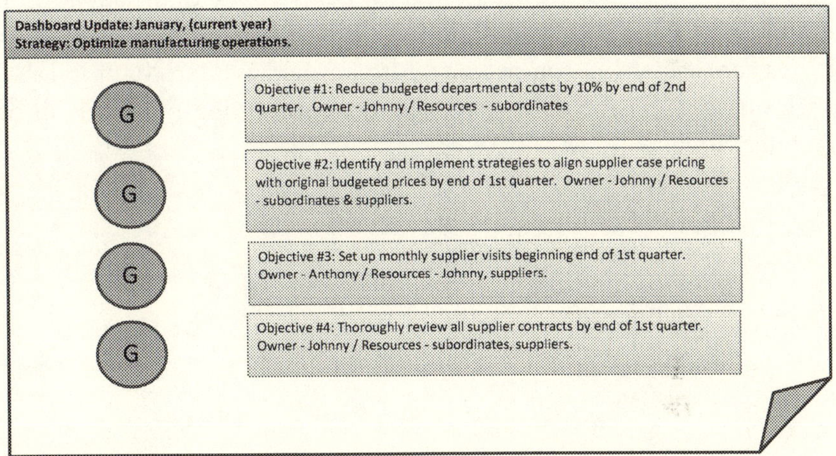

Dashboard Update: January, (current year)
Strategy: Optimize manufacturing operations.
G
G
G
G
Objective #1: Reduce budgeted departmental costs by 10% by end of 2nd quarter. Owner - Johnny / Resources - subordinates
Objective #2: Identify and implement strategies to align supplier case pricing with original budgeted prices by end of 1st quarter. Owner - Johnny / Resources - subordinates & suppliers.
Objective #3: Set up monthly supplier visits beginning end of 1st quarter. Owner - Anthony / Resources - Johnny, suppliers.
Objective #4: Thoroughly review all supplier contracts by end of 1st quarter. Owner - Johnny / Resources - subordinates, suppliers.

Leadership insights: Quantifiable leadership opportunities identified for Johnny included productivity (operating and supplier cost reductions) and quality (improving supplier case quality). Nonquantifiable opportunities included the lack of creativity, not challenging old assumptions, refraining from publicly critiquing team members, and paying attention to details.

In responding to the quantifiable opportunities noted, Johnny applied fixed cost budgeting processes, key statistically oriented process improvement, and trouble-shooting tools (such as histograms, process targets and variation, specifications, and probability determination), and root cause analysis tools such as the 5 Whys. This approach was key in developing the related dashboard cognizance and monitoring infrastructure.

Regarding the nonquantifiable opportunities, Johnny's implementation of the 5 Whys also exhibited TL attributes inasmuch as he challenged existing assumptions using creative methods. Likewise, his review of the supplier contract during the team meeting and his championing the effort to review all supplier contracts reflected his desire to pay attention to details. As indicated by comments provided by his team during the meeting close-out, it appears that "the new Johnny" will be well respected by his team.

Having set the stage for Johnny's communication, we will revisit his execution in chapter 11.

While there are more statistically sophisticated methods for quantifying and reducing process variation, the intent of the application in this section was merely to highlight the significance of incorporating IS as a core leadership competency. Also key here is the recognition that once variation has been reduced, less nonconforming product will be manufactured.

CHAPTER 7

The Buck Stops Here—Kimberly Hours

BEFORE DISCUSSING KIMBERLY Hours, regional sales director for the southeastern region, it may be beneficial to set the stage by reviewing the marketing and sales functions within a typical organization. "Marketing is the function of the company, or nonprofit organization, with the responsibility for serving customers and for dealing with intermediaries and external support organizations such as distributors and advertising agencies" (Dolan, Kosnic & Quelch 1993, 5). Despite the widespread notion that marketing is simply advertising a product, much more is involved. To better understand this, consider the instance where you have decided to incorporate your business and sell a product that you have designed and developed. Among the many questions that you will need to consider regarding the commercialization of your product are those listed (Dolan, et al, 1993).

1. Who are the customers or consumers for your product, and how do you identify that customer or consumer? Consider the geographic area (domestic or international) for your product.
2. What should comprise your product line? For example, if you develop a tennis shoe, should you also sell a shoe for running and walking, and should you develop gender-specific shoes?
3. How should you set the retail price (the price that the end user will pay for your product), and how do you ensure that this price is competitive?
4. Where should you sell your product? An online store can have the advantage of low overhead (operations cost), but some people don't shop online. Likewise, if you want to sell your product in a store, how would it be transferred from your place

of manufacture to the store for purchase, and how could that be accomplished in a way that minimizes your distribution costs?

5. Finally, you must answer perhaps the most significant question of all: How will you reach your prospective consumer base? Do you use print advertising, Web advertising, television, or some other medium? Also, should you have sales people on your team, and if so, how many do you need and in what geographic regions should they be stationed?

The first question addresses the problem of identifying the market for your product.

Questions two through five are aligned with what is also known as the *marketing mix*, which is "the tool kit ... consisting of four elements, product policy ... price policy ... distribution policy [and] communication policy" (Dolan et al., 1993, 6). Some people might argue, perhaps oversimplifying, that marketing is all about the transfer of some good from the manufacturer to the end user, otherwise known as the consumer. Building on this thinking, according to Dolan et al., "marketing that involves the sale to ultimate consumers of products which travel through a distribution channel in essentially unchanged form is called consumer, or consumer goods, marketing ... industrial marketing, on the other hand, is the marketing of products to companies, institutions, and governments" (1993, 7).

It could be argued that the best barometer of a successful marketing campaign is whether or not the product actually sells in the marketplace. However, as will be seen from the discussion below, the success of such a campaign also depends heavily on the ability of those charged with moving the product. To this end, we turn our attention to Kimberly Hours, regional sales director for Summit Consumables, as she responds to her performance evaluation.

Figure 7-1 shows how Kim began to update her conversation stage scroll resulting from the meeting with her boss. Recall that several action items were supplied by Seth, including team focused leadership opportunities as well as improving sales revenues and account management. The, 10 percent budget reduction was not identified as an action item for Kim.

Figure 7-1: Kim's Conversation Stage Scroll

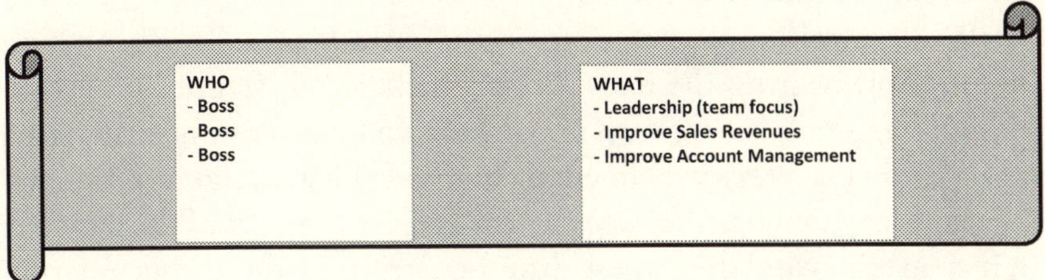

WHO
- Boss
- Boss
- Boss
WHAT
- Leadership (team focus)
- Improve Sales Revenues
- Improve Account Management

Figure 7-2 shows how Kim used information from the conversation stage of the model in the calculation scroll to prepare for the subsequent collaboration stage.

Figure 7-2: Kim's Calculation Stage Scroll

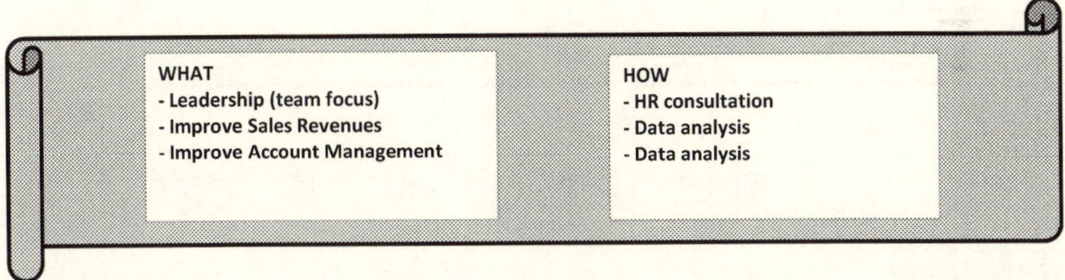

WHAT
- Leadership (team focus)
- Improve Sales Revenues
- Improve Account Management
HOW
- HR consultation
- Data analysis
- Data analysis

Unlike Jessica and Johnny, Kim elected not to engage her team to resolve quantifiable issues identified in the conversation stage of the model. Instead, her plan was to implement the necessary data analysis and subsequently engage her team in the collaboration stage to develop plans and strategies. However, consistent with the approach taken by Jessica and Johnny, Kim worked closely with the HR department and elected to issue the MLQ to all her direct reports. (See appendices A–D for MLQ details.) In addition, she took this a step further and issued the MLQ (same level rating) to the retail accounts serviced by her subordinates. In doing so, Kim assured all those at the retail level that the feedback would be kept in strict confidence and that retailer anonymity would be maintained.

Although this came as a bit of a shock to some of her team members, upon learning of the MLQ issuance, its timing was carefully calculated. Kim also set up a future meeting with her team to discuss not only the MLQ feedback but also to finalize plans and strategies to fully address issues and opportunities identified in the conversation stage and now present in the calculation scroll.

While awaiting completion of the MLQ questionnaires, Kim began implementing the data analysis included in figure 7-2 relative to improving sales revenues. Kim was able to uncover some interesting information from review of internal databases. First, as figure 7-3 shows, it became apparent that sales revenues decreased in each of the previous four quarters, with the largest drop occurring in the fourth quarter. This reduction in revenues appeared to follow regional share declines.

Figure 7-3: Regional Sales Revenues

Regional Revenue vs Share (12 months - $'s - millions)				
	Q1	**Q2**	**Q3**	**Q4**
Sales Revenue	$ 90	$ 85	$ 82	$ 75
Region Share	47%	37%	33%	28%

Notice that the relationship between lost sales revenues and regional share is not linear. That is, for every unit reduction in sales revenues, there is not a proportional or equivalent reduction in regional share. This is due to pricing adjustments that were constrained due to product *price elasticity*.

Oops! I've used a term requiring a bit of explanation. To better understand this price elasticity relationship, or lack thereof, think of a time when you were willing to pay a certain amount of money for a good or service (such as an automobile or haircut) and that, at a price above that amount, you no longer had an interest in purchasing it. Although price elasticity typically refers to quantity purchase, this simple example should help to clarify the concept.

More specifically, in the context of economics, according to Nordhaus and Samuelson, "the price elasticity of demand (sometimes simply called 'price elasticity') measures how much the quantity demanded of a good changes when its price changes [the mathematical relationship is given by] price elasticity of demand = percentage change in quantity demanded / percentage change in price" (1992, 65).

The pricing strategy for Summit Consumables is one of revenue preservation (meaning that prices may be raised despite reductions in market share). However, as with the automobile and the haircut, at some point, the consumer will determine that the value offered by the good or service no longer meets or exceeds the price for that good or service and, at that point, will refuse its purchase. To this point, "a good is elastic when its quantity demanded responds greatly to price changes and inelastic when its quantity demanded responds little to price changes" (Nordhaus & Samuelson 1992, 65).

Returning to figure 7-3, it should now be clear why reductions in sales revenues ($15 million from Q1 to Q4) do not follow, proportionately, reductions in regional share.

Being aware of the changes in sales revenues, Kim's attention now shifts to figuring out what is driving lost revenues. Because a region comprises fifteen territories, and each territory represents accounts serviced by a member of Kim's team (territory sales managers or TSMs) Kim uses the Pareto principle to further disaggregate the data. The Pareto principle may also be termed "the vital few and useful many" (Juran 1995, 47). Kim's goal with this approach is to assess each of the territories to see where the major opportunities lie in terms of those territories incurring the greatest reductions in revenues. Presumably this will yield something close to 20 percent of the territories (the vital few), accounting for 80 percent of the lost revenues. The remaining 80 percent of the territories (the useful many) should only account for 20 percent of the lost revenues and can thus be treated as a separate focus area. Figure 7-4 displays this analysis.

Figure 7-4: Prior Year Customer Account Performance

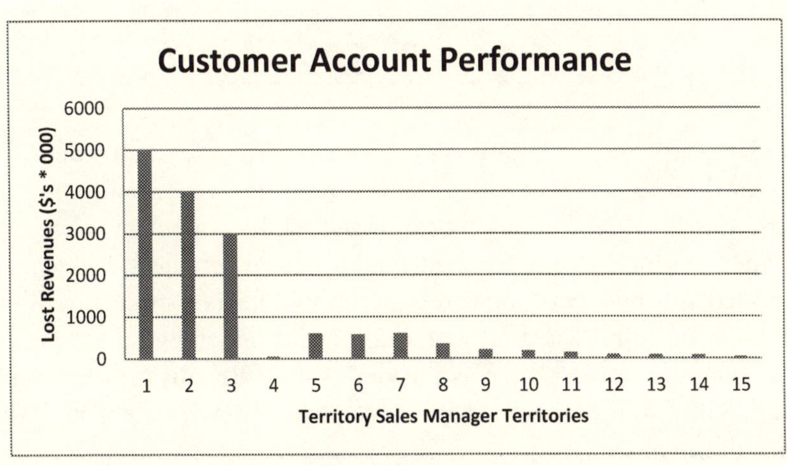

It should be clear that while territory numbers 1, 2, and 3 represent only 20 percent of the total territories (the vital few), the sum of their lost revenues is $12 million (80 percent of the total). Territories 4 through 15 represent 80 percent of the territories (the useful many) but only $3 million (20 percent) in lost revenues. The total lost revenue ($15 million) is now accounted for by this territorial analysis.

Kim is now cognizant of the key opportunity areas. (Recall that cognizance permeates the entire 5C LIM.) During Kim's early years as a TSM, she learned that store presence is the key to driving retail product acceptance and placement. So she believed that a relationship should exist between in-store product acceptance and placement and the number of sales calls made to retailers. With this in mind, Kim pulled the data for TSM calls (also known as contacts) for each of her team members, as shown in figure 7-5.

Figure 7-5: TSM Contacts

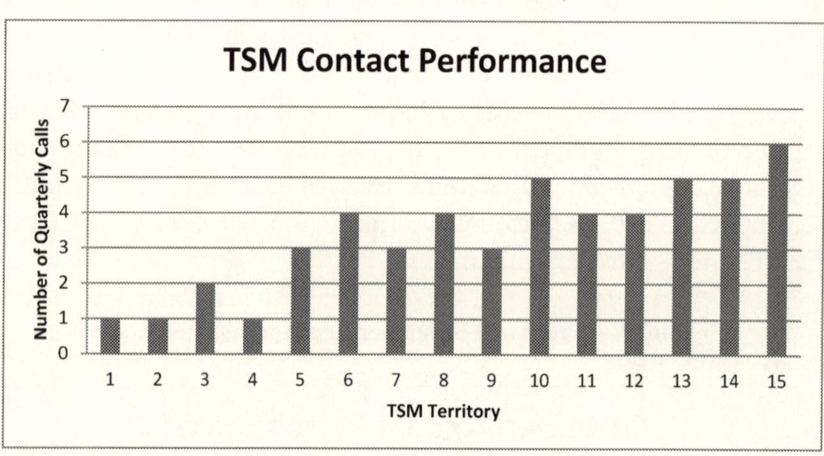

Not surprising to Kim was that the territories previously identified as contributing the greatest to the lost revenues were also among the territories in which the fewest calls were made. Namely, territories 1, 2, and 3 (which also accounted for 80 percent of the lost revenues) reflected only one, two, and three quarterly contacts respectively. While territory 4 also reflected only one call, it did not show up among the top 20 percent (also known as the vital few). With this information in hand, Kim was now looking forward to proceeding to the collaboration stage of the model.

It is always best to be in the possession of objective information when approaching an issue or topic for discussion.

Not so fast, however. It's time for leadership reflection.

7.1 Leadership Reflection

Before reviewing the MLQ feedback, Kim reflected a bit on comments that her boss previously provided regarding playing favorites. She recalled that often she hosted luncheons for her team members, but not all team members attended the luncheons. The lack of team member attendance resulted from the geographic proximity of the team member territories to the regional office. If the team members farthest away from the regional office attended the luncheons, it would involve travel expenses that Kim felt would be frowned upon by her boss. So while some team members were present, despite Kim's invitation to Skype or dial in for these luncheons, few of the TSMs operating in the extended geographical areas accepted her invitation and were thus excluded. In contrast, team members closest to the regional office were almost always physically present at Kim's team meetings. Leader member exchange (LMX) occurs when leaders focus on a subset of their subordinates, referred to as the in-group. They typically benefit in key areas, such as being more up-to-date on relevant information and aligning their actions with the desires of their leader. They also appear to be more confident in their relationship with the leader when compared to those in the out-group and are therefore more satisfied with their job, resulting in greater productivity (Northouse 2012; Barge and Schlueter 1991).

You should not take the significance of the LMX relationship lightly. Its effect is not limited to leader-subordinate interactions. According to Dubrin, "the quality of the relationship with the leader had an impact on the effectiveness of influence tactics, a poor relationship with the leader resulted in less [co-worker to co-worker assistance while] a positive relationship with the leader positively related to helping behavior" (2010, 247). Kim's LMX focused leadership style may have contributed to the lack of performance (as reflected by the lower retailer contacts) discussed earlier.

Having received the MLQ feedback, Kim was rated the lowest in the areas of idealized influence (attributes and behaviors—IIA/IIB). While a detailed review of this TL attribute is discussed in appendix

D, in summary, transformational leaders who demonstrate maturity in these areas "are admired, respected and trusted [by their subordinates]" (Avolio & Bass 2004, 101). Based on Kim's scoring, she did not appear to be among these transformational leaders. This view, as reflected in numerical MLQ ratings, was also substantiated by aggregated team responses to the three supplemental questions issued with the MLQ as seen in figure 7-6.

The responses to questions 1 and 2 seem to point to the above discussion regarding Kim's apparent LMX focus. Question 2 results also appear to identify some opportunities which, in the absence of change, might limit Kim's ability to transform the team from where it operates today to the level required to overcome critical business hurdles. The response to question 3 suggests that despite the team's lack of cohesiveness, there remains a level of respect for the team leader's knowledge.

Figure 7-6: MLQ Supplemental Feedback for Kim

Supplemental Assessment Questions:

1. What are two or three things that would help this person be more efficient?

Respect the ideas of all team members

Be more inclusive

2. One thing that gets in the way of this person's effectiveness is:

Lack of in-field participation

Be consistent in team member development

3. What I admire most about this person's leadership:

Sales knowledge

On a scale from 1–4 (lowest to highest), and driven principally by three of the fifteen territories, Kim received an average rating of 1.25 in the area of IIA. The norm table in appendix C ("percentiles for individual scores based on lower level ratings") says that a score of

1.25 for IIA is at the fifth percentile, meaning 5 percent of the normed population scored lower, and 95 percent scored higher than 1.25.

Similarly, on a scale from 1–4, Kim received an average rating of 1.75 in the area of IIB, which corresponds to the tenth percentile. The norm table in appendix C says that a score of 1.75 for IIB is at the tenth percentile, meaning 10 percent of the normed population scored lower, and 90 percent scored higher than 1.25.

Upon her review of the completed MLQ questionnaires received from the retailers, and to Kim's surprise, among those retailers responding principally from territories 1, 2, and 3, her subordinates received similar though slightly higher scores in the same areas: 1.75 and 2.21 for IIA and IIB respectively.

Two days before the meeting with her team, Kim continued to ponder the results of her MLQ feedback as well as that of her team's as received from the retailers. Given that uncanny similarities existed between feedback received by Kim in three of the fifteen territories and the retailer feedback for TSMs operating in those same territories, and that neither admiration nor respect are likely to be sustained with the absence of trust, Kim began to focus on the trust component associated with the IIA and IIB attributes. According to *Merriam-Webster*, *trust* is defined as "assured reliance on the character, strength, or truth of someone or something … confident hope … to place confidence, depend" (2007).

In the discussion regarding LMX, it was noted that the in-group subordinates appeared to be more confident in their leader (a critical component of trust). And those TSMs operating in territories 1, 2, and 3 were excluded from the in-group of TSMs. Kim believed that the first step in building trust would be to once more implement a review of all available data in an effort to justify the apparent unsatisfactory performance emanating from the cited TSM territories. During this data inquiry, Kim identified two key observations. First, as seen in figure 7-7, a key metric that Kim had been using to gauge performance is the number of products (SKUs) that the TSMs were able to persuade the retailer to accept.

Figure 7-7: Retailer SKU Acceptance by Territory

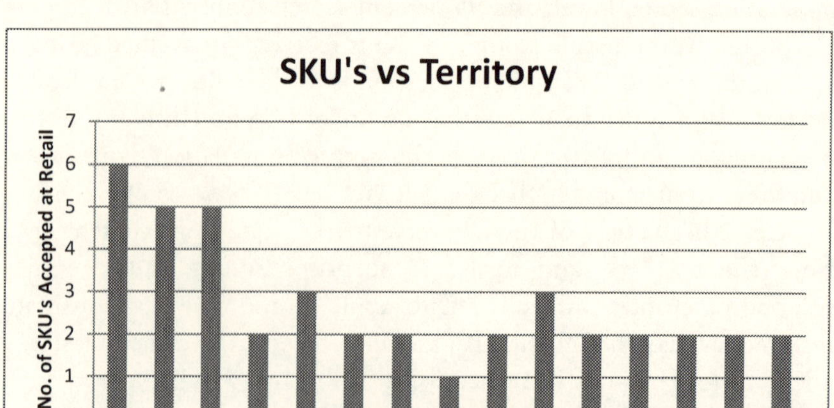

It is apparent that the TSMs in territories 1, 2 and 3 were better than those in the other territories in moving SKUs at retail. Yet over the same period, the revenue loss in those areas was significantly higher. Although major product pricing decisions were set by corporate policy, as a TSM herself, Kim believed that in order to be most effective in dealing with retailers, the ability to offer retail client product discounts should rest with TSMs. Consequently, Kim modified policy to allow her team of TSMs to have this flexibility—to offer discretionary discounts to retailers not to exceed a predefined cap. Could it be that the TSMs were offering discounts at retail in order to gain retailer acceptance of multiple SKUs? Or perhaps the TSMs were not fully aware of the significant impact that product mix could have on revenue generation.

These were only two of several questions that are most efficiently addressed in a collaborative session with the TSMs. Kim expected the TSMs to balance the pricing discounts and the product mix with overall revenue generation, which was something that she occasionally discussed during luncheons and during voluntary attendance staff meetings. However, not all TSMs were privy to these discussions.

Another key metric used by Kim was the number of new retailers (communicated as territory sales growth) brought on board by TSMs, as shown in figure 7-8.

Figure 7-8: Incremental Retailers

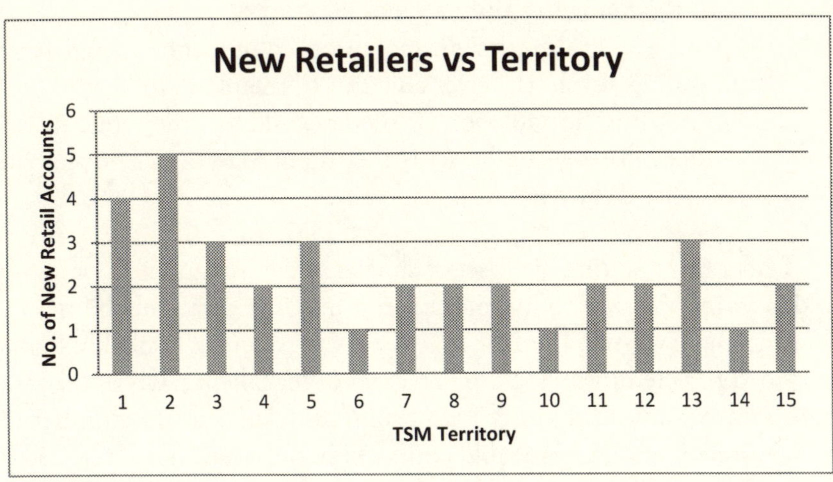

This was confusing too, because the TSMs in territories 1, 2, and 3 achieved results (securing incremental retailers) that were for the most part significantly better than the other territories. Taken in concert, these two metrics (SKU acceptance at retail and incremental retail accounts) served as the basis for TSM salary increases and annual incentives.

You may be familiar with the term *rewarding for A and hoping for B*. This describes a situation in which the person providing the reward (such as a merit increase, bonus, or incentives) is attempting to achieve a certain end but the metric used as the means, produces an effect inconsistent with the original intent. It appears Kim's metrics here parallel this reward concept. On this topic, Ken provides several examples of such metrics. Two specific examples follow:

A. "Most coaches disdain to discuss individual accomplishments, preferring to speak of teamwork, proper attitude, and a one-for-all spirit. Usually, however, rewards are distributed according to individual performance. The college basketball player who feeds his teammates instead of shooting will not compile impressive scoring statistics and is less likely to be drafted by the pros. The ballplayer who hits to right field to advance the runners will win neither the batting nor home run titles, and will be offered smaller raises. It therefore is rational for players to think of themselves first, and the team second.

B. Assume that the president of XYZ Corporation is confronted with the following alternatives:

1. Spend $11 million for antipollution equipment to keep from poisoning fish in the river adjacent to the plant; or
2. Do nothing, in violation of the law, and assume a one in ten chance of being caught, with a resultant $1million fine plus the necessity of buying the equipment.

Under this not unrealistic set of choices it requires no linear program to determine that XYZ Corporation can maximize its probabilities by flouting the law. Add the fact that XYZ's president is probably being rewarded (by creditors, stockholders, and other salient parts of his task environment) according to criteria totally unrelated to the number of fish poisoned, and his probable course of action becomes clear" (Ken 1975, 774).

It's not my intent to either corroborate or refute the realistic nature of the examples cited above, but merely to make use of them to buttress the notion of unintended consequences of certain metrics.

Kim is rewarding the TSMs for the number of SKUs accepted by the retailer and for the number of new retailers brought on board. In meeting these metrics, the TSMs disregarded the type of products being pushed at retail, and they apparently offered discretionary discounts to retailers—inappropriately—in exchange for SKU acceptance. Consequently, top line revenues were sacrificed.

Being cognizant of potential unintended consequences from certain metrics, Kim felt optimistic about the upcoming collaborative session—so much so that she issued an email to all TSMs, alerting them of the now mandatory meeting and also authorizing air travel to the regional office for any TSMs serving in territories that were not within reasonable driving distance of the office. Kim's scroll to be presented during the collaboration stage of the model is shown in figure 7-9.

The outcome linked to the HR consultation has been modified to reflect assessment results. Kim plans to discuss the results of this assessment with HR before meeting with her team. Kim's goal is to first understand how she is perceived by her team and then make use of the upcoming meeting as an opportunity to send a key message to her team based on the feedback. The key message is included in the outcomes field.

Figure 7-9: Kim's Collaboration Stage Scroll

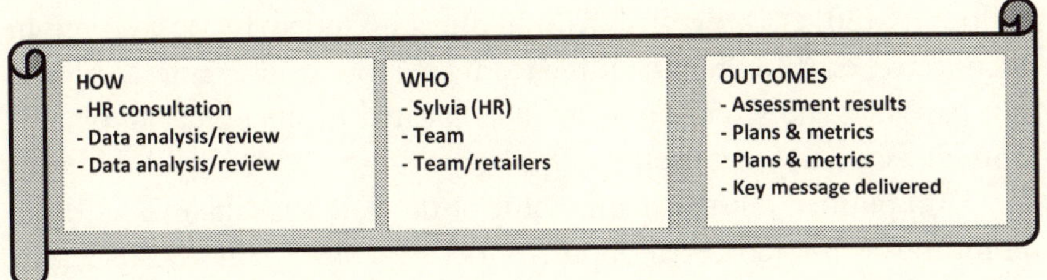

HOW
- HR consultation
- Data analysis/review
- Data analysis/review
WHO
- Sylvia (HR)
- Team
- Team/retailers
OUTCOMES
- Assessment results
- Plans & metrics
- Plans & metrics
- Key message delivered

7.2 The Meeting

During the meeting kickoff, Kim summarized the received MLQ and supplemental question feedback, focusing on themes in lieu of specifics. She circumvented what might have otherwise been an unpleasant environment resulting from her review of the results by saying, "Well, team, the good news is that I scored higher in the key TL category of idealized influence than 5 percent of those tested, and I scored higher in the TL category of idealized behavior than 10 percent of those tested."

The team, being aware of their own assessments by retailers, inquired regarding those results. Displaying maturity in the area of EI and accountability, Kim responded with: "I think it's safe to say that I have a lot of work to do regarding my leadership style. You all represent the vision that I have set for you, and that's one of the things that we need to talk about today: where we are going as a team and how we plan to get there. So let's get started, and as far as I am concerned, any opportunities with retail are opportunities that we will resolve together." The team all nodded affirmatively, Kim thanked them for the feedback, and the meeting moved forward.

Alina, a TSM in one of the territories that lagged in revenues and contacts, pointed out that the territories she failed to visit often enough were the ones located on the outer boundaries of her territorial route. However, she now recognized that those territories are just as important as the other retailers. This sounded familiar to Kim, as her LMX style failed to include in key meetings and events, some of the TSMs who were not located near the regional office.

In chapter 1, I cited a report by Mao and Venus stating: "Leaders' group based identities have also been found to spill over to their followers" (2012, 1). Because Kim in effect excluded TSMs who might incur travel expenses for attending team meetings, those same TSMs did not pay adequate attention to retailers located in the outer boundaries of their assigned territories.

Kim pointed out that while some of the data that she reviewed did point to specific territorial opportunities in retailer calls and revenues, the focus for now would be not on any specific territory but on all territories. She added that she would address TSM-specific opportunities during individual performance review discussions and pointed out that the principle focus of those discussions would be forward-looking. With this statement, Kim introduced the new, though not yet completed, key performance indicators (KPIs) shown in figure 7-10.

Figure 7-10: Kim's Proposed KPIs

Proposed Key Performance Indicators (KPI's) **Strategy: Increase Company Return on Sales (ROS)**		Evaluation Weighting
KPI #1: Sales revenue increase by 5.0% by end of 3rd quarter. Owner - TSMs/ Resources - Kimberly Hours	G	50% (TSM 40% Team 10%)
KPI #2: Increase retailer calls to 4/quarter by 3rd quarter. Owner - TSMs / Resources - Kimberly Hours.	G	30%
KPI #3: Implement sales mix techniques to ensure optimal brand mix at retail, including new products, by 2nd quarter. Owner - TSMs / Resources - Kimberly Hours	G	20%
KPI #4: Implement "field visits" 1/quarter / territory by 2nd quarter. Owner - Kimberly Hours / Resources - TSMs.	G	
KPI #5: Develop and implement visible "total team" progress report on all KPI's by end of 1st quarter. Owner - Kimberly Hours / resources - TSMs.	G	
KPI #6: TBD - TSMs to identify this measure during meeting based on needed skills, resources, etc. in support of KPI's 1 - 5.	G	

As would be expected, KPI #1 received the most attention, particularly Kim's reference to the split of the 50 percent weighting between the TSM and the team. Kim explained that for everyone's upcoming performance evaluation, a total of 40 percent of the overall evaluation would be based on increasing sales revenues by 5.0 percent in their respective territories. However, in an effort to incent the TSMs to share ideas and collaborate, 10 percent of the total evaluation would be predicated on the progress of the total TSM team.

Although some of the TSMs raised concerns regarding the feeling of being held accountable for the performance of their peers, these sentiments proved to be short-lived when Kim explained that just as Summit Consumables' success necessitated the contribution of each department in the southern region in order to succeed, each TSM should recognize the value added to the overall organization by each other TSM's contribution.

After reviewing each of the five KPIs, Kim asked the team to suggest a final KPI that would enable their successful execution of the previously discussed KPIs. After a bit of discussion among themselves, a spokesperson for the team, Alina, said that the TSMs could really use some training in the area of category management with emphasis on how to determine the appropriate mix of products that the retailer should carry, and that this training should include not only Summit Consumables' brands, but the integration of competitive brands. Kim, recalling that she had requested such training from Maria several weeks ago, thought this was an excellent idea and agreed to add the following KPI.

Provide sales mix training to all TSMs and institute best practices sharing by end of 1st quarter.

Kim listed herself as the owner and the TSMs as a resource. She immediately clarified that the TSMs would have to allow for the scheduling of the training and be willing to share best practices used in their respective territories. Consequently, they must be included as a resource. The team responded in acknowledgement and agreement. The updated dashboard is shown in figure 7-10A.

The team began to respond to Kim in a manner that she had not witnessed previously, whereby each of them began offering to share best practices with one another. They also suggested methods for the presentation of such practices. The stage was now set. Kim had not only listened to her feedback, she had accomplished something perhaps more profound: She listened to the most valuable asset in her world at Summit Consumables, her team. Upon returning to her office, Kim began to update her communication scroll, as shown in figure 7-11.

Figure 7-10A: Updated Dashboard

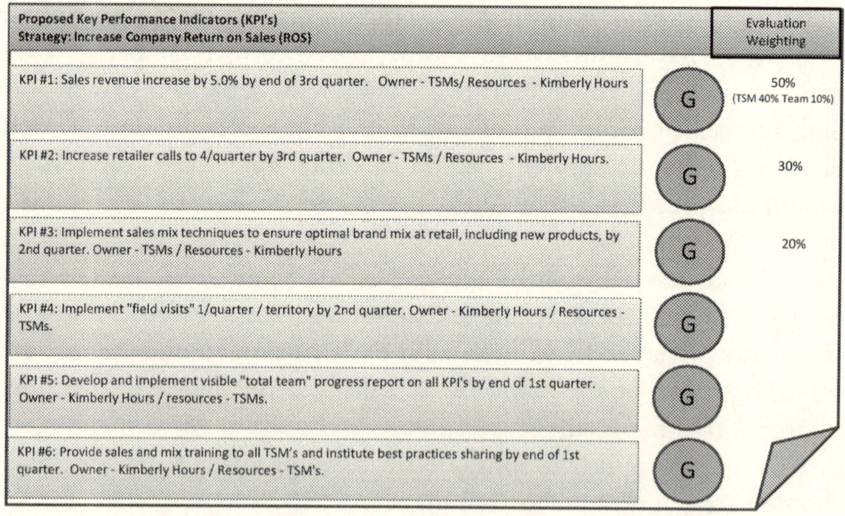

Proposed Key Performance Indicators (KPI's)
Strategy: Increase Company Return on Sales (ROS)
Evaluation Weighting
KPI #1: Sales revenue increase by 5.0% by end of 3rd quarter. Owner - TSMs/ Resources - Kimberly Hours
G
50%
(TSM 40% Team 10%)
KPI #2: Increase retailer calls to 4/quarter by 3rd quarter. Owner - TSMs / Resources - Kimberly Hours.
G
30%
KPI #3: Implement sales mix techniques to ensure optimal brand mix at retail, including new products, by 2nd quarter. Owner - TSMs / Resources - Kimberly Hours
G
20%
KPI #4: Implement "field visits" 1/quarter / territory by 2nd quarter. Owner - Kimberly Hours / Resources - TSMs.
G
KPI #5: Develop and implement visible "total team" progress report on all KPI's by end of 1st quarter. Owner - Kimberly Hours / resources - TSMs.
G
KPI #6: Provide sales and mix training to all TSM's and institute best practices sharing by end of 1st quarter. Owner - Kimberly Hours / Resources - TSM's.
G

Figure 7-11: Kim's Communication Stage Scroll

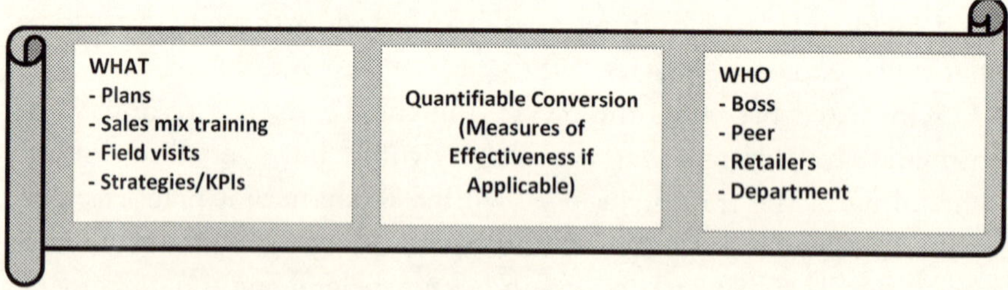

WHAT
- Plans
- Sales mix training
- Field visits
- Strategies/KPIs
Quantifiable Conversion (Measures of Effectiveness if Applicable)
WHO
- Boss
- Peer
- Retailers
- Department

Rather than communicate to a mass audience, Kim's plan was to close the loop with her boss regarding her plans, follow-up with her peer, Maria, regarding the requested sales mix training, reach out to the retailers to alert them of her impending visits with TSMs, and to post the new KPIs on the departmental intranet. Regarding the KPI posting, Kim also planned to post ongoing progress updates in the form of the traffic light indicators to complement the KPIs. Retailers were to be included in the communications process, but not all data, such as TSM evaluation weightings, would be shared with the retailers.

Closing the loop on Kim's implementation of the 5C LIM, all communication meetings were executed as planned. Recall that during

Kim's performance evaluation discussion, her boss encouraged her to schedule a follow-up meeting with his administrative assistant (Gene). To Kim's surprise, Gene informed Kim that Kim's boss had heard of the progress she was making in establishing KPIs and was looking forward to hearing more about her plans for monitoring progress.

It's not at all uncommon for bosses to become aware of actions taken by their direct reports. Typically, bosses have a far-reaching communications network and are very much in tune with activities within their areas of responsibility, particularly those representing any sort of change.

The follow-up meeting with her boss (Seth) went extremely well. He was particularly pleased with the weightings that Kim had placed alongside each of the affected KPIs. And Seth made one comment that Kim was not expecting. Before ending their meeting, he said: "Well, I guess you have figured out what you plan to do to turn things around [referring to his comments from talking about evaluation results], and if there is anything at all that I can do, please don't hesitate to let me know." Kim thanked Seth but pointed out that although she did indeed lead the charge to pull the KPIs together, it wouldn't have been possible without the input of her team.

Leadership insights: Quantifiable leadership opportunities identified for Kim included increasing revenues from product sales, which was also linked to better account management. Nonquantifiable opportunities included the lack of consideration of employee needs versus those of her own, not respecting ideas of all team members, a lack of in-field participation, and inconsistency in the area of team member development.

In responding to the quantifiable opportunities noted, Kim used budget review techniques (quarterly sales revenues versus region) coupled with comprehensive Pareto analysis such as SKUs versus territories and TSM contact performance to identify major contributors to lost revenues. She also used this analysis to identify unintended consequences of her existing performance metrics, such as "rewarding for A and hoping for B." Thus, new KPIs were identified and implemented, resulting in better alignment with desired outcomes.

Regarding the nonquantifiable opportunities, perhaps Kim's most important response was her recognition that TSMs in three territories were the unfortunate victims of her LMX (leader member exchange—in group versus out group) leadership style. Now being aware of this opportunity, Kim committed to in-field visits and providing training for all TSMs (a key TL attribute) as well as authorizing travel to now mandatory staff meetings for TSMs operating beyond reasonable driving proximity of the office. In addition, aimed at demonstrating the importance of full TSM collaboration, Kim linked 10 percent of TSM rewards (a key XL attribute) to total team performance. The inclusive and participative approach taken by Kim, coupled with her acknowledgement to her boss of the team's contribution to KPI development, should also aide attempts to build trust with her team.

CHAPTER 8

The Buck Stops Here—Maria Summers

LET'S TALK ABOUT Maria Summers, the regional product portfolio director. Several action items were supplied by Maria's boss, including leadership opportunities (focused on peer relationships), shoring up the promotions plans (northern and southern tiers), and resolving advertising issues. Figure 8-1 shows how Maria began to update her conversation stage scroll following the meeting with her boss.

Figure 8-1: Maria's Conversation Stage Scroll

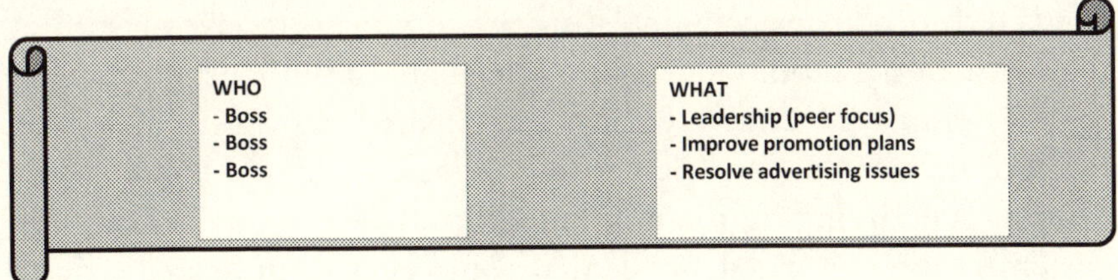

WHO
- Boss
- Boss
- Boss
WHAT
- Leadership (peer focus)
- Improve promotion plans
- Resolve advertising issues

Although Maria has much follow-up regarding collaborating with her peers, the opportunities identified in the conversation stage require only that she note WHAT is to be done. Moving to the calculation stage in figure 8-2, Maria now has considered a high-level approach to issue resolution.

Regarding the first opportunity, peer focus, Maria, in consultation with Sylvia, elected to issue the MLQ questionnaire to her peers, including Kimberly Hours in sales, and to compare the results to the percentile table comprising scores based on those operating at the same level. (See appendix C for details.) The perception of Maria's lack of collaboration with peer departments as conveyed by her boss was

Figure 8-2: Maria's Calculation Stage

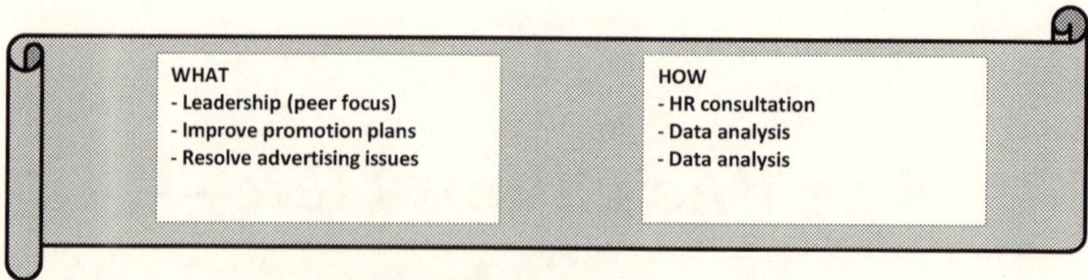

something that had plagued her since joining Summit Consumables. It had been overlooked in the past because her bottom line contributions appeared to overshadow her lack of collaboration. Indeed, it was Maria's design and implementation of the product promotion in the southern tier last year that caught the attention of her vice president and others at corporate.

Unlike actions taken by others, because resolution of the issues identified in Maria's performance evaluation required that she engage her peers, she elected not to pursue the data analysis opportunities shown in her scroll, pending receipt and review of MLQ data. But Maria did spend time contemplating the comments received regarding the southern tier promotions. She implemented a similar strategy while she was employed at a B2B firm that invited customers to redeem free products based on their visit to the company website. Upon entering identifying information into Summit Consumables' website, customers were provided a code that could later be presented at retail for redemption.

A secondary objective of this promotion was to facilitate population of the company *customer relationship management* (CRM) system.

If you are not intimately familiar with marketing jargon, you are no doubt wondering what CRM really means. Babin and Zikmund provide a great definition: "a CRM system is a decision support system that manages the interactions between an organization and its customers … a CRM maintains customer databases containing customers' names, addresses, phone numbers, past purchases, responses to past promotional offers, and other relevant data such as demographic and financial data" (2007, 170).

Maria recalled that she checked the box on key fundamental steps during the development of the southern tier promotion. She fully considered the mix of print versus TV advertising. Even though Nielsen data suggested reduced viewership of prepurchased TV advertising space, Maria felt there must be something else impacting the promotion. Instead of developing a creative strategy like at her former B2B employer, where the focus was on attributes, her design approach for Summit Consumables' message was to highlight the product benefits. Maria also implemented all aspects of the AIDA model in completing the final product advertisement. (The acronym AIDA represents attention, interest, desire and action, of which the principal objective is to incent prospective consumers to purchase the product.)

The big question that Maria has at this point is: What might be the source of the issue with her redemption-based product promotion in the southern tier? After all, it is clearly aligned with the fundamental intentions of CRM systems. Her peer Reginald Baldwin, manager of customer relations and distribution, would be able to answer all her questions in this area.

Likewise, regarding promotional issues in the northern tier (which did not rely on the website for redemption), Maria would have to speak with Jeff Hostetler, manager of market information. In looking through her tickle file (a file of items for follow-up), Maria also noticed that she had not yet responded to a request from Kimberly Hours, regional sales director. The request for sales mix training was sent several weeks back, and Maria had labeled it as a priority. A conversation with Kimberly was in order.

Despite the burning need to have these conversations, Maria remained steadfast to her original position of waiting for receipt and review of the previously routed MLQ feedback forms. In particular, she desired to approach Reginald, as well as her remaining peers, in such a way as to address any issues received in the feedback.

8.1 Leadership Reflection

Having received the MLQ feedback, Maria, like Kim, was rated the lowest in the area of idealized influence (attributes and behaviors—IIA/IIB). Transformational leaders who demonstrate maturity in these areas also "earn credit with followers [by considering] followers' needs over his or her own needs … shares risks with followers …" (Avolio & Bass 2004, 101). Based on Maria's scoring, she did not appear to be among these leaders. This view, as reflected in numerical MLQ ratings, was substantiated by aggregated team responses to the three supplemental assessment questions issued with the MLQ shown in figure 8-3. Despite the MLQ's design to measure principally leader attributes and behaviors, the rater scoring may be applied at the peer level as well, buttressed by these three questions.

The responses to question 1 seem to substantiate the discussion in the leader/follower context, whereby the leader is not sharing risks with followers. Question 2 further supports Maria's lack of teamwork or collaboration and suggests that she is not considering the needs of others over those of her own. The response to question 3 might indicate that, despite the issues identified in areas of teamwork and peer consideration, Maria's contribution to her job remains valued by her peers.

Figure 8-3: MLQ Supplemental Feedback for Maria

Supplemental Assessment Questions:

1. What are two or three things that would help this person be more efficient?

Allow peers to share in risks

Don't be afraid to ask for help

2. One thing that gets in the way of this person's effectiveness is:

Speak less in first person

Consider the perspectives of others

3. What I admire most about this person's leadership:

Job competence

Knowledge in B to B Marketing

Regarding the specific MLQ data, on a scale from 1–4, Maria received an average rating of 1.50 in the area of IIA. The norm table in appendix C reveals that a score of 1.50 for IIA is at the fifth percentile, meaning 5 percent of the normed population scored lower, and 95 percent scored higher than 1.50. Similarly, Maria received an average rating of 1.50 in the area of IIB. A score of 1.50 for IIB is also positioned at the fifth percentile, meaning 5 percent of the normed population scored lower, and 95 percent scored higher than 1.50.

Sylvia, who was present upon Maria's review of her feedback, reassured Maria that feedback is indeed a gift, and what she does with the feedback going forward is much more important than the feedback itself. Sylvia also suggested that Maria circle back to discuss the results of her peer meetings. Maria agreed to do that, thanked Sylvia for her input, and said: "You will have to excuse me now. I have some team repair work to tend to." Upon Sylvia's departure, Maria began working on her scroll for the collaboration stage as shown in figure 8-4.

Figure 8-4: Maria's Collaboration Stage Scroll

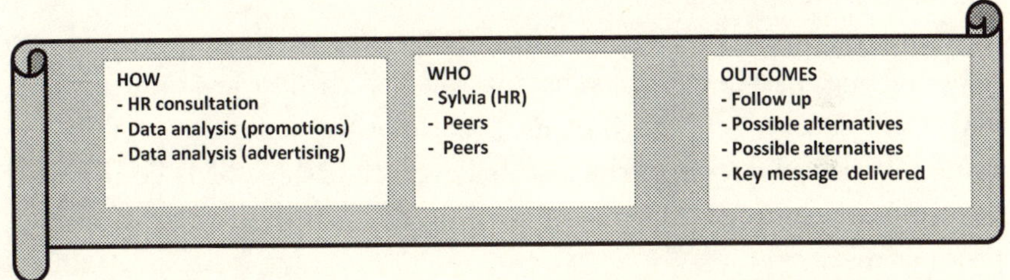

HOW
- HR consultation
- Data analysis (promotions)
- Data analysis (advertising)
WHO
- Sylvia (HR)
- Peers
- Peers
OUTCOMES
- Follow up
- Possible alternatives
- Possible alternatives
- Key message delivered

The item Follow-up appears in the OUTCOMES column of Maria's scroll, meaning that following individual meetings with her peers, Maria plans to have a follow-up discussion with Sylvia, as promised.

Recall that introduction of the 5C LIM was sequential, one stage being completed before commencing to the next. But in some cases the collaboration stage is implemented in concert with the communication stage.

To understand this better, recall our discussion of communication and the significance of the message that is to be conveyed. As with Johnny and Kim, Maria intended to send a key message reflecting her assessment results and to set the stage for how she planned to demonstrate effective listening (relative to her received feedback) while working (collaborating) with her peers to resolve the issues identified in her conversation stage scroll. Consequently, the term Key message delivered appears in the column labeled OUTCOMES in her collaboration scroll.

8.2 The Meeting

Maria's first meeting was with Kim. At the beginning of the meeting, Maria apologized for not getting back with Kim, summarized her peer feedback, and, demonstrating newfound listening skills, asked for more information regarding her request for sales mix training for the TSMs. Maria also pointed out that she had been remiss in not touching base with Kim periodically to see how things were going and that in the future she would like to have monthly one-on-ones to discuss issues, opportunities, or simply to check in with her.

Kim thought this was a great idea and asked if Maria would be OK with Kim sending some available meeting dates upon her return to the office, to which Maria agreed.

Turning now to the sales mix training request, Kim explained that sales revenues had decreased substantially over the last few quarters and, while she recognized the increased competitive environment played some role in the decrease, she also believed that the TSMs could assist in recovering some of the erosion attributed to less than optimal retailer product mix.

As you might have imagined, there is a method to how a company determines the most profitable mix of its products to sell in the market place. The only thing we have to do now is explain how it all works.

Remember our discussion regarding budgets and variable and fixed costs? If you understood that, this will be a piece of cake.

Let's assume that you have a product (call it product K) that you want to sell for $14.00 and it costs you $6.00 in raw materials and labor to make the product. You probably think that you subtract $6.00 from $14.00 and make a whopping $8.00 for each of the K's that you sell. Not so fast! The raw materials and labor account for only the variable costs. There are still fixed costs to be covered.

So now the question becomes: How do you cover your fixed costs with revenues from the sale of product K? To answer this question, we must bring into the mix (no pun intended), a term referred to as *marginal income ratio* (MIR) which is "the percent of revenue available for contribution to fixed costs and profit after variable costs have been covered [and] is given by MIR = (Price – Variable Cost) / Price" (Dolan et al. 1993, 173).

Depending on the industry, the fixed costs may be quite high or relatively low. In the example just given for product K, the MIR would be ($14.00 - $6.00) / $14.00 multiplied by 100 to get 57 percent. Assuming a sales volume of 1000 units for product K, the gross revenue in this example would be 1000 × $14.00 or $14,000. The income contribution would be $14,000 × 57 percent or $7980.

There are other applications of MIR that I encourage you to review at your leisure. The point here, however, is to present an explanation of how the sale of a product contributes to overall profitability. If a company produces several products, respective MIRs could be calculated for each product as is done in figure 8-5. From this, the optimal sales mix could be determined so that the aggregated contribution to cover fixed costs, and therefore profit, is maximized.

Figure 8-5: Product Marginal Income Ratio

Marginal Income Ratio (MIR)						
Product	**VC**	**Price**	**MIR**	**Volume**	**Gross Revenue**	**Income**
E	$ 9.00	$ 56.33	0.840	30000	$ 1,689,900.00	$ 1,419,900
F	$ 8.00	$ 36.00	0.778	10000	$ 360,000.00	$ 280,000
G	$ 12.50	$ 26.33	0.525	150000	$ 3,949,500.00	$ 2,074,500
H	$ 13.50	$ 23.34	0.422	20000	$ 466,800.00	$ 196,800
		Total Contribution to Fixed Costs:				$ 3,971,200
				Total Fixed Costs:		$ 2,765,000
				Net Income:		**$ 1,206,200**

Upon inspection of the MIRs above, we see that products E and F have the greatest marginal income ratios but only account for 43 percent ($1.7 million) of the total income contribution. Yet products G and H have much lower marginal income ratios but account for 57 percent ($2.27 million) of the total contribution.

So, what's up with that? While higher MIRs are great, sales volume may significantly magnify the total income contribution of a particular product despite its MIR. And because there is no up or down switch that the corporation can operate to control consumer preferences and therefore product sales, the correct mix of products sold at retail is imperative. With this in mind, we return to the conversation between Maria and Kim.

Now aware of Kim's needs, Maria committed to having one of her direct reports meet with Kim's TSMs to review the appropriate product mix that should be encouraged at retail aimed at maximizing revenues. Maria also suggested that, circumstances permitting, she would like to attend several of these training sessions to address firsthand any questions or concerns posed by the TSMs. Kim expanded on this idea by suggesting that she and Maria align their schedules to jointly attend the sessions, to which Maria agreed. Before exiting the meeting, Kim began to apologetically justify her MLQ feedback regarding Maria. Maria interrupted to reassure Kim that she appreciated the feedback and viewed it as a gift. She added: "How can you complain about anything of value that is received free of charge?" They both laughed and the meeting adjourned.

Turning now to the floundering promotions in the northern tier, Maria set up a meeting with her peer, Jeff Hostetler, manager of market information, to discuss the current promotional performance. Jeff was interested in working with Maria because he always thought that her prior experience in B2B marketing could benefit Summit Consumables. Recalling some of the feedback she had received, Maria began the meeting by thanking Jeff for his feedback and also saying that she appreciated Jeff's help at such a critical time and that she was looking forward to learning all Jeff could share regarding product promotional data.

Maria's biggest concern regarding the promotions was that while some minor differences existed in total product volume, there did not appear to be any way to determine which of two major promotions—B2G1 (buy two get one) or B3G2 (buy three get two)—was the most effective for two of Summit's major products, A and B. In addition, manufacturing operations was experiencing scheduling difficulty due to the unpredictable volume levels required for promoted product. If the promotional efforts yielded more consistent and predictable results, production and product category planning could be optimized. The promotional data associated with product A are shown in figure 8-5A.

Of note regarding the product data are two very important points. First, both promotion types (B3G2 and B2G1) are expressed in terms of *time in force*, measured in weeks, and *volume 1k units*, meaning that in week 3, for example, 22,000 total units were sold for the B2G1 promotion. Second, while the B3G2 promotion results in slightly less

Figure 8-5A: Product A Promotional Results Data

Prod A - Buy 3 Get 2		Prod A - Buy 2 Get 1	
Weeks In Force	Volume (1k units)	Weeks In Force	Volume (1k units)
1	5	1	0
2	11	2	50
3	19	3	22
4	30	4	19
5	41	5	26
6	51	6	42
Total	**157**	**Total**	**159**

volume (157k versus 159k), when compared to the B2G1 promotion, the trend of the B3G2 data appears to be more predictable. That is, the increases in volume appear to be related to the time in force of the B3G2 promotion.

Maria was not sure how to proceed with the analysis. At first glance, Jeff exclaimed that this would be a great opportunity to apply linear regression. Maria recalled the term regression but was not aware of its use beyond relating SAT scores to GPAs and that some colleges and universities use that type of model to predict student success.

As a bit of background, figures 8-6 and 8-7 reflect the data and the respective plot for a typical example of linear regression used to predict college GPA scores.

On the horizontal (x-axis) are SAT scores, and on the vertical (y-axis), are GPAs. The aim here is to allow a student's SAT success to predict his or her college success as measured by achieved GPA. The points on the chart represent the actual scores. While only a few points are shown on this chart, regressions used to predict this and similar relationships typically involve many data points.

In our example, the featured data point represents a college GPA of 2.9 and an SAT score of 1100. The line sloping upward from left to right represents a prediction of college GPAs. To determine the relationship, select any SAT score from the x-axis, move vertically to the prediction line then move to the left to select the GPA on the y-axis. This suggests that a student scoring 1500 on the SAT is predicted to achieve a college GPA of between 3.5 and 4.0. Not rocket science right?

Figure 8-6: GPA and SAT Data

SAT	GPA
1100	2.9
1290	3.2
1400	3.4
1550	3.9
920	2.1
1080	2.3
1010	2

Figure 8-7: Linear Regression Plot

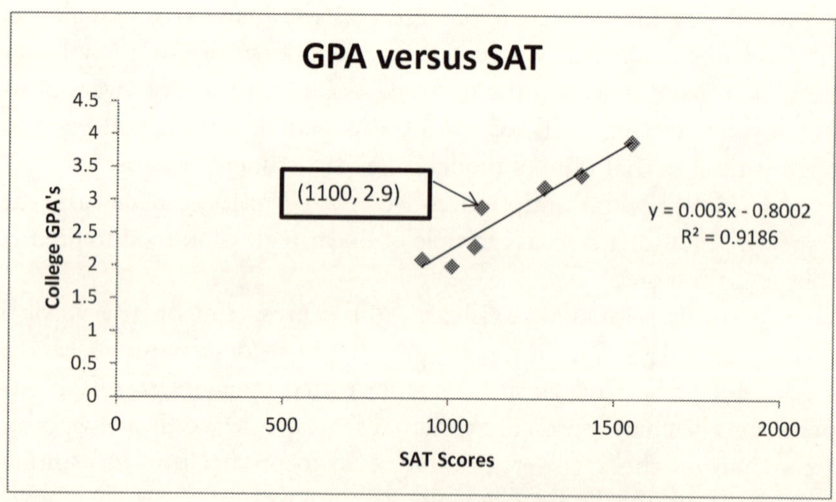

I know, you are thinking that the 0.5 range is rather large, and you would prefer to be more accurate in your prediction. Well, another way to predict the GPA is to apply the formula y = 0.003x – 0.8002, which is also listed in the box on the chart. If we selected the SAT (x-value) of 1500, multiplied this by 0.003, and then subtracted 0.8002, the corresponding GPA (y-value) would be 3.699. There's a more precise predictor of the actual GPA.

Notice also that a few of the points used to construct the prediction line do not actually fall on the line itself, for instance1100 and 2.9. This is because the prediction line is just that—a *prediction* of SAT scores.

So how do you determine the strength of this prediction line? Great question! One way to address this question is to understand the relationship between the values and the prediction line. Generally speaking, the greater the R^2 value (a statistical measure pronounced R-squared), the stronger the correlation between the data points and the prediction line. A more statistically correct definition of the R^2 value is that "the R^2 value, also known as the coefficient of determination, measures the percentage of variation in the values of the dependent variable [in our example GPA] that can be explained by the change in the independent variable [in our example SAT scores]" (Berk & Carey 2010, 323).

Two basic components are needed to complete a regression model. The first is a data set such as the SAT and GPA scores; the second is application software such as Excel, which can walk you through the process. The key point to remember is that when you desire to determine if there is a relationship between two variables, regression analysis might very well provide the answer.

Now that you are an expert in linear regression, its application is made even clearer as Jeff completes the linear regression analysis for both product A promotions based on the data provided in figure 8-5A above. These regressions are shown in figure 8-8.

Figure 8-8: Linear Regressions Product A - B3G2 and B2G1

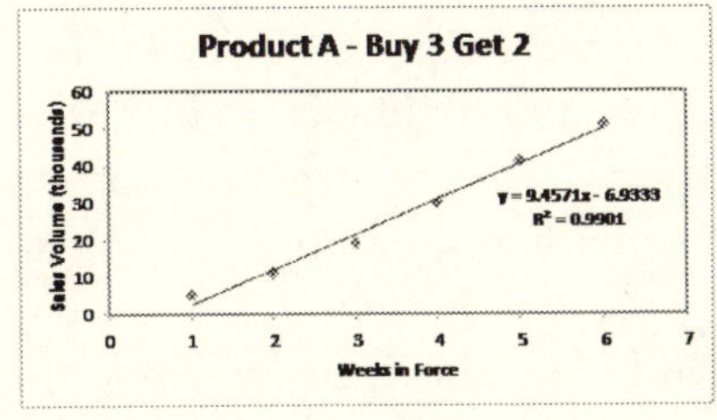

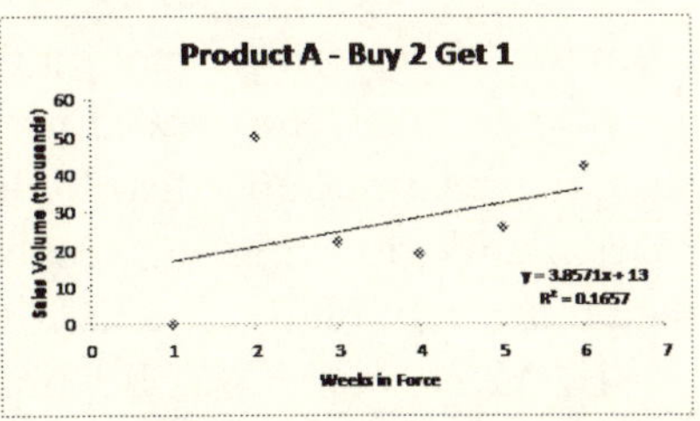

A review of these charts suggests that the B3G2 promotion yields an R^2 value of roughly 99 percent while the B2G1 promotion for the same product yields an R^2 value of roughly 17 percent. There does appear to be a strong correlation between the B3G2 promotion and customer preferences over time. So if the aim is to provide a more predictable product A demand, the B3G2 promotion may be the best option.

Likewise, for the product B promotional results data (see figure 8-9), the B2G1 promotion on the surface appears to yield more predictable and increasing results.

Figure 8-9: Product B Promotional Results Data

Prod B - Buy 3 Get 2		**Prod B - Buy 2 Get 1**	
Weeks In Force	Volume (1k units)	Weeks In Force	Volume (1k units)
1	9	1	4
2	12	2	9
3	14	3	12
4	20	4	19
5	7	5	23
6	23	6	32
Total	**85**	**Total**	**99**

Looking at the regressions for product B shown in figure 8-10, it is also clear that the B2G1 promotion offers greater predictability, boasting an R^2 value of 98 percent versus the same of 27 percent for the B3G2 program.

With Jeff's help, Maria now has a better handle on the market's reception of her two promotion types for each of products A and B.

Maria's next stop was to visit Reginald Baldwin, manager of customer relations and distribution. Upon entering Reginald's office, Maria thanked him for his feedback and asked if he might be able to shed some light on the southern tier promotion issues.

To Maria's surprise, Reginald said that the issue was not the promotion; it was, instead, the retailer's dislike of the new, less durable cases used for product shipping. He shared specific information suggesting that some retailers have conveyed their frustration with the flimsy cases and that after spending time preparing product for returns, little time is left to implement the code redemption program.

Figure 8-10: Linear Regressions Product B - B3G2 and B2G1

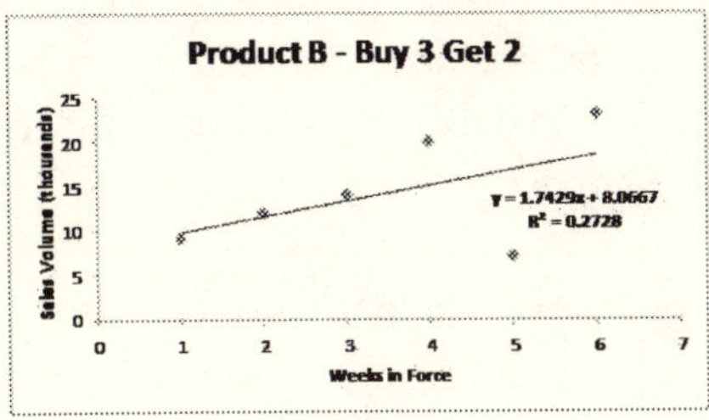

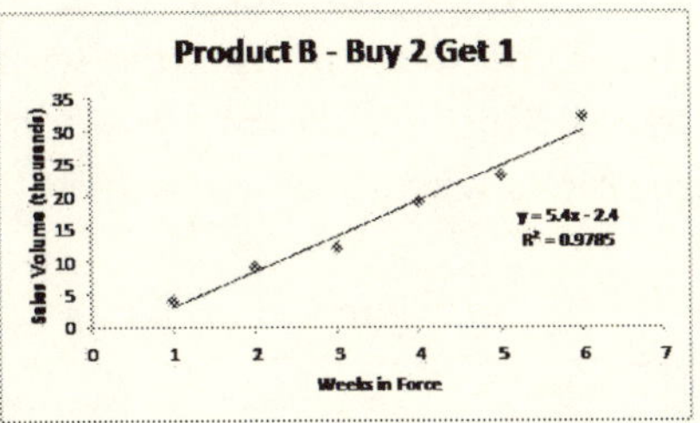

He also pointed out that the legacy inventory management system was down (out of service) almost as much as it was up (in service). Consequently, product had to be re-cased off-line using employees who were not fully trained, resulting in some mix-ups being reshipped to retail. Prior to exiting, Maria thanked Reginald for his insights.

Back in her office, Maria read an email from Jessica (director of manufacturing operations) requesting a meeting to talk about production scheduling issues that appear to be exacerbated by unpredictable product demand at retail. Maria, now being sure of the best approach for the B2G3 and B2G1 promotions, responded to Jessica's email with alacrity.

Maria also contacted several retailers for the purpose of validating comments shared by Reginald. All retailers operating in the southern tier that Maria contacted expressed worry regarding the new shipping cases, which were also being used for the casing of promoted products before shipment and the receipt of mixed and incorrect product. Consequently, those same retailers appeared to have given up on uncasing promotion products and were, instead, rejecting shipments with little to no inspection.

With this information, Maria sent an email to Johnny Goode (senior buying analyst) requesting his game plan for resolution of the flimsy case issue. Her thinking at this point was that both northern tier promotions (for products A and B) could be salvaged, and the southern tier promotion might be turned around as well if the case issues could be solved.

Maria reached for the telephone to contact Earl Easy (see the next chapter) regarding the legacy inventory system upgrade. But the phone rang before she could pick it up, and it was Earl. He asked if it would be possible for the two of them to meet to discuss his plan for executing the legacy system replacement project.

Maria's communications scroll is shown in figure 8-11. It reflects her intention to circle back with her boss regarding her plans and strategies for promotions and to meet with Earl and Johnny and to follow that by meeting with Kim. In addition, Maria will implement monthly meetings with Kim as reflected by the go-do.

Figure 8-11: Maria's Communications Stage Scroll

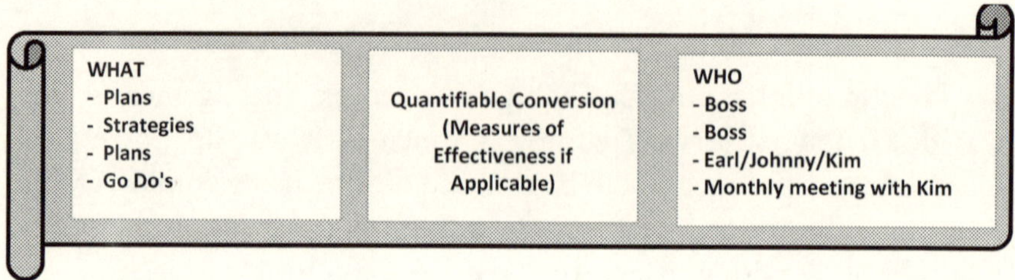

Leadership insights: Although the opportunities identified for Maria were not as easily quantifiable as those for Jessica, Johnny, or Kim, her lack of leadership, particularly in the area of inconsistent product promotions, profoundly affected the company's advertising and product growth strategy. Likewise, the inconsistent results achieved in the promotions affected production scheduling in manufacturing operations. Many of the nonquantifiable issues identified concerned Maria's relationships with her peers. Her feedback suggested she didn't value the input from her peers, nor did she allow her peers to share in risks.

In response to the quantifiable opportunities, Maria used statistical linear regression (including use of the R^2 value) to identify the most effective promotion to use (B2G1 or B3G2). This strategy maximized company financial resources and concurrently minimized scheduling disruption to manufacturing operations.

Regarding nonquantifiable opportunities, by considering the needs of her peers (a key TL attribute), Maria applied analytical marketing techniques such as the marginal income ratio (MIR) to provide a comprehensive overview to Kim about planned TSM category management training. Moreover, in completing the promotion regressions, Maria worked closely with one peer, Jeff Hostetler, and she also valued the input received from another, Reginald Baldwin, regarding the impact that failing cases might have on product promotions.

Cognizance was not discussed, particularly in the context of dashboard type infrastructure, in relation to Maria. Instead, Maria spent a great deal of time seeking to gain knowledge (a close synonym of cognizance) regarding the B2G1 and B3G2 promotion issues.

CHAPTER 9

The Buck Stops Here—Earl Easy

Shifting discussions now to Earl Easy (IT manager), figure 9-1 shows how he began to update the conversation stage scroll following the performance discussion with his boss (Frank). As was the case with others, there were several action items supplied by Frank, including leadership opportunities (particularly being out of touch and aloof) as well as bringing the website and infrastructure upgrade projects back on track. Consistent with others' approaches, Earl worked with the HR department to issue the MLQ.

Figure 9-1: Earl Easy's Conversation Stage Scroll

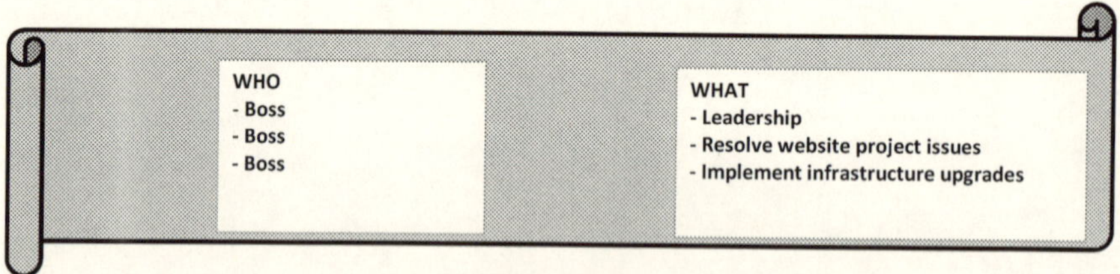

WHO
- Boss
- Boss
- Boss
WHAT
- Leadership
- Resolve website project issues
- Implement infrastructure upgrades

And as with the others, the timing for issuance of the MLQ was carefully calculated. Earl also set up a meeting with his direct reports to discuss the resolution of website project issues and infrastructure upgrades, to occur after receiving the MLQ feedback.

Moving now to the calculation stage, figure 9-2 shows Earl's plan to move forward.

The output from this stage may be several actions to be taken to the collaboration stage that, when implemented or otherwise addressed, are expected to resolve the current stage inputs. Note also that even though the website and infrastructure upgrade projects are viewed as separate issues or opportunities, the resources and approach required for their resolution are the same and involve Earl's direct reports.

Figure 9-2: Earl's Calculation Stage Scroll

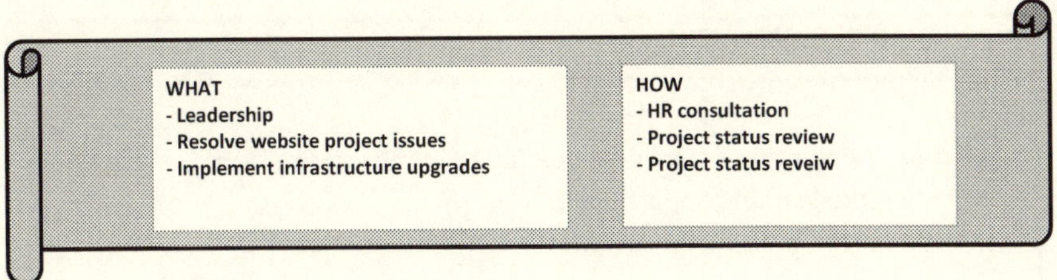

Recall that not all issues that move into the calculation stage will necessarily be quantifiable (as is a10-percent budget reduction). The purpose of this stage is to consider pro and con arguments aimed at addressing any item identified in the conversation stage, not to simply mechanically apply mathematical or deductive logic.

9.1 Leadership Reflection

In the previous chapter, Earl initiated contact with Maria regarding the inventory management system operational issues. While this demonstration of accountability was consistent with effective leadership, as will be seen in this section, it was also out of character for Earl. To this end, Earl's supplemental feedback to complement the MLQ rater feedback is shown in figure 9-3.

It appears Earl might do well to define subordinate objectives and responsibilities better, challenge them more, link results to rewards better, and hold each person accountable for assignment outcomes. Another key bit of feedback, although listed as a strength, is that Earl is perceived to be an easy boss to work for in that he tends to allocate ratings contingent on factors other than performance.

According to MLQ feedback, Earl was rated lowest in contingent reward (CR). (See Appendix D.) On a scale from 1–4, as substantiated by supplemental feedback, Earl received an average rating of 1.29 (the lowest possible score) in contingent reward (CR), which corresponds to the fifth percentile, meaning 5 percent of the normed population scored lower, and 95 percent scored higher than 1.29.

Figure 9-3: MLQ Supplemental Feedback for Earl

Supplemental Assessment Questions:
1. What are two or three things that would help this person be more efficient? Provide more learning opportunities Provide more clarity regarding objectives & responsibilities **2. One thing that gets in the way of this person's effectiveness is:** Does not reward for success Does not challenge his direct reports, no-one is held accountable **3. What I admire most about this person's leadership:** Very easy going Freely gives out top performance ratings to everyone

"Transactional [CR] leadership clarifies expectations and offers recognition when goals are achieved … the clarification of goals and objectives, and providing of recognition once goals are achieved should result in individuals and groups achieving expected levels of performance" (Avolio and Bass 2004, 102).

By the same standard, Earl received an average rating of 1.50 in the area of individualized consideration (IC), which corresponds to the tenth percentile, meaning 10 percent of the normed population scored lower, and 90 percent scored higher than 1.50. Leaders exhibiting IC "pay attention to each individual's need for achievement and growth by acting as a coach or mentor … followers are developed to successfully higher levels of potential …" (Avolio and Bass 2004, 102).

So we are saying that on the one hand, Earl essentially hands out unearned performance evaluation results, and on the other hand, Earl is critiqued because he doesn't reward for success. (See supplemental feedback.) What's up with that? The answer is simple. Earl fails to exhibit behaviors consistent with necessary XL, such as linking rewards to goals and objectives (CR), while failing to focus on the needs of his direct reports as evidenced by his low IC rating in TL.

During our review of the performance appraisal, we discussed at length the relationship between the CR component of XL and how such behavior actually facilitates optimal leadership. It is incumbent upon leaders to make clear the expectations (the goals and objectives) for subordinates, which may be viewed as telling them what to do. How and why subordinates achieve the goals and objectives may be linked to motivation and inspiration provided by the leader. According to Avolio and Bass some of the qualities XL includes are: "provides assistance in exchange for efforts, discusses who is responsible for what, makes clear [the] rewards for efforts, focuses attention on mistakes and attention [is] directed to failure" (2004, 102). TL includes: "inspire, instill pride, sense of purpose, displays confidence, talks optimistically, articulates a vision [and] questions assumptions" (2004, 101).

So it should be clear that effective leaders must both say what is to be accomplished and present vision and strategies on how to get it done. Supporting this point, Avolio and Bass stated that "the transactional process, [contingent reward] in which the leader clarifies what the associates need to do for a reward, is nevertheless viewed … as an essential component of … effective leadership" (2004, 21). Recall too that CR is one of only two XL constituents, so it accounts for 50 percent of the total perceived style rating.

The other constituent for XL is *management by exception active* (MBEA). Bennet (2009) cited works of multiple authors who argued that contingent reward was, in itself, related to TL (Avolio and Bass 2004, 6).

In the upcoming meeting, Earl has the opportunity to respond to the received feedback, not in a retaliatory manner, but in such a way that demonstrates his desire to challenge and build the skill sets of his direct reports and to provide clear direction regarding what is to be done, by when, and by whom.

Earl's plan was to first engage his entire team to review his assessment results. This would be followed by one-on-one meetings to discuss key projects and to collaboratively set key milestones and objectives. Going into the collaboration stage, Earl prepared the scroll as shown in figure 9-4.

Figure 9-4: Earl's Collaboration Stage Scroll

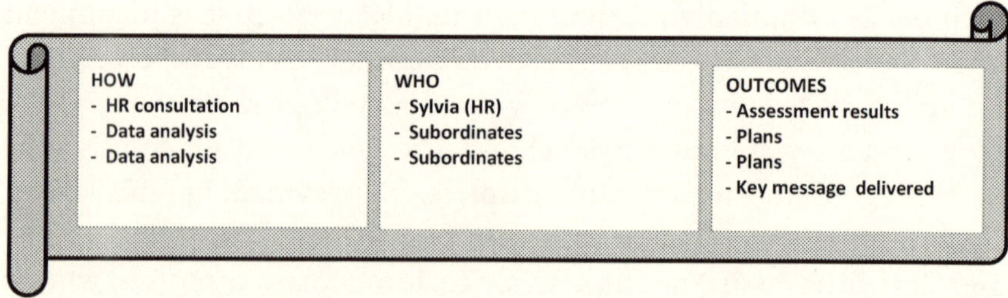

HOW
- HR consultation
- Data analysis
- Data analysis
WHO
- Sylvia (HR)
- Subordinates
- Subordinates
OUTCOMES
- Assessment results
- Plans
- Plans
- Key message delivered

During the collaboration stage, the leader may choose to send a key message, particularly as such relates to feedback, to all those attending the meeting or other such collaboration forum. The outcome linked to the HR consultation has been modified to reflect assessment results. The significance here is that Earl plans to discuss the results of his assessment with HR before meeting with his team. Earl's goal is to first understand how he is perceived by his team and then leverage the upcoming meeting as an opportunity to send a key message (also included in the outcomes field) to his team based on such feedback.

9.2 The Meeting

To kick off the meeting, Earl summarized the received MLQ and supplemental question feedback, focusing on themes in lieu of specifics. Like the others, he circumvented what might have otherwise been an unpleasant environment resulting from his review of the results by saying, "Well team, the good news is that I scored higher in the key TL category of individualized consideration than 10 percent of those tested, and I scored higher in the XL category of contingent reward than 5 percent of those tested." He continued in seriousness: "I believe that I know exactly what I need to do to not only challenge and coach each of you more, and I mean that in a positive way, but I also understand the importance of making a clear link between our key objectives and allocation of rewards."

The team, believing that their performance evaluations might be negatively impacted by the feedback they provided, seemed a bit on edge. Earl, anticipating this response, assured the team that based on the work that had to take place over the next several months, there would be ample opportunity for everyone to do well on the next performance evaluation—provided, he added, that key project milestones are met.

Surprisingly, the team appeared to rally around this comment. Perhaps this was their first exposure to challenge offered by Earl. After all, the water cooler conversation had dubbed him "easy Earl." Earl suggested that the best approach for addressing the critical projects (website and infrastructure upgrades) was to meet individually with those affected. He adjourned the meeting after setting up separate meetings with his direct reports.

We now join Earl the next morning in a meeting with Justin Dean, his direct report responsible for the infrastructure upgrade and replacement project. Summit Consumables currently uses a legacy system for managing inventory of raw materials for several key products and for cased product storage and retrieval. Legacy systems are typically high maintenance devices and may even require intricate patching and modifications for sustained use. Justin has been working on the project for several months and appears to be in heated disagreement with the finance department regarding contractor selection.

Summit Consumables requires that any new capital project, in order to be deemed viable, must meet certain payback, NPV (net present value), and IRR (internal rate of return) criteria, with the principal focus being on NPV. However, all criteria must consider the cost of capital or *hurdle rate*, as it is commonly known (all to be discussed shortly).

Justin has been debating with Finance suggesting that the most important of these requisite criteria should be the NPV and payback and that the IRR is not necessary. The contractor that Justin would like to accept, according to Justin, "blows away" the NPV and payback when compared to the other two bids.

Here comes the Finance 101 tutorial.

Let's say that you are the owner of a freight delivery company. Your business is expanding, so you are trying to decide between two alternative truck purchases. You can select only one, not both. In financial terms, this is a mutually exclusive approach. The first alternative (project X) is a larger truck that can haul 1.5 times more volume than the other delivery truck but requires an initial purchase price of $180,000. Use of this truck is expected to generate annual cash flows (incoming money from truck hauling operations) as indicated in figure 9-5.

The other truck (project Y) carries an initial purchase price of $106,000 but generates slightly less annual cash flows due to its smaller capacity, as also indicated in figure 9-5. As the owner, you have decided to consider these cash flows for a four-year period.

Figure 9-5: Alternative Truck Purchase Data

		Project X		Project Y
Year		Cash Flow		Cash Flow
0	$	(180,000.00)	$	(106,000.00)
1	$	36,000.00	$	18,500.00
2	$	52,000.00	$	21,560.00
3	$	60,000.00	$	34,000.00
4	$	63,000.00	$	52,000.00

The question now becomes: How does one determine which project will add the most value to the business based on its cash flow contribution? A simple approach would be to determine the *payback period* for each project, compare them, and select the one that has the highest payback. The payback period, according to Brigham and Gapenski, is defined as "the expected number of years required to recover the original investment" (1991, 323). In other words, how long would it take, in years, to repay the 180,000 expended for the new truck in project X? If I add the first 3 years of cash flows (year 1: $36,000, year 2: $52,000 and year 3: $60,000), the result is $148,000. However, I have not yet fully paid back the $180,000 as I am still $32,000 ($180,000 – $148,000) short. Not to worry. If I then divide this remaining $32,000 by the cash flow amount ($63,000) in the next available year, I get 0.51 years. So the total payback period for project X is the fully used three years of cash flows plus the 0.51 of the fourth year. Adding the two, I get a payback for project X of 3.51 years.

Applying this approach to projects X and Y, the payback periods would be 3.51 years and 3.61 years respectively. So you may be thinking, OK, I'll select project X, and it's a wrap. Well … not so fast. While these two project options are mutually exclusive, there does remain another option. What if instead of investing in a new delivery truck, you invest the money in a bank's interest-bearing account that offers a better payback or return for the same time period as the best project alternative? Keep in mind that you are in business to make a profit, and whether it's investing in business infrastructure (a truck purchase in this case) or investing money (capital) into a bank or other investment, the desired outcome should be the same—an increase in profits.

To understand the bank investment approach, consider the following question: Assuming you were guaranteed 5 percent interest by a bank investment, would you prefer to receive $784 today or $1000 five years from now? If you said that you would be comfortable with either scenario—good job! If not—this question has to do with time value of money (which is used interchangeably with *discounted cash flow* analysis). In other words, when money is invested into an interest-bearing investment, it will grow (on a *compounding* basis) over time.

In our scenario, at 5 percent interest, the $784 would grow to be $1000 in five years. Thus, there is neither a financial loss nor a financial gain by accepting $784 now or $1000 in five years as long as the interest rate remained at 5 percent. The $784 represents the present value (PV) of $1000 at 5 percent interest in five years. Conversely, the $1000 represents the future value (FV) of the $784 at 5 percent interest in five years.

How do you find the PV and FV? Great question! The formula for FV is "$FV_n = PV(1 + k)^n$ [where n is the number of years and k is the interest rate]," and the formula for finding the PV is "$PV = FV_n (1 / 1 + k)^n$ [where n is the number of years and k is the interest rate]" (Brigham and Gapenski 1991, 178).

You may also hear the term *discounting* used interchangeably with PV. When I was pursing my MBA, we used a Hewlett-Packard 10B calculator to determine both PV and FV. More contemporary methods for solving these types of problems include the use of application programs such as Excel.

So now that we know how to find the PV and FV for a specified amount of cash, we can also find the same for a stream of cash flows. Returning to our example, as shown in figure 9-6, we see the sum of the PVs of each of the cash flows from the two alternative projects. This time, however, we have modified PV such that it now reflects NPV (where the N represents *net*), which requires that once the PVs for each cash flow is determined, we sum these discounted cash flows to get the NPV for the project.

In the PV and FV example, we used an interest and discount rate of 5 percent. In capital projects (such as with the truck delivery example), the term *interest rate* is replaced with any of the terms *opportunity cost, hurdle rate*, or the *cost of capital.* "Cost of capital [which will be used in subsequent discussion in lieu of interest rate] refers to the opportunity cost of making a specific investment. It is the rate of return that could have been earned by putting the same money into a different investment with equal risk. Thus, the cost of capital is the rate of return required to persuade the investor to make a given investment" (investinganswers.com).

Many financial textbooks further disaggregate the cost of capital into specific components, also referred to as the *weighted average cost of capital* (WACC). Further inquiry into this area is encouraged but left to you to implement.

Figure 9-6: Payback, NPV and IRR Results for Projects X and Y

		Project X		Project Y	
Year		Cash Flow	Present Value	Cash Flow	Present Value
0	$	(180,000.00)	$ (180,000.00)	$ (106,000.00)	$ (106,000.00)
1	$	36,000.00	$ 34,285.71	$ 18,500.00	$ 17,619.05
2	$	52,000.00	$ 47,165.53	$ 21,560.00	$ 19,555.56
3	$	60,000.00	$ 51,830.26	$ 34,000.00	$ 29,370.48
4	$	63,000.00	$ 51,830.26	$ 52,000.00	$ 42,780.53
Payback (years)		3.51		3.61	
NPV ($'s)		5111.76		3,325.61	
IRR		6.12%		6.13%	

From figure 9-6, it is clear that the best decision involving the two mutually exclusive projects is to select project X based on the value of the NPV of the cash flows. Cash flows, as used here, could result from revenues received from use of an asset, such as the dump truck discussed earlier, or the avoidance of costs incurred for maintenance of an existing system, such as a legacy IT system.

Two remaining financial measures are worthy of discussion here. The first of these is *internal rate of return* (IRR). In summary, and perhaps at the risk of oversimplifying, as long as the calculated IRR for a particular project is greater than the cost of capital, it should be accepted. And in mutually exclusive situations, the project yielding the highest IRR (above the cost of capital) should be accepted. In financial jargon, "the IRR is defined as that discount rate, r, which equates the present value of a project's expected cash inflows to the present value of the project's expected costs" (Brigham & Gapenski 1991, 327). "The formula for IRR is: $0 = P_0 + P_1/(1{+}IRR) + P_2/(1{+}IRR)^2 + P_3/(1{+}IRR)^3 + \ldots + P_n/(1{+}IRR)^n$ [whereby] P_0, P_1, … P_n equals the cash flows in periods 1, 2, … n, respectively; and IRR equals the project's internal rate of return" (investinganswers.com). In other words, the IRR is the level at which the NPV is equal to zero.

So, as also shown in figure 9-6, the IRR of roughly 6 percent is greater than the cost of capital of 5 percent and therefore suggests that either project would be financially acceptable and thus viable. It should be noted that some companies may elect to elevate the required project IRR such that it exceeds the cost of capital by a given margin – say 2 percent.

Although not a focal point for discussion in this book, you should also be aware of the *modified internal rate of return* (MIRR). In comparison to the IRR, "the MIRR has a significant advantage … [as it] assumes that cash flows from all projects are reinvested at the cost of capital, while the regular IRR assumes that cash flows from each project are reinvested at the project's own IRR" (Brigham & Gapenski 1991, 336). As was the case with NPV, Excel or other application software may be used to calculate the IRR. Moreover, most corporations or businesses use software specifically designed to calculate financial measures, such as payback, NPV, IRR, and PI, within their capital budgeting processes.

As the second and final additional financial measure, we now look at *profitability index* (PI), which is given by "PI = PV benefits / PV costs" (Brigham & Gapenski 1991, 328). PV benefits in this equation is the sum of the positive present value cash flows, whereas PV costs are the sum of the cash outflows, meaning cash going out, such as the initial cost for the project or asset. In our example, there were four cash inflows occurring in years 1 through 4, and one cash outflow occurring in year 0. So the PI is 1.03 for both projects. The payback, NPVs, IRRs and PI for projects X and Y are shown in figure 9-7.

Are you totally confused? It appears that two of the four financial measures (profitability index and IRR) for both projects are roughly the same, so how do I know that either one is really a more feasible alternative over the other? Great question!

Figure 9-7: Payback, NPV, IRR and PI Results for Projects X and Y

Year		Project X Cash Flow	Project X Present Value	Project Y Cash Flow	Project Y Present Value
0	$	(180,000.00)	$ (180,000.00)	$ (106,000.00)	$ (106,000.00)
1	$	36,000.00	$ 34,285.71	$ 18,500.00	$ 17,619.05
2	$	52,000.00	$ 47,165.53	$ 21,560.00	$ 19,555.56
3	$	60,000.00	$ 51,830.26	$ 34,000.00	$ 29,370.48
4	$	63,000.00	$ 51,830.26	$ 52,000.00	$ 42,780.53
Payback (years)		3.51		3.61	
NPV ($'s)		5111.76		3,325.61	
IRR		6.12%		6.13%	
Profitability Index		1.03		1.03	
Cost of Capital		5.00%		5.00%	

In our example, we assumed that the cost of capital was fixed at 5 percent. As long as that is the case and the projects are mutually exclusive (meaning that you may select one or the other but not both), "logic suggests that the NPV method is [the best measure], since it selects that project which adds the most to shareholder wealth … if a project has a positive NPV then its cash flows are generating an excess return [which] accrues solely to the firm's shareholders" (Brigham & Gapenski 1991, 326, 331).

For the remainder of discussion in this section, we will focus on NPV, as it appears to be recognized as the most acceptable measure for capital budgeting and mutually exclusive project decision making. Thus, in our example because project X has an NPV of $5,112 it would be selected over project Y with an NPV of $3,326.

Now that you are an expert in financial decision making, we return to the conversation between Earl and Justin.

Summit Consumables has set certain criteria for project acceptance, including payback, NPV, and IRR, with the principal focus on NPV. Justin is in heated disagreement with the finance department regarding their reluctance to accept what Justin believes is a viable contractor proposal for the replacement of the legacy inventory management system. Recalling the key message that Earl desired to convey during meetings with his direct reports, he expressed his concern to Justin regarding the project delay and pointed out that while slight delays are understandable, execution of this initiative was of paramount importance for both him and Justin. He asked to see all information shared with finance.

In response, Justin presented the information shown in figure 9-8. The negative cash flow at year zero represents the initial outlay, or cost for the new system, whereas the cash flows in years one through four represent the savings when compared to the current scenario requiring legacy system maintenance, including system patching and modifications.

Figure 9-8: Inventory System Replacement Project Alternatives and NPVs

Inventory System Replacement Project						
		Contractor A		Contractor B		Contractor C
Year		Cash Flow		Cash Flow		Cash Flow
0	$	(10,000,000)	$	(10,000,000)	$	(12,000,000)
1	$	5,000,000	$	1,000,000	$	3,000,000
2	$	4,000,000	$	3,000,000	$	2,000,000
3	$	3,000,000	$	4,000,000	$	4,000,000
4	$	1,000,000	$	6,000,000	$	7,000,000
NPV (K=5.0%)	$	1,804,238	$	2,065,035	$	1,885,470

Justin pointed to the NPV of $2,065,035, at k = 5.0 percent, which represents the cost of capital that Justin used several years ago when working with finance on another project. Justin's view was that although all NPVs were positive, this one was of the greatest magnitude and should therefore be selected over the remaining proposals regardless of any change in cost of capital.

The word from finance was that Justin was not considering the entire financial picture and that their preference was contractor A's proposal, given changes in the cost of capital requirements to k = 10 percent. Earl pointed out that while he believes the contractor B proposal to be a viable option, the assumption that Justin is making is that the NPV is not sensitive to a different cost of capital and would remain the same at varying k levels. He suggested that Justin rerun the numbers assuming cost of capital levels of 5 percent, 10 percent, and 15 percent just to understand how the NPV behaves under those conditions. This analysis is reported in figure 9-9.

Figure 9-9: Contractor Proposals as a Function of Various K's

Inventory System Replacement Project						
		Contractor A		Contractor B		Contractor C
Year		Cash Flow		Cash Flow		Cash Flow
0	$	(10,000,000)	$	(10,000,000)	$	(12,000,000)
1	$	5,000,000	$	1,000,000	$	3,000,000
2	$	4,000,000	$	3,000,000	$	2,000,000
3	$	3,000,000	$	4,000,000	$	4,000,000
4	$	1,000,000	$	6,000,000	$	7,000,000
NPV (K=5.0%)	$	1,804,238	$	2,065,035	$	1,885,470
NPV(k=10.0%)	$	788,198	$	491,770	$	166,519
NPV(k=15.0%)	$	(83,297)	$	(801,419)	$	(1,246,679)

Of note here is that at k = 10.0 percent, the respective NPVs are $788,198, $491,770, and $166,519 for proposals A, B, and C. This was quite revealing to Justin as he was not aware that the NPVs were as sensitive to varying values of k. Earl also pointed out that the IRR associated with contractor A yielded 14 percent while contractor B yielded an IRR of 12 percent and contractor C yielded 11 percent. Likewise, the PI for all projects exceeded 1 as indicated in figure 9-10.

Figure 9-10: Contractor Proposals NPV's, IRR's and PI's

Inventory System Replacement Project						
		Contractor A		**Contractor B**		**Contractor C**
Year		Cash Flow		Cash Flow		Cash Flow
0	$	(10,000,000.0)	$	(10,000,000)	$	(12,000,000)
1	$	5,000,000.0	$	1,000,000	$	3,000,000
2	$	4,000,000.0	$	3,000,000	$	2,000,000
3	$	3,000,000.0	$	4,000,000	$	4,000,000
4	$	1,000,000.0	$	6,000,000	$	7,000,000
NPV (K=5.0%)	$	1,804,238	$	2,065,035	$	1,885,470
NPV(k=10.0%)	$	788,198	$	491,770	$	166,519
NPV(k=15.0%)	$	(83,297)	$	(801,419)	$	(1,246,679)
IRR		14.49%		11.79%		10.54%
PI (k=10%)		1.08		1.05		1.01

Although not the principal criterion for Summit Consumables, this IRR supported the finance position that the proposal from contractor A should be preferred. Analysis of the cash flows for the contractor A proposal reveals a payback of 2.33 years (not shown in the figure), which is also lower than the remaining proposals.

In response to Justin's question regarding why the IRR did not change despite the changes to k, Earl pointed out that the IRR is a measure of the return driven by the actual cash flows that corresponds to the NPV being zero. So it has no sensitivity to k.

At the conclusion of the meeting, Justin thanked Earl for his push regarding the project timeline and also expressed his appreciation that Earl took time to explain how changes in projected cost of capital could influence a project's NPV. Earl acknowledged this by also stating that he plans to ask all his direct reports to complete their desired personal development plans (identification of areas aimed at building their individual capabilities) by month's end. Justin appeared even more appreciative at hearing this news.

Earl was pensive en route to his meeting with Tonya McCoy, his direct report in charge of the website upgrade project. He considered the nonquantifiable opportunity cost of lost team effectiveness and efficiency resulting from his lack of alignment of team rewards with project success. He also thought about his failure to use their strengths while bolstering their weaknesses. Recalling key tenets of EI, particularly self-awareness and regulation, his thought pattern quickly shifted to staying on message in the next meeting.

Earl asked Tonya to give a bit of background on the website project and to discuss why it was delayed. Tonya replied that Maria's team had not been forthcoming with information for the website. (Recall that Maria is regional product portfolio director.) For example, Tonya sent an email requesting the content and theme several weeks ago, but no one responded. Earl asked if Tonya followed up, and Tonya indicated that she had not. Earl admonished, "When work needs to be done, you can't simply say that because a key customer didn't respond to your email, you are OK with being late on delivery."

As the two were engaged in conversation, Tonya received an email from Maria, who also copied Earl, stating that she was just made aware of the request from their team and that the requested information would be provided by week's end.

Earl asked Tonya to share with him the requirements and specifications document that was sent to Maria's team. Tonya seemed a bit puzzled by this request and said that she had simply sent Maria's team an email requesting them to respond with what they wanted to be included in the website. At this point Earl began to recall MLQ feedback that he had received, pointing to his lack of employee development. He asked Tonya for a marker to draw on her whiteboard and began drawing the diagram seen in figure 9-11 as espoused by O'Brian. (1990, 93).

Figure 9-11: The Traditional Information Systems (IS) Development Cycle

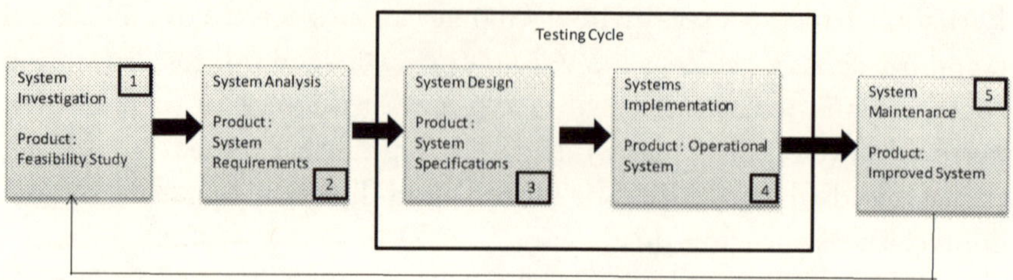

Earl explained that, despite the apparent complexity of the system, whether a website or a system to collect manufacturing operations data, there needs to be some level of structure to determine the current problem and identify and create viable solutions, followed by a means to validate the system and a process to monitor and improve it.

Earl asked Tonya if she knew the difference between a company website and a business information system. Ahead of Tonya's response, he quickly suggested that, in a broad sense, technically there are no measurable differences. According to O'Brien, an information system is "a set of people, procedures, and resources that collects, transforms, and disseminates information in an organization" (1990, 6).

With this as a backdrop, Earl discussed the flow diagram from left to right, beginning with the investigation in stage 1, which includes structured problem definition. He pointed out that there needs to be some plan for filtering potential alternative information system approaches. Also included in this first phase is the feasibility study to include cost benefit analysis and constraints.

Moving to stage 2, the systems analysis stage, this is where end user requirements are developed. In the case of creating or upgrading a website, information required would include that needed for user interface in addition to that required by Summit Consumables. Some people refer to this work as *defining system functionality* or *specifications.*

While this stage may also be termed deciding what a system should do, stage 3, systems design, "specifies how the system will accomplish this objective." The objective is to develop the system specifications required to address system requirements, including the completion of the logical and physical system design as per applicable design standards.

Next comes stage 4, system implementation, which includes software development and acquisition and testing. System design and system implementation occur on an iterative or testing mode basis.

Stage 5, maintenance, also viewed as monitoring, is aimed at continued assessment of the system post implementation. Any errors identified during the monitoring phase are corrected (O'Brien, 1990).

The O'Brien model is but one of several models used in the IT project implementation space. For example, Brewer and Dittman identified several models for use in the IT product and systems development cycle. Among those was "the waterfall model" as pictured in figure 9-12.

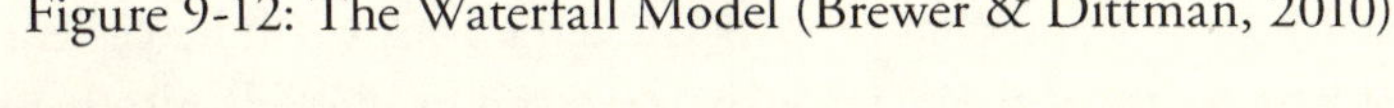
Figure 9-12: The Waterfall Model (Brewer & Dittman, 2010)

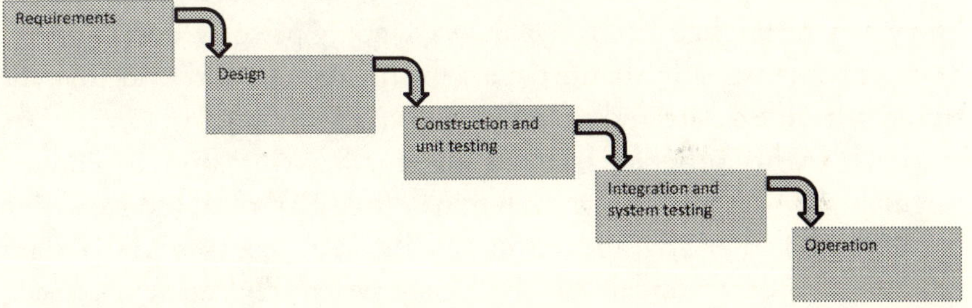

Note the similarities between this model and the one previously discussed. The principal difference is that while both models offer a path to systems development, the waterfall model is more sequential, offering little opportunity for iterations and system maintenance.

Other models include the evolutionary prototyping model, the spiral model, the iterative and incremental model, the scrum model, the RUP model" and the XP model, each of which offers its own strengths and weaknesses (Brewer & Dittman 2010). While Earl refers to the O'Brien model, any one of the just-mentioned models could have been presented in his discussion.

Earl suggested that Tonya study both traditional and more contemporary information system design steps to facilitate design and implementation of the website upgrades. He also stressed the importance of documentation, particularly in the system requirements and specifications phases. Finally, he reminded Tonya of the "triple constraint … associated with every project whereby … the customer requirements (scope), the amount of time available to produce the system in support of the requirements (time), and the limit of money available (cost) [are all constraints]" (Brewer & Dittman 2010, 14).

He also pointed out that as the project moves forward, Tonya should be mindful when considering the triple constraint that if she did not keep the contract IS folks on track, it would not be as simple as having them work overtime. Doing so would result in overtime pay, which would more than likely impact the project's overall cost. Likewise, if the scope grows, which would not be surprising considering the specific project being addressed, the growth would more than likely negatively impact the project's timeline, cost, or both.

Earl ended by saying he would like to see a detailed plan and timeline by week's end that reports the data Tonya will be collecting to populate the stages of the previously reviewed model. He also wanted to know how he might assist Tonya in her ongoing personal development. Tonya enthusiastically thanked Earl for his request and said that she would schedule a date and time for their next meeting.

Back in his office, Earl read an email asking him to contact Reginald ASAP. Upon doing so, Reginald told Earl of the conversation between he and Maria and encouraged Earl to contact Maria right away to provide an update on the legacy system replacement project. Earl responded accordingly as was previously discussed in the context of accountability.

Fast forwarding, we find Earl in his office finalizing the communications scroll as shown in figure 9-13.

Accordingly, Earl's aim was to communicate to his boss, subordinates and applicable peers, the overarching strategy his team's work would be linked to, the objectives that support that strategy, and to reinforce his earlier request for completion of employee development plans. Using his communication scroll and staying true to the key message that he intended to convey during the collaborative stage, Earl completed the dashboard shown in figure 9-14.

Figure 9-13: Earl's Communication Stage Scroll

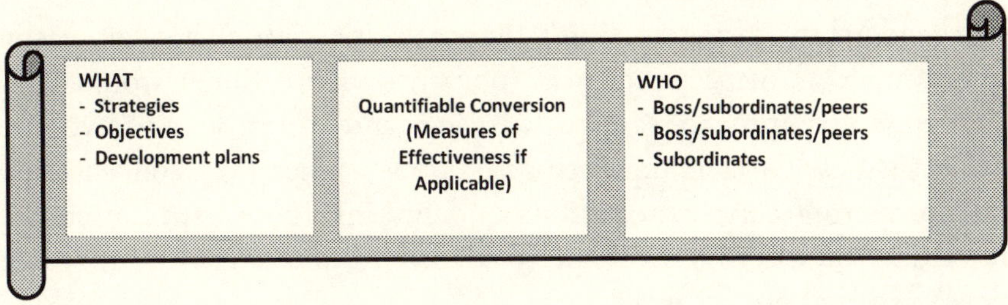

WHAT
- Strategies
- Objectives
- Development plans
Quantifiable Conversion (Measures of Effectiveness if Applicable)
WHO
- Boss/subordinates/peers
- Boss/subordinates/peers
- Subordinates

Figure 9-14: Earl's Dashboard

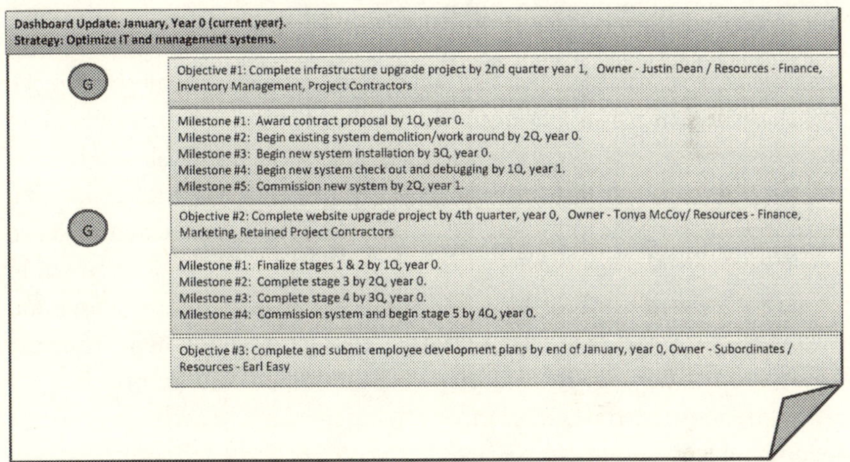

Dashboard Update: January, Year 0 (current year).
Strategy: Optimize IT and management systems.
G
Objective #1: Complete infrastructure upgrade project by 2nd quarter year 1, Owner - Justin Dean / Resources - Finance, Inventory Management, Project Contractors
Milestone #1: Award contract proposal by 1Q, year 0.
Milestone #2: Begin existing system demolition/work around by 2Q, year 0.
Milestone #3: Begin new system installation by 3Q, year 0.
Milestone #4: Begin new system check out and debugging by 1Q, year 1.
Milestone #5: Commission new system by 2Q, year 1.
G
Objective #2: Complete website upgrade project by 4th quarter, year 0, Owner - Tonya McCoy/ Resources - Finance, Marketing, Retained Project Contractors
Milestone #1: Finalize stages 1 & 2 by 1Q, year 0.
Milestone #2: Complete stage 3 by 2Q, year 0.
Milestone #3: Complete stage 4 by 3Q, year 0.
Milestone #4: Commission system and begin stage 5 by 4Q, year 0.
Objective #3: Complete and submit employee development plans by end of January, year 0, Owner - Subordinates / Resources - Earl Easy

Unlike dashboards we've seen before, Earl's cognizance dashboard not only reflects the high-level objectives, but it also includes critical milestones that must be accomplished en route to achieving those objectives. Because the legacy project extends beyond the current year (listed as year 0) into the second year (listed as year 1), he has listed the quarter for accomplishing the work and the year for such accomplishments. Given the likely delay in both projects, and in response to his lack of XL previously exhibited, Earl believed that specificity was an important enabler for project success.

Notice the term *retained contractors* in the second objective. These are the contract resources Earl's team manages. Earl also requested his team to complete and provide personal development plans by the end of January.

Leadership insights: Earl's opportunities were not as easily quantifiable as those for Jessica, Johnny, or Kim. But it would be a challenge for him to resolve infrastructure upgrade and website project issues. Earl's nonquantifiable opportunities were concentrated on not setting clear expectations and linking those expectations to rewards. Likewise, he did little to identify and strengthen employee developmental opportunities.

Regarding the infrastructure upgrade project opportunity, Earl used key financial concepts—time value of money, NPV, IRR, payback, profitability index, and cost of capital—to assist Justin in selecting the correct project alternative for moving forward.

Similarly, he used IT systems development cycle and project management techniques to assist Tonya in refocusing the website project.

In responding to the nonquantifiable leadership opportunities, Earl made use of his interactions with his team as "teachable moments" to talk about the importance of meeting project deadlines (a key XL attribute); also about following up, as required, to ensure schedule, cost, and scope compliance.

He allocated time (a key TL attribute) to explain to Tonya the importance of the "triple constraint" project management concept. To assure further project success, Earl developed and communicated a comprehensive strategic plan. It included the overarching strategy, specific objectives, and associated milestones for each project. Also included in this monitoring and cognizance infrastructure was a specific objective that required Earl's direct reports to submit development plans. This further addressed feedback concerns and exhibited a key TL attribute.

CHAPTER 10

The Buck Stops Here—Kenneth Bethone

WE'LL TURN OUR attention next to Ken Bethone (regional call center manager).

As a purchaser of consumable goods, you've no doubt seen the 800 number stamped on a package you are directed to call if you want to contact the manufacturer. (This number may actually begin with 877, 866, or something else). Ever wonder who takes those calls? If you were calling to offer comments regarding any of Summit's Products, you would speak with one or more of fifteen associates employed in Ken Bethone's area. That is, if you remain on the line long enough to speak with a live person.

Figure 10-1 shows how Ken began to update the conversation stage scroll precipitated by the discussion with his boss, Victor. As was the case with others, Victor supplied Ken with several action items including reducing caller wait time as well as reducing reporting error rates. In addition, Victor challenged Ken to exhibit leadership in building team member skills. Like the others, Ken, working with the HR department, elected to issue the MLQ (see appendices A–D). Unlike those previously discussed, Ken issued all three MLQ forms: higher level ratings, peers, and subordinates. And as with the others, his timing was carefully calculated, as he also set up separate meetings with his boss, customers, and subordinates for a time after he received the 360-degree feedback.

Moving now to the calculation stage, figure 10-2 shows Ken's plan to move forward, listing the best methods for tackling the previously identified issues and opportunities.

Figure 10-1: Ken's Conversation Stage Scroll

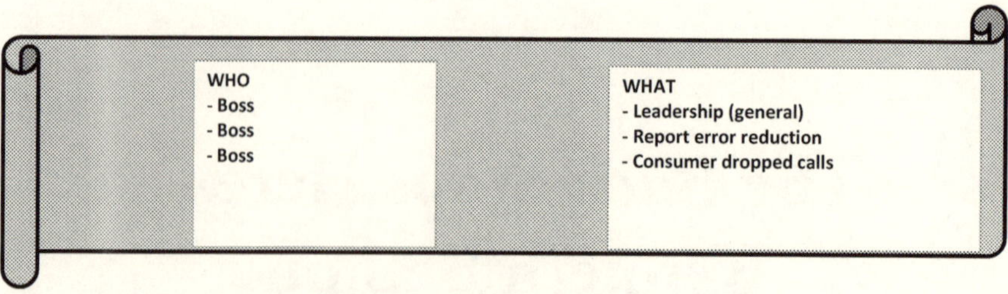

WHO
- Boss
- Boss
- Boss
WHAT
- Leadership (general)
- Report error reduction
- Consumer dropped calls

Figure 10-2: Ken's Calculation Stage Scroll

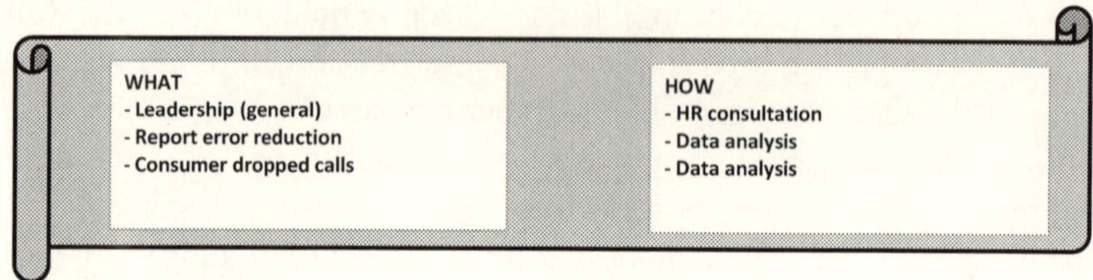

WHAT
- Leadership (general)
- Report error reduction
- Consumer dropped calls
HOW
- HR consultation
- Data analysis
- Data analysis

The output from this stage may be several actions to be taken to the collaboration stage that, when completed, are expected to resolve the current stage inputs. Regarding the item Leadership, not all issues that move into the calculation stage will be as quantifiable as, say, a 10-percent budget reduction. The intent of this stage is not to simply apply mathematical or other deductive logic, but to consider pros and cons aimed at addressing any item identified in the conversation stage.

10.1 Leadership Reflection

To this point, we have been concerned with certain leadership attributes and behaviors (transformational and transactional) with the underlying assumption that success in those attributes or behaviors corresponds to greater levels of employee commitment, success, and satisfaction. This then poses the following question: How does one determine the efficacy of good to great leadership? According to Avolio and Bass: "transformational and transactional leadership are both related to the success of the group. Success is measured with the MLQ by how often the raters perceive their leader to be motivating, how effective raters perceive their leader to be at interacting at different levels of the organization, and how satisfied raters are with their leader's methods of working with others" (2004, 102). Ken's supplemental MLQ feedback is presented in figure 10-3.

Figure 10-3: MLQ Supplemental Feedback for Ken

Supplemental Assessment Questions:

1. What are two or three things that would help this person be more efficient?

Better leadership, associates' efforts are at minimum
Do your current job well instead of looking for the big promotion
Adjust communications style to his audience

2. One thing that gets in the way of this person's effectiveness is:

Stick up for his employees more
Try to see himself through the lens of others
Spend time building our skill level and we will work harder

3. What I admire most about this person's leadership:

Very analytical, great process knowledge
Can count on him when you need time off to deal with personal issues

The feedback suggests that Ken, contrary to how he perceives himself, could do well to beef up his leadership skills or at least his exhibition of leadership skills. There also appears to be a perception that Ken is looking to move to the next level, possibly looking past his current assignment. Additionally, there appears to be a lack of trust in Ken's support for his employees. Like other leaders at Summit Consumables, Ken appears to lack key TL attributes such as building the skills of the team and acting in a selfless manner.

Despite the unfavorable qualitative feedback offered, Ken's principal concern is to validate his belief that he is an effective leader, which he also believes to be supported by comments regarding his analytical ability. Recall that Ken elected to implement the MLQ on a 360-degree basis. Therefore; he received feedback from his boss, his boss's peers, his departmental peers, and his direct reports.

Regarding the quantitative portion of the feedback, while the feedback may be compared to an aggregated percentile table, Ken's disaggregated scores in the area of extra effort (EE) ranged from a low of 1.33 (direct reports, who completed the lower level ratings forms) to a high of 1.67 (his boss and boss's peers, who completed the higher level ratings forms). As the name implies, EE is all about influencing others to go above and beyond (see appendix D).

On a scale from 1–4, Ken received an average rating of 1.33 in the area of EE from his subordinates which corresponds to the tenth percentile, meaning 10 percent of the normed population scored lower, and 90 percent scored higher than 1.33. For this same attribute, the rating provided by higher level raters (his boss and boss's peers), was 1.67, also corresponding to the tenth percentile, and may be interpreted as scoring lower than 90 percent of the normed population. In the area of leadership outcomes, effectiveness (referred to as EFF in appendix D), which measures effectiveness in representing employees as well as representing oneself, Ken was rated 1.50 by his subordinates which corresponds to the fifth percentile and 2.00 from higher-level raters, which corresponds to the tenth percentile. In the final area for leadership outcomes, satisfaction (referred to as SAT in appendix D), which measures how satisfied others are with Ken's leadership style, he was rated 1.00 by his subordinates, corresponding to the fifth percentile, and 2.00 from higher-level raters, corresponding to the tenth percentile.

For obvious reasons, Ken was disappointed by these results. However, he also recognized that, as his boss Victor pointed out to him during his performance evaluation discussion, the buck stopped with him. He and only he could rectify his leadership shortcomings. And it was up to him to make use of the collaboration stage of the 5C LIM to begin to change his perceived leadership style narrative.

Ken also recognized that there was no way that things could change overnight, yet he was looking forward to getting started. Figure 10-4 shows Ken's collaboration scroll, including the key message that he plans to send to all.

Unlike the previously discussed leaders, Ken's first meeting was with his boss. As a reminder, while the outcome of Ken's discussion with HR is his assessment results, it is Ken's application of those results that allows him to send his key message during subsequent meetings with others.

Figure 10-4: Ken's Collaboration Stage Scroll

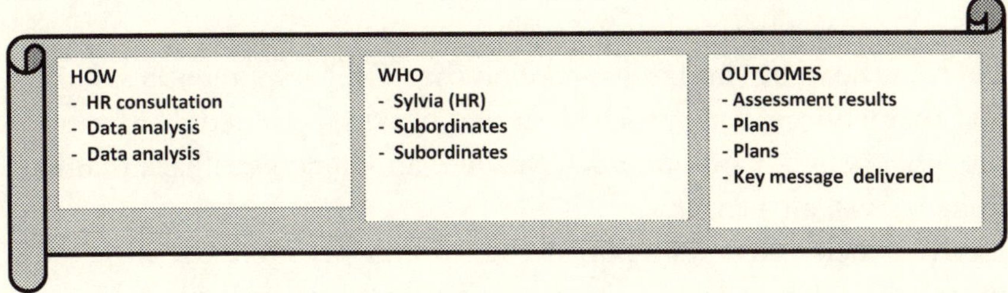

HOW
- HR consultation
- Data analysis
- Data analysis
WHO
- Sylvia (HR)
- Subordinates
- Subordinates
OUTCOMES
- Assessment results
- Plans
- Plans
- Key message delivered

10.2 The Meeting

Ken began his meetings with an unscheduled drop-in on Victor, who ushered him in and asked how things were going. Ken, recalling how the performance evaluation ended, offered his apologies for that meeting. He assured Victor that he intended to do all that he could to turn his department around and to further develop his leadership skills. He also assured Victor that the effect of his efforts to improve his overall departmental performance would be measurable (qualitatively and quantitatively) on a 360-degree basis.

Not only did Victor find these comments refreshing, he felt that Ken was not simply blowing smoke but would do all he could in earnest to bring his commitments to fruition.

A word is in order here regarding credible leadership and trust. Albert Einstein wrote: "Whoever is careless with the truth in small matters cannot be trusted with important matters." Ken made some strong commitments in his discussion with Victor. And just as it is important for Ken to follow through on these pledges for the sake of improving departmental performance, follow-through is also required for his credibility with Victor. Inasmuch as the MLQ is concerned, the "traits expected to correlate with … transformational leadership scores include … honesty, integrity … credibility, and originality" (Avolio & Bass 2004, 83). Moreover, Kouzes and Posner conducted research that indicated that honesty was the number one characteristic admired in leaders. The respondents represented "six continents: Africa, North America, South America, Asia, Europe, and Australia" (2007, 31). Thus, a leader's word may also reflect his or her credibility.

We now return to discussions regarding Ken.

The next meeting was with Ken's direct reports. As indicated in his collaboration scroll, he had to rely on his team to assist in resolving two critical issues: consumer dropped calls and report errors.

Ken began by sharing his take on the MLQ assessment results. He said that while he was surprised, he was not disappointed that his team thought enough of him to provide candid and honest feedback that was, in his words, a true gift.

Ken then asked the team if they would be interested in helping resolve the issue of dropped calls using a Six Sigma approach. None of his associates were familiar with this concept, nor were they aware that Ken was a Six Sigma Black Belt.

Oops, did I use the term *Six Sigma*? What is that? you ask. Believe it or not, you have already reviewed some of the key concepts of Six Sigma, particularly in the discussion regarding Johnny Goode. That's right—it's all about structured problem solving, individual resolve, and a little bit of statistics. Well, maybe a lot of statistics.

We begin with a high level definition based on a comprehensive literature review that includes relevant Internet searches. Six Sigma is a quality oriented management philosophy the origin of which is attributed to a Motorola engineer and statistician led by Deming's idea of process variation. The general operational approach is to set audacious objectives, measure progress via data collection, and implement analysis techniques en route to creatively eliminating defects and nonconformities in the company's products and services.

As a result of its application, documented accounts suggest that companies enjoy a competitive advantage, including reduced costs, better business results, and improved quality. This high-level method is used by applying two fundamental improvement maps, for which the acronyms are DMAIC and DMADV. DMAIC stands for define, measure, analyze, improve, and control. DMADV means define, measure, analyze, design, and verify.

Emphasizing the obvious, the first three components of both methods are identical. However, DMAIC emphasizes improvement and control while DMADV is aimed at designing and verifying. So, what's up with that?

As I will discuss with a statistical example shortly, Six Sigma is most commonly known for significantly reducing defects, thereby approaching perfection of products and services. Consequently, defects measured in an existing manufacturing process, such as with automobile parts, are best reduced using the DMAIC application. And yes, you guessed it! Yet to be implemented processes, including those that have been scrapped and replaced with new processes, are great candidates for the DMADV approach (esixsigma.org; Eckes 2001, 5; searchcio.techtarget.com; villanovau.com; Evans & Lindsay 2005, 18–19; whatissixsigma.net).

Now that you have a good understanding of the philosophical underpinnings of Six Sigma, let's see a statistical example. Hold on tight, because this could get a little tricky!

During the discussions regarding Johnny Goode, I introduced you to the normal distribution and the symbol σ, pronounced sigma, which we defined as the process standard deviation, or simply process variation. We also saw that the values that lie between –3σ and +3σ account for 99.7 percent of all values and those between –2σ and +2σ account for 95 percent of all values. Those between –1σ and +1σ account for 68 percent of all values.

We also saw that on the extreme left and right sides of μ, (pronounced "mew" and representing the process mean, which is ideally where the process target should be), lies –3σ and +3σ respectively. Likewise, we saw in our example regarding the weights of a certain component that with a process mean of 40 lbs. and a σ equal to 10 lbs., the weights of the components that lie between –3σ and +3σ ranged from 10 lbs. to 70 lbs. Assuming a total of 1,000 units, then according to our formula, 99.7 percent or 997 would be within the allowable specification (assuming specifications were set at +/– 3σ) and 3 per 1,000 (or 0.3 percent) would be defective. If instead of 1,000 units we made 1,000,000 units, then our number of defective units would still equal 0.3 percent but the actual number of defective units would be 3,000 (0.3 percent × 1,000,000), or 3,000 defects per million. The value 6σ says that, relative to the process target, there are –6σ to the left of that target and +6σ to the right of that target. And instead of 6σ being equal to 99.7 percent, it is now equal to 99.999 percent, which—you guessed it—is 3.4 defects per million. Simple, right?

Now here's the tricky part. The assumption for 6σ used in the Six Sigma example, is that the process mean can actually shift 1.5 standard deviations (1.5σ) to the left or right of the target. Statistically, the 3.4 defects per million corresponds to 4.5σ. While there is a 6σ span from the target to the closest specification limit (lower and upper specification), the accepted assumption is that processes tend to shift to the left and right up to 1.5σ, So the longer-term view of the process is 4.5σ. Another way of stating this is that "a six-sigma quality level corresponds to a process variation equal to half of the design tolerance while allowing the mean to shift as much as 1.5 standard deviations from the target" (Evans & Lindsey 2005, 36). So the key takeaway from this statistical discussion is that using the Six Sigma quality approach significantly reduces defect levels and places the engaging company on a path to perfection.

As a final point in this area, in chapter 2, "The Corporation Speaks," I mentioned that Ken was a Six Sigma Black Belt. Now that we understand the basics of Six Sigma, we also know that someone must be qualified and capable of leading the respective improvement efforts. A Six Sigma Black Belt is one who has been trained in the methodologies, can appropriately leverage statistically oriented analysis tools, is fluent in the application of DMAIC and DMADV processes, can effectively communicate to lay audiences, possesses good leadership skills, and should be a self-starter (esixsigma.org; Eckes 2001, 5; searchcio.techtarget.com; villanovau.com; Evans & Lindsay 2005, 57; whatissixsigma.net).

Whew, enough already! OK, now that you have acquired a fundamental understanding of Six Sigma, we will return to discussions regarding Ken.

As mentioned, in the meeting with his direct reports Ken responded to the received feedback, not in a retaliatory manner, but in such a way as to demonstrate thorough collaboration how he might inspire his team to become more effective. Ken summarized his feedback but also indicated that he was not concerned with who said what but with how the department could become a more cohesive and effective team. Recognizing the need for resolution of the issues identified in the conversation stage of the 5C LIM, he solicited the team for their participation in seeking process improvement regarding dropped calls and report errors. All his associates volunteered to take part in the efforts, so Ken divided them into to two teams—eight people for the dropped calls, and the remaining seven for resolving the report error issues. Ken, as a Six Sigma Black Belt, assumed the role of project leader for both efforts, and the data analyst was assigned to support both teams with needed data obtained from the automated collection systems.

Note I used the word *project leader* here. It is standard Six Sigma practice to approach a process improvement initiative as a project. Likewise, it is also the typical practice that Six Sigma teams "are cross-functional [in that] they cut across boundaries of different departments or functions" (Evans & Lindsay 2005, 56). However, given that the project is contained within and controlled by the call center personnel, all team members were sourced by the call center—Ken's department.

The following discussion focuses on dropped calls. I also encourage you to implement a comprehensive review of DMAIC application because the intent here is to stress only certain aspects of a much more detailed, albeit straightforward quality improvement process.

Ken's initial focus for the team was in the "define" area. Relying heavily on his black belt training, he understood the importance of focusing on the customer (also termed the voice of the customer) en route to resolving the dropped call issue.

Information reviewed, based on calls received, suggested that a key quality characteristic for Summit Consumables' consumers contacting the call center was wait time—that is, the time required for a consumer to progress from hearing the phone greeting to actually speaking to a call center associate. Thus, the *critical to quality* (CTQ) measure was waiting or holding time (as measured in seconds), and the related CTQ specification (the level desired) was fifty seconds. With this information, a defect rate could then be calculated which is simply the percentage of calls that exceed the fifty-second specification.

Typically, resulting from customer engagement, the consumer affairs departments offer coupons to customers who are dissatisfied with product performance. These coupons may be redeemed for the purchase of additional company products. While this action may not make the customer as happy as if the need for the call not been present (meaning the product met or exceeded customer expectations), receiving a coupon may satisfy the customer enough to remain loyal to the product. Recall from chapter 5 that an unhappy customer can impact the bottom line, because "market research done by Ford showed that a happy customer tells on average eight people the good news about the product, but a dissatisfied customer tells on average more than twenty people of the ordeal with the product" (Aguayo 1990, 14). Thus, the importance of keeping the customer happy, or at a minimum, satisfied, is paramount to the company and can be achieved only through truly understanding where the gaps are in doing so. Information gained from customer calls is a great source for gauging customer product satisfaction.

The next step Ken initiated was to define the existing call center customer engagement process, as shown in figure 10-5, with the aim of determining the problem statement.

Figure 10-5: Call Receiving, Routing, and Engagement Process (CRREP)

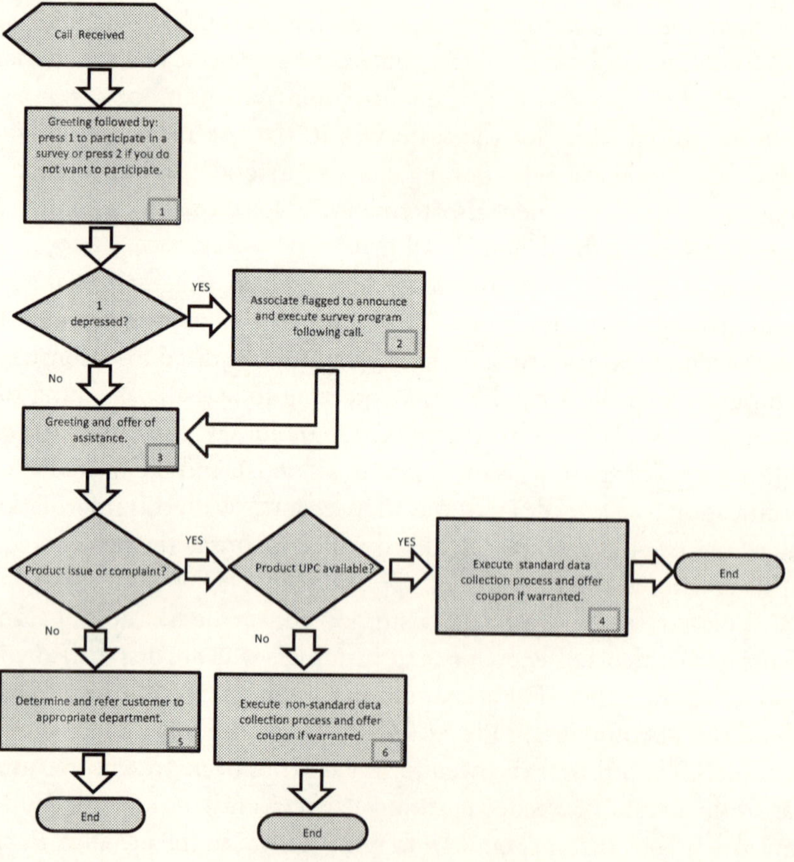

A close review of the flow chart and detailed discussions with the data analyst resulted in the following problem statement: "The call receiving and engagement process is not customer focused, resulting in dropped calls." The principal goal will be to improve the call service level, thereby reducing dropped calls.

During the "measure" stage, concentration shifted to determining where calls were being dropped. Facilitating this effort was identification of an initial sample of 1000 received calls. The plan was to take advantage of existing data collection systems to trace the flow and timing for each of the 1000 calls through the CRREP, paying attention to the time required to process each call, and the number of calls entering a process block compared to the same exiting that block. In addition, survey results would be retrieved and reviewed for those customers who elected to participate in the survey program following the handling of their call.

We move now to the analysis phase, the opportunity to apply the high-powered statistics that you have been waiting for to assist in dissecting the problem and data to reveal the root cause (or causes). You know—multivariate statistics, factor analysis, principal components analysis, cluster analysis, canonical correlation, multidimensional scaling, ANOVA, MANOVA, discriminant analysis, and similar funny-sounding statistical tools. Or, in this specific example, simply use Pareto analysis, also known as the vital few and the useful many. (See chapter 7 and the discussion of Kimberly Hours for a refresher if desired.)

Referring once more to the CRREP shown in figure 10-5, an analysis of 1000 calls received yielded the data provided in figure 10-6. Analysis of this chart suggests that the majority of the dropped calls occurred in process stages 4 and 6. (By the way, the Universal Product Code (UPC), listed in the decision block just prior to process stages 4 and 6, is used for product identification. It is typically displayed on the product label in the form of vertical black bars of varying widths on a white background.)

The total number of dropped calls (231) occurring in process stages 4 and 6 accounts for 77 percent of all dropped calls, leaving roughly 23 percent of the remaining dropped calls to be spread among the remaining stages. Does this close to 80 percent to 20 percent relationship sound familiar? If so, then you also know that these two areas (stages 4 and 6) should be the focal point for improvement efforts.

Figure 10-7 represents another way of looking at the data in the context of percentage. It is always a good idea to view data in many formats, particularly when preparing to communicate conclusions to an audience. As indicated in this chart, based on the 1000-call sample, roughly 1 percent of the calls are dropped in process stage 1, and

Figure 10-6: Consumer Hang-ups vs. Process Stage

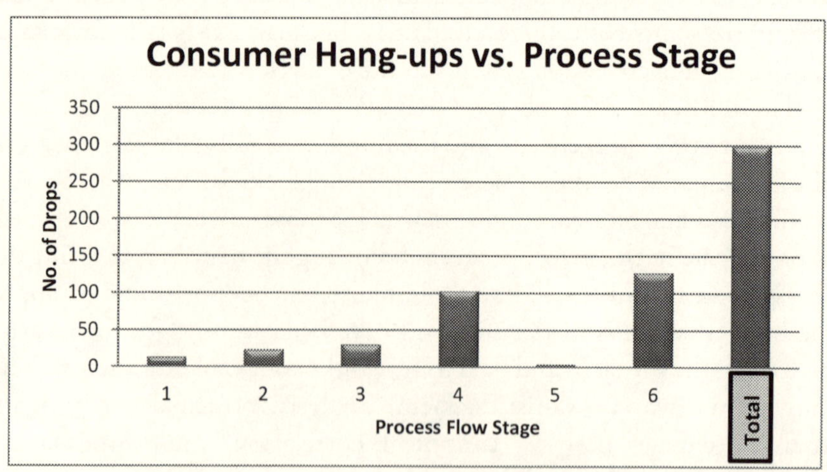

a *cumulative* 4 percent of the 1000 calls are dropped through process stage 2. This continues through the flow chart, with the total cumulative percent of dropped calls equaling 30 percent exit process stage 6. With this knowledge, the problem statement could be refined to reflect the quantifiable opportunity. It might be restated as follows: "The call receiving and engagement process is not customer-focused, resulting in 30 percent of all received calls being dropped."

Figure 10-7: Percent of Hang-ups vs. Process Stage

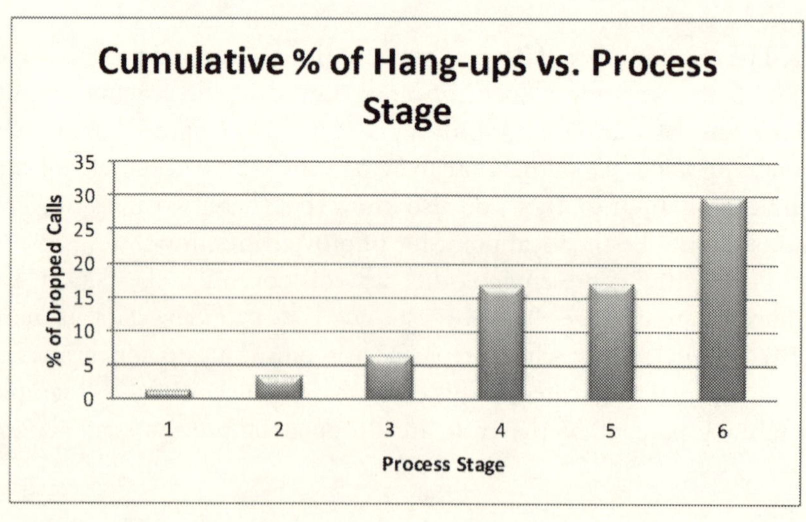

Although additional statistical sampling and tools might be used to validate the 30 percent dropped calls over an extended period of time, the intent here is to only reflect an attempt to refine the problem statement.

Based on these two charts, the process stages in which the majority of calls are being dropped are quite evident. However, this represents only the first level of analysis. We still don't know why the calls are being dropped.

Figure 10-8 takes a deeper dive into the root cause of the dropped calls because it plots the average time per caller in each of the stages. Now we are getting closer to a solution, or at least to a better definition of a solution.

An analysis of the chart suggests that the average call wait time in stage 1 is 12 seconds. (Also recall that the dropped calls here were only 1 percent of the total.)

Figure 10-8: Average Consumer Wait Time vs. Process Stage

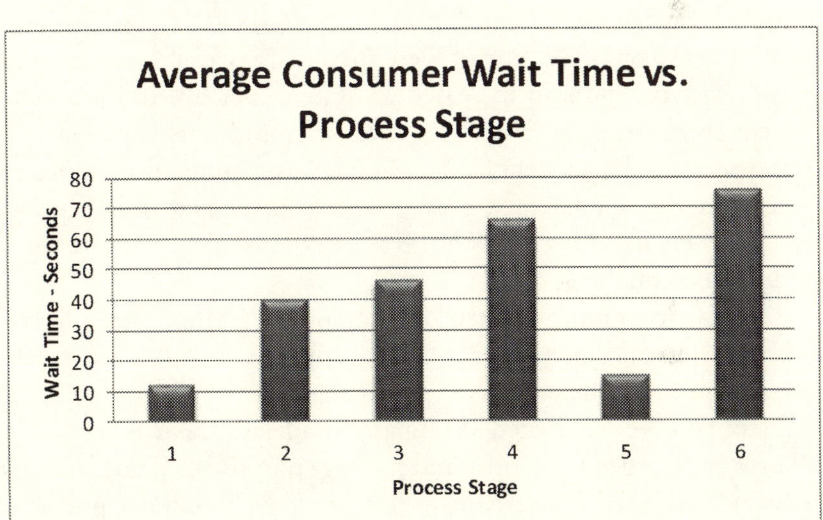

If you are among those wondering what the heck wait time has to do with dropping 1 percent of the calls with a wait time of only twelve seconds in process stage 1 versus the specification of fifty seconds, you are on the right track! But the answer is simple. It has nothing to do with the fifty-second specification.

The real issue is that when consumers contact Summit Consumables, some don't want to hear an IVR—that's interactive voice response, by the way. What they want is to speak with a live person. However, look at process stages 4 and 6, where the average wait time jumps precipitously to 66 and 76 seconds respectively. This certainly suggests that further analysis would be productive, perhaps exploring with tools such as 5 Whys, cause and effect/fishbone diagraming, and possibly other tools that facilitate drilling down to the root cause for the delays occurring in process stages 4 and 6.

With this information in hand, focus can shift to the final two blocks in the DAMIC methodology (improve and control). Although not discussed here, you are encouraged to review these two blocks in your leisure, along with some of the tools that may be used therein.

Fast forwarding, we find Ken in his office reviewing the completed work regarding both project assignments, approached using the Six Sigma improvement (DMAIC) process. A few points became readily apparent to Ken. First, his cooperative attitude, as reflected by his willingness to allow associates to have time away from work to address personal business, was a contributing factor to the lack of achievement in both project areas. Because of these absences, associates who reported to work had to handle an increased volume of calls due to the absence of their peers. Second, despite the lack of commitment exhibited by some associates, his current staffing model, assuming all were present 100 percent of their assigned work time, was inadequate for efficiently and effectively handling the volume of work for which his department was held accountable.

Ken also recognized the need for employee training, particularly in the area of responding to consumer calls (process stage 6) who did not possess a UPC for the purchased product.

Have you ever contacted a company and heard the message, "This call may be recorded for quality and training purposes?" If you have and you wondered what that actually meant, you now have the opportunity to witness how, in some instances, this information may be used.

Ken's data analyst reviews random samples of conversations that associates have with consumers who contact Summit Consumables. Based on that review, which was also shared with Ken, several associate training opportunities were identified.

Ken also recognized that valuable time was being lost post call completion because associates were required to transfer some data from the online system to an offline system in order to complete required reports. This data transfer often resulted in transposition errors. Thus, Ken's communication scroll, as shown in figure 10-9, conveyed his intention to implement critical discussions with his subordinates and boss.

Figure 10-9: Ken's Communication Stage Scroll

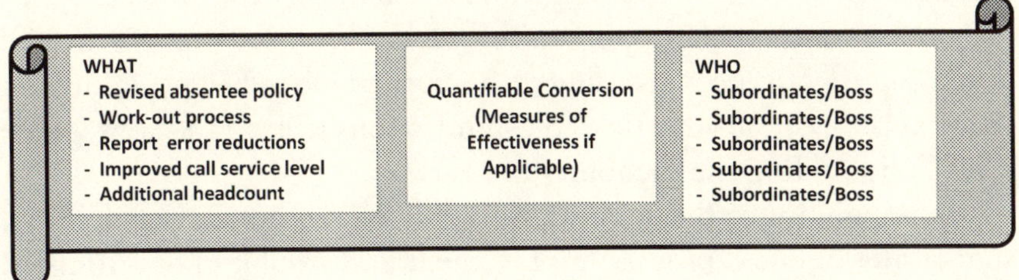

WHAT
- Revised absentee policy
- Work-out process
- Report error reductions
- Improved call service level
- Additional headcount
Quantifiable Conversion (Measures of Effectiveness if Applicable)
WHO
- Subordinates/Boss
- Subordinates/Boss
- Subordinates/Boss
- Subordinates/Boss
- Subordinates/Boss

As indicated, he planned to require his associates to make use of their vacation time to address personal business in situations where all other paid time off (PTO) had been exhausted. Likewise, he would be challenging them to work with a paid consultant to learn how to implement a work-out process to streamline their work processes such that the maximum focus can be placed on the delivery of core departmental work. (See chapter 5 for a refresher on work-outs.)

Ken also planned to request additional headcount aimed at bringing his department in line with industry standard levels. Ken's strategy was to announce that the number of new hires would be decided contingent on needs determined upon completion of the work-out process.

With this potential headcount request, and implementation of employee training, he also planned to communicate plans for a 45 percent reduction in report errors and to improve the call service level from its current 70 percent to an unprecedented 99.7 percent. Aimed at mitigating some of the issues regarding the request for additional headcount, Ken planned to also say that the work-out process is expected to expose the need for fully integrated systems that, if implemented, would eliminate the need for data reentry, positively impacting the resource needs.

Returning for a moment to Ken's MLQ supplemental feedback, some of the comments provided suggested a lack of team support, insufficient skill building, lack of focus on his current job, and the need for clearer communications. And, while only sustained efforts can shift perspectives, Ken's leadership, as evidenced by his communications plan, is certainly a step in the right direction.

Before the meeting with his boss, Ken will complete the dashboard cognizance infrastructure, which is not shown but is left as an exercise for you to complete.

Leadership insights: Quantifiable leadership opportunities identified for Ken included report error reduction and reducing consumer dropped calls. Nonquantifiable opportunities included improving his overall leadership effectiveness, focusing on his current job in lieu of looking for the next promotion, adjusting communications style to the appropriate level, and building the capability of his team.

In responding to the quantifiable opportunities noted, Ken used key statistically oriented process improvement and trouble-shooting tools, such as the Six Sigma DMAIC process, business process tools, such as flow charting and root cause analysis tools, such as problem statement development, to plot the path forward.

Regarding the nonquantifiable opportunities, Ken's implementation of business and process improvement tools afforded him the opportunity to identify training needs for his direct reports and to enlist their support in issue resolution (both key TL attributes). Like Earl and Johnny, he used this interaction as a "teachable moment," providing leadership through the lens of a Six Sigma Black Belt, meanwhile being mindful of the importance of clear communication during the implementation of the Six Sigma process improvement approach. Aided by root cause analysis to resolve the consumer dropped call issue, Ken also identified opportunities for more structure, meaning less leniency, in employee attendance (a key XL attribute).

This discussion regarding Ken concludes the character focus for this book. Wait a minute! you exclaim. What happened to the discussion regarding Joseph Brilliant? Didn't he also receive a performance evaluation? Yes, but that's a topic to be addressed in a forthcoming book in the *All the Way to the Top* book series.

In the next chapter, we will transition from functional leadership to exhibition of presentation leadership. Facilitating this discussion I will introduce, and cover in detail, the 5Ps – purpose, preparation, perception, persuasion and power. Taken in aggregate, these 5Ps allow for the demonstration of power in action.

CHAPTER 11

The Presentation

"MANY PEOPLE—EVEN THE most accomplished public speakers feel everything from slight nervousness to outright terror before they give a presentation … one study revealed that an alarmingly high number of people would rather have unnecessary surgery than give a speech" (*Harvard Business Review*). This chapter is not intended to coach you in developing cool PowerPoint slides; many resources and presentation templates exist to assist in that area. It is instead aimed at addressing a much more fundamental yet essential component of presenting effectively—the exhibition of leadership ahead of and during the formal presentation.

We will begin the discussion of presentations after paying our customary homage to *Merriam-Webster (via merriam-webster.com)* in the areas of oration, speech, and presentation. What do oration and speech have to do with delivering a PowerPoint presentation? you ask. Well, simply put—everything! To this end, *oration* is defined as, "an elaborate speech" (merriam-webster.com). *Speech* is defined as "… the act of speaking…talk, conversation …the power of expressing or communicating thoughts by speaking" (merriamwebster.com). Now for our final definition, *presentation defined is*: "the act of presenting…the act power or privilege…symbol or image that represents something … a descriptive or persuasive account (as by a salesman of a product) … an immediate object of perception, cognition, or memory" (merriam-webster.com). We will return to these definitions at the end of this section. For now I'd like to set context through the sharing of excerpts from some of the most famous speeches of all times.

The first of these was given by Abraham Lincoln during his first presidential inaugural address on March 4, 1861.

Fellow-citizens of the United States: In compliance with a custom as old as the government itself, I appear before you to address you briefly, and to take in your presence the oath prescribed by the Constitution of the

United States to be taken by the President before he enters on the execution of his office ... I do not consider it necessary at present for me to discuss those matters of administration about which there is no special anxiety or excitement ... apprehension seems to exist among the people of the Southern States that by the accession of a Republican administration their property and their peace and personal security are to be endangered (Abraham Lincoln, www.loc.gov).

Speaking to the United States following his election, and amidst the Depression, Franklin Roosevelt, during his March 4, 1933, inaugural address said:

This is a day of national consecration ... and I am certain that on this day my fellow Americans expect that on my induction into the Presidency I will address them with a candor and a decision which the present situation of our people impels. This is preeminently the time to speak the truth, the whole truth, frankly and boldly. Nor need we shrink from honestly facing conditions in our country today. This great Nation will endure as it has endured, will revive and will prosper. So, first of all, let me assert my firm belief that the only thing we have to fear is fear itself (Franklin D. Roosevelt, www.millercenter.org).

Mahatma Gandhi, as an advocate for India's freedom from British rule beginning in 1915, said:

Let me place before you one or two things... I want you to understand two things very clearly ... I ask you to consider it from my point of view, because if you approve of it, you will be enjoined to carry out all I say ... let me assure you that I am the same ... as I was in 1920 ... I attach the same importance to nonviolence (Mahatma Gandhi, Daley 2013).

Susan B. Anthony, speaking regarding women's suffrage on January 23, 1880, said:

Friends and fellow citizens ... I stand before you under indictment for the alleged crime of having voted at the last presidential election, without having a lawful right to vote ... it shall be my work this evening to prove to you that in thus doing so, I not only committed no crime, but instead simply exercised my citizen's right, guaranteed to me and all United States citizens by the National Constitution beyond the power of any State to deny (Susan B. Anthony, Daley 2013).

And finally, in his address to the nation on the war in Vietnam on November 3, 1969, Richard M. Nixon said:

Tonight I want to talk to you on a subject of deep concern to all Americans and to many people in all parts of the world—the war in Vietnam ... I believe that one of the reasons for the deep division about Vietnam is that many Americans have lost confidence in what their Government has told them about our policy. The American people cannot and should not be asked to support a policy which involves the overriding issues of war and peace unless they know the truth about that policy (Richard M. Nixon, www.presidency.ucsb.edu).

Upon reviewing the above excerpts, one thing becomes quite apparent: Each of the speakers seeks to achieve an end. Abraham Lincoln sought to assuage concerns regarding the potential loss of the most fundamental human needs—to maintain their families, homes and properties, and their lives. Franklin Roosevelt sought to transform the nation's view of its current situation of depression (after the stock market crash) to one of prosperity and renewal. Mahatma Gandhi sought to reassure the India Congress Committee of his unwavering belief in nonviolence as a means through which change may be effected. Susan B. Anthony sought to defend herself against allegations of crime resulting from her voting. And finally, expressing policy concerns, Richard Nixon sought to reconcile division in the nation regarding the Vietnam War.

While there was much more to be conveyed within each of the speeches, the fundamental purpose of each speech was immediately clear. Thus, *purpose*, the first of our 5Ps, is defined as "something set up as an object or an end to be attained" (*Merriam-Webster* 2007). You may recall being present in a meeting or other environment during which the speaker seemed to ramble on until you had to wonder where his speech was headed. Usually, this means the speaker has not made the purpose of the speech clear.

In a corporate or business setting, the purpose for a speech or presentation is often made clear by the requester of such. Purpose, used in the context of the 5Ps, is all about defining what you are presenting and why. Are you seeking approval, disseminating goals and objectives to your team, advocating a position or recommendation, or simply providing an update? As evidenced by the excerpts provided above, whether you are being asked to provide a solution to a critical business issue or simply provide a status update, your purpose should be clear and evident at the outset of the presentation.

You now must implement the necessary steps—mechanical, qualitative and quantitative—for fleshing out your presentation through *preparation*—the second of our 5Ps. In this book's introduction, I mentioned comments offered by General Colin Powell. I repeat them here: "There are no secrets to success. It is the result of preparation, hard work, and learning from failure." According to *Merriam-Webster*, *prepare* defined is: "to make or get ready … to get ready beforehand … to put together … to put into written form" (2007). Good preparation necessitates that each of the following questions and points be addressed.

1. Who are the *participants* expected to attend the presentation? Knowing who they are will allow you to modify your delivery to fit the audience. You've no doubt heard the adage "When in Rome, do as the Romans do." Well, as the presenter and center stage speaker, there is little that can be more damaging to your presentation than speaking around, over, or above your audience. This is sometimes the case when a highly technical individual is asked to present to a nontechnical audience.
2. What *perspectives* might the key participants and stakeholders bring to the presentation that may be in conflict with those of your own? Similarly, if you are but one of several presenters to the same audience, it is also important to be aware of the topics that will be covered by your peer presenters. In the event you are presenting the same topic, the worth of your delivery may result from a comparison with the peer who addresses the same topic. So if flexibility exists regarding the purpose of your presentation, being cognizant of this potential may afford you the opportunity to either modify your presentation or collaborate with the other presenter(s).

   In preparing for any presentation, it is always important to be aware of the water cooler conversation as it pertains to your particular topic. Said differently: How is the issue you are going to be presenting being talked about by the key stakeholders?

   Time and circumstances permitting, once you are able to identify dissenting perspectives and opinions, you can then visit those stakeholders to not only better understand their positions, but to also determine how rigid they might be in those positions—and possibly shift their thinking such that it is more compatible with yours.

Alternatively, if applicable, modify your position to one more aligned with the expectations of your audience. Reaching out to your audience ahead of the presentation is a critical step because the last thing you want to occur during your presentation is for it to be derailed by new information surfacing, particularly if it might serve to undermine one or more of your key arguments.

Knowing and understanding the perspectives of the audience has been a strategy executed by many great leaders. Indeed, during the preparation of Lincoln's inaugural address, he recognized that discussions of "matters of the administration" took a back seat to concerns of "property, peace and personal security." Likewise, Roosevelt recognized during the preparation of his inaugural address that the nation had grave concerns or "fears" when considering its then current state.

3. What is the *timeline* for the presentation, and how much time is allocated to you? On occasions, I have attended a presentation where the presenter's slides contained one or more errors (typically misspellings) and some other errors. My personal experience suggests that when a presentation is pulled together at the last minute, the risk for typographical errors or erroneous data to be included is increased almost exponentially. As the presenter, you should always know the date of the presentation and should allow enough time in your preparation timeline for that date to be compressed. Despite our good intentions, the typical brain functions best when it's not under the gun to deliver. Likewise, if your presentation is scheduled for ten minutes, don't design a presentation that requires exactly ten minutes for you to completely cover all your slides. Invariably, you will either receive a question or unexpectedly ad lib a bit, resulting in your presentation running over the allotted time.
4. What is the *story* that you want to tell? Reynolds said of storytelling, "good stories have interesting, clear beginnings; provocative, engaging content in the middle; and a clear conclusion" (2008, 80). Now that you understand the purpose of your presentation and have identified the attendees as well as their perspectives on the topic, it is time to pull it all together.

While it may seem a bit redundant, even though the purpose of your presentation was given to you, it is still a great idea, if not a requisite action, to restate it up front in your presentation. The intent of this discussion is not to show you how to design presentation slides. But early on in your presentation, certainly not later than a slide in, you should restate the purpose. Don't include every word that you plan to share during the voice over (your actual speaking), as this will make for a busy slide. But do provide enough information so that those who prefer to read your purpose slide have a good understanding of the presentation purpose.

Once your purpose has been clearly defined, the next step is to share a bit of background about the issue to be addressed. For example, if the purpose of your presentation is to resolve issues with floundering sales in a certain region, you might want to show historical data leading up to the current situation. In doing so, you would be sure to point to any interesting or assignable causes that you might be able to make use of for turnaround later in your presentation.

All the while, you are walking your audience through the issues and leading them to your next focus area. In this case, you might consider discussing alternative courses of action that have the potential to resolve the depressed sales issue. But you want to do so succinctly, addressing no more than three total options and the pros and cons associated with each. (Often the pros and cons discussion includes reference to a cost/benefit analysis or other quantitative or qualitative means for alternative differentiation.)

During a presentation, there is often insufficient time to discuss a lot of information. Nor is there sufficient time to discuss a little information in great detail. Consequently, the options should be reviewed at the right level of detail, based on your execution of the strategy previously discussed (knowing your audience and their perspectives).

Next you advance your recommended course of action. Since this represents the pinnacle of your presentation, it is extremely important that you think it through so that it will be seen as the no-brainer option that will withstand the pressures of critique, scrutiny, and questions posed by the audience.

So, you're done right? Not so fast! Although you have shared the issue and its respective solution, you have not yet discussed the implementation plan. This is one of the key points that speakers often overlook—solution implementation feasibility.

While a comprehensive review of a feasibility study is beyond the scope of this book, a few critical points are noteworthy. In particular, depending on the type of project or alternative, aspects of its feasibility might include: technical, economic, schedule, and operational. As the topic headings imply, the technical feasibility study has to do with technology and risks; economic feasibility has to do with resources and respective constraints;, schedule feasibility has to do with the time required to execute the recommendation and lastly, operational feasibility concerns problems or issues (if any) associated with the alternative such as management resistance. (cs.toronto.edu).

This is not at all to suggest that the presenter provide a comprehensive feasibility analysis report during the presentation. It is, however, incumbent upon the presenter to share enough information to achieve comfort among the audience that the recommended path forward has been fully vetted.

At this point, you have completed the fundamental requirements of story development. Some presenters include as the final slide a Q&A prompt. While this is a good practice, my experience suggests that rarely will the audience allow you to reach the end of the presentation before asking questions or seeking clarification.

5. What is the role of your *slides*? During your presentation, you should by no means simply read your slides. Your audience could do that by receiving a copy in email. Instead, you should allow your slides to guide your conversation with the audience. For example, if on one of your slides you wanted to display the difference in NPV's for two project alternatives, you might simply show the NPV for each project. But during your discussion, you might want to review the cash flow sequence or the fact that you

also considered IRR and PI as well as payback. In this way, the attention is on you, the presenter, and not your slides.

So how do you commit to memory all the information that you want to share without putting it on a slide? Great question! Something that has worked well for me is the "notes" feature in PowerPoint to capture what is to be said, and making the mental connection between the slide and the words in the notes section. Typing what you are going to say in the notes section as closely as possible to how you plan to communicate it during the actual presentation will go a long way toward eliminating the perfunctory delivery of attempting to recall and convey data or numbers in a manner inconsistent with your typical communications style. Repetition is a great way to solidify the connection between notes pages and actual slides.

6. *Test drive* your story over and over again! Many guinea pigs (people to listen to your dry run) are available upon whom you can rely for unbiased feedback. An administrative assistant is always a good choice for this approach along with peers and family members. Select a mix of those who know absolutely nothing about your topic and those closest to and most knowledgeable about it.

   The value of this approach is twofold. First, by selecting someone who knows nothing about your topic, you can assess whether or not your story is logical and generally cogent. Despite the rhetorical and typical nature of inaugural addresses, there have been instances where there were clear points that allowed the audience to get it despite having little to no firsthand knowledge of the subject matter. One example is Roosevelt's "the only thing we have to fear is fear itself" comment. Likewise, regarding Kennedy's January 20, 1961, inaugural address, consider his words: "my fellow Americans: ask not what your country can do for you—ask what you can do for your country" (Daley 2013). I submit that very few listeners, or readers, failed to comprehend the gravity of those spoken words.

   Second, selecting someone who is very close to your topic serves as a sort of acid test and fact check. Despite our best intentions, we are all fallible human beings, and as such, we may not get it right all the time. Telling your story to someone who has been-there-done-it often reveals holes in your story that you may not have recognized or anticipated.

Who cares? you say. No one in the audience will know as much as I do about my topic. Don't kid yourself! Typically, particularly in possibly contentious situations, those attending a presentation may ask a person with whom they associate, or more often someone who works for them, to join the attendee in the presentation to sort of keep the conversation honest. Or sometimes an attendee may review the key topic areas of your presentation before attending, in hopes of becoming an "overnight expert." So as the presenter, you should never go into a presentation thinking that you can simply gloss over a topic without anyone noticing.

7. What are your *knowledge limitations*? Don't become an overnight expert. Similar to the second point discussed in item 6, often, in an effort to impress or otherwise fly solo, presenters attempt to incorporate information in a presentation about which they have only superficial knowledge. There are two issues with this. First, while it may seem easy to have a conversation with an expert on a topic and believe you understand its ins and outs, recalling that information in the heat of the battle (meaning during a live presentation) is something different. For example, if you were told that a certain process change, such as reducing the variation of an input part, actually improved the quality of a product, which should result in fewer customer complaints, this may seem simple enough to regurgitate during a presentation. But what if someone in the audience asked you to talk about the statistical confidence level that assertion was based on, or to discuss whether the statistical inference was predicated on parametric or nonparametric statistics? How would you respond? Better approaches would be to avoid this comment altogether or to build into your presentation enough time for an expert to offer a slide or two on the topic. If the latter approach is taken, remember that it is your presentation and you are working with a defined time slot. Thus, some coaching of the additional participant may be in order.

A slight spin on the foregoing comments is to recognize that invariably and despite your most diligent efforts questions will be asked and comments offered to which you may not have the correct answers. When that happens, just respond with something like "Good question. I haven't looked at that but will certainly consider it," or "Perhaps we can talk more about that following my presentation."

These and similar responses work well for questions that are not germane to the logic used in your presentation. As long as the question or comment doesn't significantly weaken your proposed position, the audience should be accepting of your use of one of these, or similar, responses. However, use them in a measured and calculated manner.

I once attended a conference where several participants holding PhDs offered presentations. I recall two particular presenters. The first of these was someone who studied computer science. The other was in the field of business management and strategy.

During the first presentation, in reply to almost every question, the presenter responded: "That question is beyond the scope of my research," even replying to questions that appeared to be germane to the key points discussed.

During the second instance, I asked a question about psychometric modeling. I believed that if the presenter had considered this model, it may have significantly changed the presented perspective. In response to my question, the presenter said, "Here's my card. Give me a call and perhaps we could discuss a collaboration over a cup of coffee."

While I'm not exactly sure what the presenter meant, I was pretty sure that the audience recognized a potential hole in his presentation exposed by my question, which, by the way, was not at all intended to undermine what was otherwise a great presentation. (I never made use of the card he gave me.)

So diligently prepare, anticipate some tough questions, use certain responses in a meaningful way, and know when to play the "Let me get back to you" card.

8. *Location*, location, location. Where will the presentation be delivered? Several years ago, I was asked to introduce a revered Harvard professor at a location with a seating capacity for over 3500 attendees (speaking to a crowd this large would be a first for me). Initially, the thought of delivering this introduction sort of made my stomach feel a little queasy. However, that queasy feeling was short-lived, as one of the first things that I did was to arrange a practice session at the facility. Visiting it afforded me the opportunity to test out the sound system, begin to create eye focus with certain sections of the theatre seats (which I linked to certain points in my introductory speech), observe the lighting, and become familiar with the location of the lectern relative to the curtain from which I would emerge. Most importantly, it gave me comfort that on the evening of the event, I would be introducing a renowned Harvard professor in a facility I had not only become acquainted with but in which I had also repeatedly practiced.

   My introduction was comprehensive (and I admit it was a bit long), but with the practice under my belt, I was feeling pretty good. Following the real time introduction, the professor gave me a big hug and the applause was tremendous. To top it off, the next morning I received in my in-box a copy of an email addressed to my then boss's boss raving about my introduction and also praising my "excellent representation of the company." That the sender of the email held a senior executive level position in a field where public speaking ability served as a make-or-break core competency was simply icing on the cake when considering the complimentary comments.

   I attribute at least 80 percent of the success of that delivery to having visited and practiced in the facility ahead of the event and to getting others to listen to and critique my story before the event. Much of the remaining 20 percent may be ascribed to my speech writer.

> Although the discussion of location in this section referred specifically to a speech *delivery*, I followed a similar strategy for *presentations* as well, particularly when the location was one with which I was unfamiliar.

These steps may not occur in the sequential order listed. For example, you may learn of the location for the presentation immediately when it is requested. The key point, however, is that you use these steps as predecessors to the remaining three of the 5Ps.

Think about the following references and scenarios to see if you can determine the common theme. Some of them may sound dated. But I believe them to be germane to the core point.

- Kenny Rogers's song "The Gambler."
- The movie *Jerry Maguire*, where Dorothy Boyd said: "You had me at hello."
- A salesperson who says to you, following a locked-in deal on a new car; "I would have reduced the price another few hundred dollars if you had just held out for a little while longer."
- A co-worker says, "Wow, looks like the boss is in a pretty foul mood today."

The answer brings us to the third of the 5Ps, which is perception. All four scenarios had to do with someone failing to observe a verbal or nonverbal cue that, if caught, may have influenced someone's next action.

In the Kenny Rogers song, it has to do with a gambler reading the faces of poker players and those players doing likewise.

In the Tom Cruise movie *Jerry Maguire*, Tom's character (Jerry) walks into the house where Renee Zellweger's character (Dorothy) is present, and he says hello and proceeds to talk about how he really cares for her and wants his wife back. As he continues to talk, Dorothy interrupts him, saying, "Shut up … you had me at 'hello'."

The salesperson, if pushed for a greater discount, would have caved by several hundred dollars. (And the boss, whether verbally or nonverbally, may have exhibited a petulant disposition.)

Merriam-Webster defines perception as "an act or result of perceiving … awareness of one's environment through physical sensation … ability to understand …" (2007). During a presentation, there will be many nonverbal cues and possibly some verbal ones that the presenter should recognize. Dubrin says of nonverbal and verbal communications: "effective leaders are masterful nonverbal as well as verbal communicators" (2010, 356). Your leadership responsibility should not diminish while presenting. To the contrary, there is perhaps no greater visible opportunity in which to display it.

The presenter's nonverbal communications are just as significant. If, for example, the presenter responds uncertainly to a question, the asker and possibly other attendees may observe the presenter's manner of responding, resulting in a lack of speaker credibility.

Dubrin also says: "a self-confident leader not only speaks and writes with assurance but also projects confidence through body position, gestures, and manner of speech" (2010, 356). Dubrin points to several observable attributes of a confident leader (speaker):

- Standing with toes pointing outward rather than inward
- Using an erect posture when walking, standing or sitting
- Speaking at a moderate pace, with a loud, confident tone
- Smiling frequently in a relaxed, natural-appearing manner
- Maintaining eye contact with those [in the audience]
- Gesturing in a relaxed, nonmechanical way, including pointing toward others in a way that welcomes rather than accuses ..." (2010, 357).

It follows that despite all the preparation to nail the purpose and adequately prepare, insufficient maturity in perception or perceptiveness can make or break an otherwise great presentation. But even after you have defined the purpose, adequately prepared your presentation, and learned all there is about perception, what then? Have you completed all that is necessary to deliver a stellar presentation?

The answer is not quite. Many times, despite your best efforts at preparation, there remain those who see the world a bit differently. And unless those attendees buy in to your views and perspectives, your job may not be complete. So you as the presenter have an accountability to persuade others to see things just as you do, which represents the fourth of our 5Ps of presenting – persuasion.

From our early years, when we induced our parents to see things our way by not grounding us or buying us that special toy despite our undeserving behavior, we were learning and fine-tuning our persuasiveness. According to *Merriam-Webster* that means "to win over to a belief or course of action by argument or entreaty …" (2007). Here *argument* does not refer to the emotional discussions that may result from disagreement.

To better understand the distinction, let us consider a philosophical approach to argumentation. An argument consists of *premises* followed by a *conclusion*. These premises may be viewed as statements leading up to a claim of some sort. The premises are often referred to as *propositions*. The claim may also be termed the *conclusion* and is typically preceded by words such as *therefore* and *consequently*.

For example:

It is raining outside.

Rain is wet.

Therefore; the ground is wet.

In this simple argument, "It is raining outside" and "Rain is wet" acts as the premises, and "Therefore the ground is wet" serves as the conclusion.

Statements may also have *truth value*, which tests whether or not the statement is true based on what we know and understand to be correct about the world in which we live. A statement asserting that the sun is green, while it is indeed a statement, and could also be predicated on one or more premises, has very little truth value because the sun is not green.

Arguments may be deductive or inductive. Their validity links to the premises used. An example of a deductive argument is:

All human beings need water for survival.

You are a human being.

Therefore, you need water to survive.

This argument is valid because the premises lead to the conclusion. It is also sound because, according to our world views, the argument (including the premises and conclusion) is also true. Validity and truthfulness are not synonymous. Whereas validity, in this context, refers to whether or not the argument structure is correct, truthfulness refers to the correctness or incorrectness of the argument itself.

In contrast, an inductive argument seeks to gain buy-in that the conclusion most likely follows from the premises. These arguments cannot be termed valid or invalid as was the case with deductive arguments. An example of an inductive argument would be:

Some school age children born in the South play two different musical instruments.

Consequently, school age children born in the South play two different musical instruments.

This argument generalizes that school age children in the South play two different instruments, which may or may not be true when considering all school age children born in the South (Copi 2002; cse.buffolo.edu).

Other key terms associated with arguments are not discussed here, such as *inductive argument cogency*, a further analysis of deductive arguments and the premises included therein. Further inquiry in this area is encouraged. However, the key takeaway from this philosophical discussion is that the art of persuasion is predicated to a large degree on the presenter's ability to offer sound and logical arguments, and also to assess arguments offered by others for their validity and truthfulness.

On June 12, 1987, Ronald Reagan, using logic and sound reasoning, exhibited one of the greatest acts of persuasion ever documented when he challenged General Secretary Gorbachev to dismantle the Berlin Wall. Here is a key excerpt from the speech:

There is one sign that the Soviets can make that would be unmistakable, that would advance dramatically the cause of freedom and peace ... General Secretary Gorbachev, if you seek peace, if you seek prosperity for the Soviet Union and Eastern Europe, if you seek liberalization ... come here to this gate ... Mr. Gorbachev, open this gate ... Mr. Gorbachev, tear down this wall (Daley, 2013).

At the time, many believed—and some continue to believe today—that the dismantling of the Berlin Wall, which occurred shortly after Reagan's request, exhibited not simply the power of persuasion but also the power of the United States of America.

Interestingly, many dictionaries list the word *influence* as having a close relationship to *persuade.* Ivancevich and Matteson also noted a relationship between influence and power, stating that "power is the potential to influence, while influence is power in action" (1993, 383).

Therefore, the adept presenter will recognize the opportunity to demonstrate power—leveraging persuasion and influence—during the presentation. Its execution represents the fifth of the 5Ps: *power in action.*

Unlike some leadership attributes, such as emotional intelligence, power, as used here, is not an individual attribute. It is, instead, predicated on interpersonal interactions.

With every presentation comes the opportunity to interact with others, which also allows for demonstration of interpersonal skills. Power may be categorized as legitimate, reward, coercive, expert, and referent. And while the first three may be viewed on an organizational level, our focus here is on expert and referent power (also known as personal power).

Expert power, as the name implies, suggests that the leader has special expertise in a particular field. *Referent power* suggests that the leader possesses charismatic personality traits. A presenter exhibiting both of those kinds of power is more likely to achieve power in action during a speech or presentation (Ivancevich & Matteson 1993; Dubrin 2010; Bateman & Zeithaml 1993).

To further solidify the concept of power in action, consider some comments that I heard while listening several years ago to an audio program on verbal skills building. "When Cicero spoke, people marveled. When Caesar spoke, people marched" (Cato, Roman Politician, Elster 1995). This is a clear example of power in action.

Staying true to my belief in Ernest Hemingway's aphorism to show people everything but tell them nothing, figure 11-1 reflects the relationship between and among the 5Ps.

Figure 11-1: Interdependence of the 5Ps

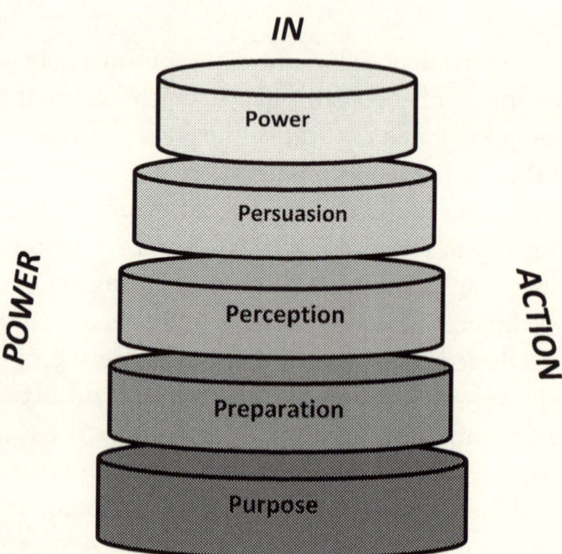

Viewing the diagram from bottom to top, note that purpose is the first stage, followed by preparation, perception, persuasion, and ending with power. This diagram could also be viewed as analogous to a powerful rocket inasmuch as each stage facilitates implementation of and shares interdependence with the next stage function and implementation. Just as the first stage of a rocket is required to generate the thrust for liftoff, so the purpose of a presentation is required in order to have any chance of success. Likewise, the middle stages of our 5P rocket must be fully completed and operational, thus enabling a successful mission (presentation). The fifth and final stage may be viewed as the command module through which the presentation mission (execution of power in action) is ultimately accomplished.

It is my hope that the linkage between oration, speech and presentation, as was introduced at the outset of this chapter, is now quite clear. The relationship between oration and speech should be obvious. And persuasive, perception and power were all used to define speech and presentation. Thus, through their definition, we have accounted for three (3) of the 5Ps discussed above. The remaining two (purpose and preparation) are assumed to be very fundamental enablers for delivering effective presentations.

If the linkage (oration → speech → presentation) did not resonate with you, the key takeaway from this discussion about power in action is that as the presenter, you are standing center stage among your audience, and you are the one who will be perceived as having the answers. It's simply a matter of making use of your expert and referent power to demonstrate power in action as you move the audience to where you know they should be as reflected by the story that you tell and the conviction with which you tell it.

11.1 The Oration Begins

Each year Summit Consumables Incorporated selects individuals from among the company's leadership ranks to visit the corporate office and provide a presentation to senior members of the management staff. Summit has historically used these meetings to corroborate management recommendations for promotable candidates. However, due to the current corporate environment, this year's meetings will be used instead to give a last look at those candidates who may not make the cut given the impending plan to downsize. Although local management was directed to keep this approach hush-hush, word leaked out, and the big fear across the company is receiving an invitation to participate in the presentations. This year, among those selected for presentations are Maria Summers, Kimberly Hours, Johnny Goode, Jessica Wright, and Earl Easy. Additionally, the presentations are scheduled to be held in the auditorium at the Georgia facility (the physical location of the selected presenters). Before the scheduled presentations, the attending management was provided a copy of excerpts from the prior year's performance evaluations and respective employee ratings.

Upon learning of the others invited to present in the upcoming meeting, Maria reached out to everyone. During the initial preparation meeting that she scheduled, she suggested that rather than providing individual presentations, given the overlapping nature of their work, they should consider providing a collaborative presentation. She proceeded to discuss how despite her marketing experience, she had always wanted to learn more about the departments that make it happen, from sales to manufacturing and manufacturing support. A collaborative effort, Maria believed, would facilitate this learning.

This idea was well received by the participants, so much so that Kim suggested Maria kick things off at the formal presentation, to which all agreed. Jessica suggested that once they complete their draft presentations they meet at least a couple of times in the auditorium (the location of the actual presentations) before the formal delivery date just to fine-tune things and ensure smooth transitions. Johnny added that it might be a good idea to have at least one direct report from each department in attendance during the dry runs to assure accuracy of any detailed information planned for sharing in the formal presentation. Earl followed, suggesting that each of the presenters play the role of devil's advocate by anticipating and asking questions of one another.

Kim responded that while she would definitely contribute to the practice sessions, she would not be available for the formal presentation because of a personal conflict. She asked Maria if she would mind presenting on her behalf. Maria agreed, and the meeting continued with each participant seeking calibration regarding the purpose of the presentation. (During this meeting Maria learned of the negative cost impact that the lack of predictability in promotions was having on Jessica's manufacturing operations. This cost resulted from the frequent equipment changeovers required to produce various SKUs involved in the northern tier promotions.)

We now fast forward to the presentations. Just before kickoff, Dave Sterling, chairman of Summit Consumables, walked into the auditorium and sat down in the front row, just a few feet from the presenters. Let us now listen in on each of these presentations with an eye toward the concepts and strategies we have discussed.

Maria opened up the presentation with these comments: "I recognize that this is a pivotal time for Summit Consumables. There are many threats to the very core of our business—our products. However, one area that I believe remains strong is our capacity to identify and meet, as yet unmet consumer needs. Our R&D department has been, and I am sure will continue to be great at doing that. Yet, unless and until we can effectively promote and deliver our products while concurrently minimizing the cost to manufacture those products, we will continue to fight an uphill battle. It is in this vein that I plan to share with you how we, marketing and sales, working in concert with manufacturing, procurement, and IT, plan not only to promote and sell our products, but also to deliver those products with quality." Reviewing the agenda, Maria added: "To this end, this afternoon we plan to discuss Kim's efforts to revive sales revenues. I plan to talk about refocusing the promotional efforts. Johnny will then talk about some critical plans for not only responding to short-term cost issues but for focusing on the longer term as well. Earl will discuss some infrastructure upgrades that we are all quite excited about. And Jessica will close the presentation with a discussion regarding manufacturing operations."

Following Maria's review of the agenda, one of the senior members serving in marketing said flippantly: "Yeah, I hear that the whole problem with the promotion is those weak cases, and it has nothing to do with our department."

To this comment, Maria responded: "While there were no doubt some issues with cases, which Johnny will discuss shortly, that was certainly not the only contributing factor to the promotional issues, as you will see momentarily."

Maria then asked if there were any additional questions before she began, but Dave Sterling responded: "No, Maria, the floor is yours."

Maria continued: "Kimberly was unable to join us this afternoon. However, I would like to point out that I am very excited by the work that she is doing, which I will cover now."

With this statement, Maria began sharing the revenue chart Kim provided and, at a high level, the root cause analysis work that Kim had implemented, leading up to the development of the sales team's KPIs. Maria specifically called attention to Kim's sixth KPI, which read: "Provide sales and mix training to all TSMs and institute best practices sharing by end of 1st quarter." Maria added: "While the sales and mix training is certainly not the panacea for all revenue declines, it is something that my team should have provided much sooner, and we are now making a concerted effort to not only provide the training but also assess the efficacy of that training. I believe the key takeaway from the work that Kim's team is planning is that through TSM development and retailer engagement, Summit Consumables should realize increased revenues and strengthened relationships with its key regional accounts."

Dave Sterling commented: "I appreciate the quantifiable nature of the sales revenue objectives."

Following Maria's response to a few more questions regarding the Pareto charts presented, she transitioned to discussions regarding the ostensible lack of product promotion predictability. She began by covering the B3G2 and B2G1 promotions in the northern tier for products A and B and how the issue was not the promotion itself but the lack of understanding of which promotion was objectively predictable.

While reviewing these charts, Maria pointed out that she was not at all an expert in the subject but did have enough understanding to know that the best option was the B3G2 promotion for product A and the B2G1 promotion for product B. She added that the selection was predicated on the linear relationship between volume and the promotion as well as, in her words, "something referred to as the R^2 value, which is generally used to corroborate the predictability." She also pointed out that she did have the expert (Jeff Hostetler, manager of market information) on standby if necessary, who could delve deeper into the statistical area if necessary.

To this Dave Sterling responded: "We trust you. Please continue."

Maria pointed out that more predictable product promotions would positively impact manufacturing costs because of reduced equipment downtime, changeovers, and consequential material waste. She ended discussions regarding the northern tier promotions by recommending that any effort to reposition TV advertising space based on Nielson ratings be delayed until the northern tier promotion predictability had stabilized.

Maria shifted discussions to the southern tier promotion and said that while she was continuing to fully vet the promotion from a marketing perspective, there were a couple of issues beyond her control that appeared to impact the promotion as well. To elaborate on these, she turned the floor over to Johnny, to be followed by remarks offered by Earl and closing out with Jessica sharing her view of manufacturing operations.

Johnny began: "Thanks Maria. Let me begin by saying that while I certainly appreciate Maria not throwing me under the bus, the truth is that a significant contributor to the lack of success with the promotions in the southern tier is a result of failing cases, an issue for which there is no excuse, and one for which I am fully accountable. What I would like to do now is explain what happened, share with you the strategies that we have put in place to circumvent future similar issues, and review plans to optimize our case supplier's process, resulting in the potential for significant cost savings.

"First, resulting from the procurement of cases with insufficient crush strength, which is the amount of weight required to cause case deformation, many of the retailers in the southern tier were fed up with receiving product that was either damaged or incorrectly cased. Earl will discuss the incorrect casing in a moment. As a result, they refused quite a bit of our product and returned opened case product as well, some of which was not damaged, but they returned it anyway out of frustration.

"So how did we get to where we are shipping product with weak cases? The answer is simple. A few months ago we switched suppliers in favor of one offering lower cost per case. One of the clauses in the contract with the new supplier required us to provide process improvement recommendations which would result in an even lower cost per case. Unfortunately, and I take full responsibility for it, we never submitted any process improvement recommendations. And due to the lack of control of the supplier's process, we continued to receive weak cases and pay a higher cost for those same cases."

Dave Sterling said: "Are you kidding me?"

Johnny responded: "I wish I were." He proceeded to discuss his plan to assure the receipt of cases that meet the desired crush strength levels in the future through in-process segregation occurring at the supplier, and also his plan to reduce costs longer term by implementation of process improvements and reducing the supplier in-process crush target.

To this, Dave Sterling added: "Let me make sure I understand. We are already receiving weaker than desired cases, and you are saying that you want to lower the supplier's crush strength target even more. What am I missing here?"

Johnny responded by referring to a chart derived from that shown in figure 6-10. He explained how a reduction in supplier variation would yield more consistent case crush strength levels, allowing for a downward shift in the crush strength target while concurrently reducing the inclusion of a very expensive ingredient, thereby resulting in significant cost savings per case.

Dave Sterling said, "This all sounds good but, last time I checked, there was no process variation button that you just turn down. How do you plan to do this?"

Exhibiting a smile of confidence, Johnny explained: "We have already begun to enlist the support of those closest to and most knowledgeable about the case manufacturing process at the supplier, and as we speak, we're running a pilot test incorporating some of their recommendations. And I have to tell you, it's looking pretty good."

Johnny proceeded to share his dashboard, using a chart derived from figure 6-12 and subsumed by objective #2, reflecting the timing for this initiative as well as the remaining objectives in his department.

Dave Sterling simply nodded and sat back comfortably in his chair. Johnny, recognizing this body language added: "While I would love to take the credit for the approach, I must admit that it only surfaced after a team meeting with my department, and they deserve all the credit."

Dave Sterling said, "Perhaps they do, but I'm sure your leadership played a critical role in getting to this point."

Johnny responded by saying, "Well, please keep in mind that I want to have a long future with Summit Consumables." Following an audience chuckle, Johnny continued. "OK, what I've covered focused on the supplier, but based on my conversation with our finished goods area, we are having a lot of issues with our legacy inventory system. I'm pleased to report that Earl is all over the issue and has both a short and long-term plan for resolution. Earl would you like to come forward?"

Earl got up to continue the discussion. "As Johnny mentioned, the existing inventory system is outdated and well beyond dependable repair. In the short term, we have negotiated a lease agreement with Automated Conveyor Company, the inventory management system vendor, for equipment that can be used to replace the offline hand casing operation, and we have implemented a patch that should at least temporarily eliminate the product mix-ups once the product cased offline is reintroduced to the automated case storage and retrieval system."

Harvey Macklin, executive VP of finance, responded, "It sounds like you're talking about a capital project, and you know that we have asked that all capital projects, especially those not meeting our hurdle rates, be delayed due to budgeting constraints."

Earl had anticipated this question. He showed a chart patterned after figure 9-10. Looking directly at Mr. Macklin, he added: "Mr. Macklin, you are 100 percent correct. However, the project that we are recommending has a very strong financial upside, including an NPV of $1.8 million at a cost of capital equal to 5.0 percent, which remains positive, coming in at $788 thousand at a hurdle rate as high as 10.0 percent. Not to mention an IRR of 14.5 percent, a PI of 1.08 and a payback of 2.33 years."

Mr. Macklin, now displaying a huge smile, nodded affirmatively, but asked: "So what took so long? Didn't we know that there were case-handling issues last year?"

Earl explained. "That, quite frankly, is on me. We did know about the issue, but there was a bit of confusion regarding the financial ROI, which I should have recognized much earlier but, as you see here, we have since rectified that. And in addition, we have negotiated an agreement with Automated Conveyor that not only meets the company's financial criteria but also allows us to have on site OEM support, including installation, start-up, training, and maintenance for twenty-four months following initial commissioning.

"Thus far, we have talked about the product at the retail level as well as plans for optimizing supplier processes. However, as we all know, the first process step in getting product into cases for shipment to retail is to manufacture that product. If there are no further questions or comments for me, Jessica is going to walk us through her plans in that area."

Looking at Dave and others seated just in front of her, and in a relaxed manner, Jessica began. "Allow me to share with you my vision for manufacturing. I see an agile operation, where the application of qualitative and quantitative problem solving-tools is overshadowed only by the teamwork and workforce engagement used in the deployment of such tools. And that is not simply within the boundaries of manufacturing operations. But just as we have demonstrated interdepartmental collaboration today, I want to continue the relationship with marketing, IT and procurement, and quite frankly any other group that can help me out." The audience chuckled with Jessica at that comment.

"So what does the vision look like on my end? It starts with my cognizance of and willingness to listen to the voice of manufacturing operations. And that voice is all of manufacturing operations, from the floor sweeper to the repair technician."

Dave Sterling said, "Jessica, that all sounds good, but I have to ask—What are you going to do specifically so that you are on top of your business?"

Exhibiting a confident smile, Jessica responded: "Great question! It begins with implementation of my personal dashboard as you see here." She showed a chart derived from figures 5-11 and 5-12. "My key focus areas are employee safety, product quality, process compliance, and cost."

Jessica explained the dashboard, and when she finished, she received a question from Bill Jennings, senior vice president of technology.

"Jessica, I have a question. What do you mean by process compliance? If you just work with the QA department, as you have said, and have them take product samples, there should be no product quality issues. When I ran manufacturing operations, that's how we did it."

Jessica stepped a bit closer to the edge of the stage, and responded after establishing eye contact with Bill. "At the risk of oversimplifying, Bill, an analogy here would be baking a cake. As much as I'm sure we would all enjoy taste testing samples of the cake, if you add the right ingredients—flour, eggs, sugar, and so on—and you have the right temperature and bake it for the right amount of time, assuming your raw ingredients meet specifications, the cake has to turn out right. No, we're not baking cakes, but we are delivering a finished product employing processes that should yield a consistently high quality product if we assure process compliance. Did that answer your question?"

"Yes it did," Bill replied. "That's a fresh way of looking at it that we never thought of before. Please continue."

"OK, in addition to my personal dashboard, I've also created an objectives-based dashboard as you see here." She displayed a chart derived from figure 5-10. "It includes the strategy, objective, the accountable, support resources, and the time by which the objective is to be completed."

Next Jessica discussed changes to her staff and department meeting format that, although not reflected on her objectives-based dashboard, includes quarterly department meetings, inviting hourly workers to participate in her weekly staff meetings, and using the famed GE work-out process to streamline the work of her salaried staff.

"As a final note," Jessica continued, "just last week I communicated key portions of this very same presentation to my entire department, including my hourly employees, and it is my sincere belief that we are now all on the same page." She asked if there were any other questions or comments before turning the meeting back over to Maria.

When Maria returned to the stage, she exhibited an erect posture, with her toes pointed outward. Maintaining eye contact, she spoke in a loud, confident tone. "I think I speak for all of us when I say that we sincerely appreciate all of you taking your time to allow us to share our strategies and plans. And while I think it's safe to say that many opportunities exist from marketing to sales to IT to procurement and manufacturing, I also believe it's true that we're all over it, as Johnny says. Thank you again."

The audience chuckled a bit and then, following Dave Sterling's lead, applauded. Breaking the applause was a comment offered by—yep, you guessed it—Dave Sterling.

"You know, I've sat through many presentations, some exciting, some stressful, and some long and boring. But this presentation exhibited by far the greatest level of teamwork and collaboration that I think I have ever witnessed. I'm really looking forward to each of you being around long enough to execute the strategies that you have presented here today. And if you should run into barriers that appear to be insurmountable, don't hesitate to contact me. For each of you, I'm just a telephone call away. Good job!"

We conclude this chapter by emphasizing that despite the issue or opportunity precipitating the need for *your* presentation, by zeroing in on the purpose, implementing good preparation, and demonstrating perceptiveness and persuasion, you should be adequately positioned to exhibit power in action.

CHAPTER 12

Another Look at the 5C Leadership Improvement Model

THIS BOOK BEGAN with a discussion of leadership and offered examples using various author perspectives on the topic. I introduced you to the performance appraisal and the corporate structure by means of the fictional Summit Consumables Incorporated. I introduced several Summit employees and later made use of them to demonstrate execution of the 5C LIM (conversation, calculation, collaboration, communication and cognizance) in response to a performance evaluation. In doing so, various analytical business and improvement tools were used to facilitate implementation of certain leadership strategies.

In this chapter we revisit each of the employees you were introduced to in order to show how various aspects of the 5C LIM may have been used, proactively, to obviate critical leadership development issues and opportunities previously identified. The approach taken here is to focus on a single stage of the 5C LIM to initiate the discussion and to build on this stage, bringing in other 5C LIM stage components as applicable to certain employees. In doing so, the integrated nature of the 5C LIM should become obvious to you.

We begin nonsequentially in the area of conversation with Earl Easy. His feedback suggested that he was "somewhat aloof and needed to take charge." One simple but effective leadership tool within the 5C LIM to apply to this problem is conversation.

Recall that both projects in Earl's purview (website upgrade and inventory management system replacement) were behind schedule, and Earl was apparently unaware of the delays. The importance of having a conversation with your team cannot be overstated. These may be as formal or informal as necessary to provide the level of awareness (cognizance) to keep critical projects and initiatives on or ahead of schedule. It is also during a conversation that employee development opportunities are identified. After all, as was evidenced in discussions between Earl and his direct reports, it is the leader's responsibility to continuously grow the skill sets of those being led. Being cognizant of such development opportunities is paramount for effective leadership.

Beyond employee development, another critical instance evidencing of the lack of cognizance among Summit's players was the discussion regarding Jessica Wright. Not only was she unaware of the quality and productivity issues occurring in her area of responsibility, she apparently also lacked cognizance regarding her budget. As you may recall, the corporate office at Summit transferred around $4 million of costs into her operations budget. While this may represent an extreme example, the point to be made is that, particularly within the leader's domain, a keen awareness of all aspects of the business is also paramount.

Jessica's implementation of her personal dashboard was a big hit during the presentation and certainly facilitated her overall manufacturing operations awareness of the most critical metrics.

Similarly, we saw that Ken missed opportunities to proactively improve the core functions of his organization: error-free reports and dropped consumer calls. But in Ken's case, his lack of cognizance regarding the ineffectiveness of his leadership style could have been avoided if he had engaged his team in candid and productive conversations much earlier. And remember Ken's surprise upon learning that he was not on the fast promotion track despite thinking he was. This too, could have been made clear if he had engaged in the right conversation with his boss much earlier in the performance cycle.

Johnny exhibited a lack of cognizance as well, particularly regarding the supplier price increases and the contract that was not reviewed in detail and in his failure to notice the email that was sent to him from Anthony addressing process improvement suggestions related to that contract. As seen in this example, the impact of the absence of a conversation can be profound.

Another key lesson learned in this area is about communication in the general sense. Recall the discussion regarding the email that Anthony sent to Johnny and Earl's discussion with Tonya regarding the email that she sent to Maria. While the initial communication attempt was made in both cases, there was no evidence of a follow-up conversation being conducted by either Anthony or Tonya. Had such a conversation taken place, perhaps the situations would have been somewhat mitigated. And Kim saw how insufficient communications can lead to lost revenues, feelings of alienation among team members, and inadequate TSM training.

Finally, we saw countless examples of where the absence of team collaboration between peers and subordinates resulted in important issues and opportunities. While the most obvious instance may have been exhibited in the form of peer feedback supplied to Maria, more subtle instances occurred as well. You may recall the effect on the southern tier promotion resulting from issues existing outside of Maria's immediate circle. In this instance, both Johnny and Earl could have and should have reached out to (communicated with) Maria in an effort not only to alert her of the issues with weak cases and mixed-up product, but to also collaborate with her so that she could proactively address the promotional issues.

Another missed opportunity for collaboration was in manufacturing operations, whereby the QA manager did not reach out to Jessica regarding consumer complaint levels. Although the QA manager is not a central character in the book, you should recognize that the accountability to communicate and collaborate rests with everyone across the organization.

Returning once more to the discussion in chapter 4 regarding overlap of the 5C LIM core stages, see figure 12-1. We have discussed the interdependence of conversation collaboration, cognizance, and communication, but have not yet discussed calculation. This is by design, not an oversight.

Recall that in the examples that used scrolls, *calculation* was characterized as a method through which issues and opportunities identified in the conversation stage were addressed. It was thus reflected in the scrolls as a HOW mechanism. Further, we saw that the calculation stage was not constrained by mathematical algorithms or formulas, but expanded to accommodate logical reasoning and argumentation as well. So the calculation stage may be further explained as a means for contemplating how to engage in a conversation, how to execute collaboration, and how to disseminate an appropriate communication. This view of calculation is supported by revisiting its definition from

Figure 12-1: Core Stage Overlap Core 5C LIM Stages

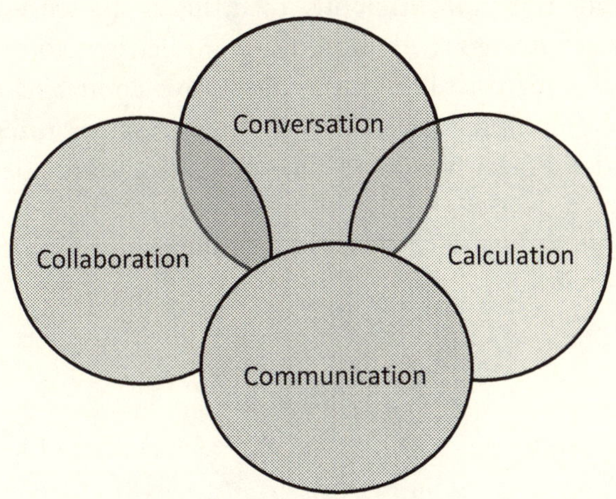

Merriam-Webster: "the process or an act of calculating … to determine by mathematical processes … to reckon by exercise of practical judgment … to design or adapt for a purpose by forethought or careful plan …" (2007). Of particular note is the reference here "to design or adapt for a purpose by forethought or careful plan."

For example, consider the situation in chapter 3 regarding Ken's response to his boss, Victor, during the performance evaluation discussion. There were several opportunities for Ken to exercise forethought and careful planning before responding. Granted, Ken's responses occurred on a real time basis with little time to actually plan. But just as a driver executes a sudden lane change to avoid a head-on collision or slams on the brakes to avoid impact with an animal crossing his path, such calculated responses can and do occur in an instant.

In a much less challenging environment wherein you are the person providing the feedback, or even if you are the receiver and such a conversation allows time for thought, your capacity to calculate how to either deliver or receive the feedback is greatly magnified. Likewise, calculating how to collaborate with, for example, a difficult person or group also demonstrates the functionality of this 5C LIM stage.

Finally, regarding the relationship between calculation and communication, consider Jessica's intent to communicate her plans department wide. Obviously, her discussion with her boss in this regard would be different from what she communicates to her entire department, including the hourly workforce. This approach to communicating her plans and strategies differently to different audiences within her department is analogous to the adage, "When in Rome, do as the Romans do," which is all about a calculative approach. Figure 12-2 captures the graphical representation of this discussion regarding the role of calculation relative to the remaining stage components.

Figure 12-2: Calculation Integration

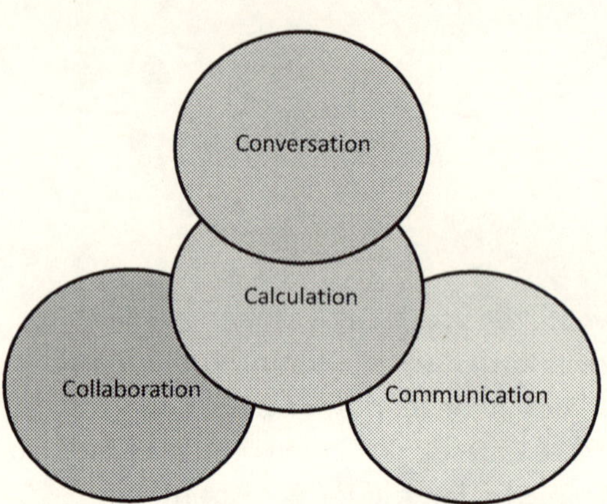

Although subtle, the revised representation reflects the connectivity regarding the role that calculation plays in execution of all 5C LIM core stages.

You may conclude that calculation is aligned with the four domains of emotional intelligence I presented in section 1.4: self-awareness, self-management, social awareness, and relationship management. And, to some degree, this thinking is correct. There is, however, a slight divergence here in that while EI domains discuss *what* is to be done, calculation as discussed here is more aligned with *how* it is to be accomplished.

It could be argued that, generally speaking, the 5Ps of presenting may be supplanted by the 5C LIM, whereby purpose is subsumed in the conversation stage, preparation is subsumed in the calculation stage, perception and persuasion are subsumed in the collaboration stage, and power (in particular power in action) is addressed by the communication stage. And while this may indeed be a robust argument, the 5Ps may provide a more lucid path for presentation development.

To learn more about how the 5C LIM, 5Ps and other leadership strategies presented in this book can help you get all the way to the top, visit www.leadershiplmc.com.

Thank you for reading this book, and it is my sincere hope that you gained as much delight and insight from reading it as I did in preparing it.

Be sure to look for the companion books: *The 5C Leadership Improvement Model* and *The 5Ps for Exhibiting Presentation Leadership* as well as other books under the *All the Way to the Top* series. Until we meet again ... so long and happy leading!

APPENDIX A

Measuring Instrument

A.1 Instrument Introduction

MANY INSTRUMENTS (SUCH AS THE FFM) may be used to measure leadership style. Critical to the instrument chosen, however, is its reliability and validity. Leedy and Ormond offered support for this perspective, stating: "regardless of the type of scale a measurement instrument involves, it must have both validity and reliability for its purpose" (2013, 89). Likewise, "although individuals may have different views in terms of what constitutes psychometric adequacy, most people can agree that a measurement is only useful to the extent that it provides meaningful information about individuals" (Briesch, Chafouleas, & Swaminathan 2014, 14). Creswell added to the discourse, stating: "to use an existing instrument [the author should] describe the established validity and reliability of the instrument [which includes] reporting efforts by authors to establish validity" (2009, 149).

Figure A1.1 reflects the interconnectedness of the relationships between the instrument of choice and the critical components of validity, reliability and objectivity.

Figure A1.1: Instrument Efficacy

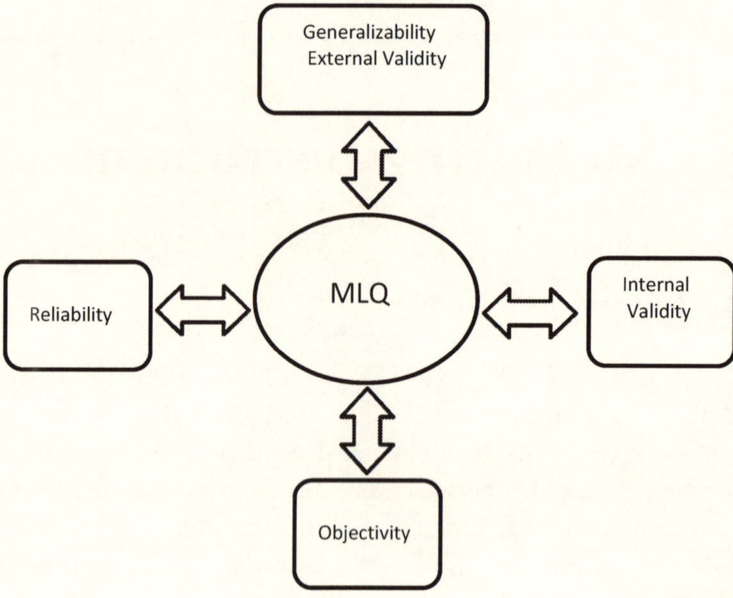

Before I can talk about instrument validity and reliability, let me first visit the multifactor leadership questionnaire (MLQ) in the context of Full Range Leadership Theory (FRLT). Pioneering authors of leadership theory such as Bass and Avolio determined that more was needed than leaders simply providing rewards for subordinate behavior characterized by XL. They also identified the need to understand how leaders influence followers to set aside self-interests for the good of their organizations through optimal levels of performance.

Early expansions in leadership theory included five TL factors, three XL factors, and one nontransactional laissez-faire leadership component (Antonikass et al., 2003, 264). The contemporary FRLT model maintains the five TL factors, as discussed previously: idealized influence, idealized behaviors, inspirational motivation, intellectual stimulation and individualized consideration. However, there are two XL factors, defined as contingent reward (CR) and management-by-exception: Active (MBEA). The other leadership style, Passive Avoidant, is also comprised of two attributes (management-by-exception: Passive (MBEP) and Laissez-Faire (LF)). The MLQ questionnaire (see appendix B) is designed to assess each of the three leadership styles through select questions that are subsequently combined via the MLQ5X scoring form (again, see appendix B) for determination of applicable descriptive statistics.

A.2 Measuring Instrument Validity

We begin with discussions of external instrument validity. Leedy and Ormond characterized external validity as "the extent to which the research study's results apply to situations beyond the study itself" (2013, 103). According to Avolio and Bass, "in numerous studies, transformational leaders were found to generate higher commitment in their followers" (2004, 36). Thus, what is being measured by the MLQ can be traced to a valid form of real world effective leadership. Likewise, testing conducted by Bogler determined "that teachers' satisfaction increases as they perceive their principals' leadership style as more transformational and less transactional" (2001, 677). Fuller et al. (1996), as cited by Avolio and Bass, reported in a meta-analysis greater follower compliance if their leaders were more transformational than transactional (2004, 36). The list of scholarly writings substantiating the external validity of the MLQ is far-reaching. Therefore, discussions in this section shift to construct validity.

"The extent to which an instrument measures a characteristic that cannot be directly observed but assumed to exist based on patterns in people's behavior [is termed construct validity]" (Leedy & Ormond 2013, 90).

Creswell addressed the topic of construct validity by asking, "do items measure hypothetical constructs or concepts" (2009, 149). According to Barge and Schlueter, "the MLQ possesses good construct validity … as seen in the previous studies, transformational versus transactional leadership was found to be more highly correlated with a variety of outcomes" (1991, 551).

Armstrong and Nuttawuth, following the implementation of tests including confirmatory factor analysis, modification indices, and chi square testing of the nine factor model (meaning the MLQ version referenced in this book) concluded, "after acknowledging the MLQ criticisms by refining several versions of the instruments, the version of the MLQ, Form 5X (Bass and Avolio, 1997), is successful in adequately capturing the full leadership factor constructs of transformational leadership theory" (2008, 10). In the end, there appears to be substantial support for the MLQ's construct validation.

Regarding predictive validity, according to Barge and Schlueter, "the MLQ demonstrates good predictive validity. Bass and Avolio (1990) report transformational leadership scores were strongly correlated with the extra effort of followers, satisfaction, and the effectiveness of the organization" (1991, 550).

A.3 Measurement Instrument Reliability

Leedy and Ormond defined reliability as "the consistency with which a measuring instrument yields a certain, consistent result when the entity being measured hasn't changed" (2013, 91).

Bass and Avolio (1991), as cited by Barge and Schlueter, concluded that although "the alpha reliability coefficients for the self-rating form were consistently lower than those for the rater form, with reliabilities ranging from .60 to .9, reliability of the two forms existed" (1991, 550). (Note that this book assumed use of the rater form for data collection.) Bass and Avolio concluded that "reliabilities for the total items and for each leadership factor scale ranged from .74 to .94 … all of the scales' reliabilities were generally high, exceeding standard cutoffs for internal consistency recommended in the literature" (2004, 49). Barge and Schlueter also "report[ed] the MLQ Rater Form demonstrated good internal reliability with all factors above an alpha of .82, with the exception of management-by-exception (.79) and laissez-faire leadership" (1991, 549). Also in this area, Bennett cited research conducted by Lowe, Kroech and Sivasubramaniam (1996) that assessed five factors of the MLQ: charisma, individualized consideration, intellectual stimulation, contingent reward, and management by exception. The resulting "mean Cronbach scale obtained for the five scales tested were 0.92, 0.88, 0.86, 8.82 and 0.65 respectively" (Bennett 2009, 6). Bennett also cited work by Dumdum, Lower and Avolio (2002) which assessed "twelve scales" of the MLQ concluding that "internal reliability was good as the mean Cronbach … for eleven of the twelve scales was above 0.7 and the final one was 0.69" (2009, 7).

Another reliability measure is called Test-Retest Reliability. And according to Bass and Avolio (1990) as cited by Barge and Schlueter, "test-retest reliabilities were provided by a study using the ratings by 193 followers and 33 leaders measured 6 months apart … the rater form test-retest reliabilities ranged from .52 to .82 and from .44 to .74 for the self-rating form" (1991, 550).

In conclusion, the above research sufficiently supports the validity and reliability of the MLQ for its intended purpose—measuring FRLT. This support is therefore the basis for its reference throughout this book.

APPENDIX B

Multifactor Leadership Questionnaire

BECAUSE OF COPYRIGHT constraints, only five each of forty-five rater questions or items are shown on the following two rater forms.

Multifactor Leadership Questionnaire
Rater Form

Name of Leader: .... Date: ....

Organization ID #: .... Leader ID #: ....

This questionnaire is used to describe the leadership style of the above-mentioned individual as you perceive it. Answer all items on this answer sheet. **If an item is irrelevant, or if you are unsure or do not know the answer, leave the answer blank.** Please answer this questionnaire anonymously.

Important (necessary for processing): Which best describes you?

____ I am at a higher organizational level than the person I am rating.
____ The person I am rating is at my organizational level.
____ I am at a lower organizational level than the person I am rating.
____ Other than the above.

Forty-five descriptive statements are listed on the following pages. Judge how frequently each statement fits the person you are describing. Use the following rating scale:

Not at all	Once in a while	Sometimes	Fairly often	Frequently, if not always
0	1	2	3	4

The Person I Am Rating. . .

1. Provides me with assistance in exchange for my efforts 0 1 2 3 4
2. *Re-examines critical assumptions to question whether they are appropriate 0 1 2 3 4
3. Fails to interfere until problems become serious 0 1 2 3 4
4. Focuses attention on irregularities, mistakes, exceptions, and deviations from standards 0 1 2 3 4
5. Avoids getting involved when important issues arise 0 1 2 3 4

MLQ Multifactor Leadership Questionnaire
Scoring Key (5x) Short

My Name: .... Date: ....

Organization ID #: .... Leader ID #: ....

Scoring: The MLQ scale scores are average scores for the items on the scale. The score can be derived by summing the items and dividing by the number of items that make up the scale. **If an item is left blank, divide the total for that scale by the number of items answered.** All of the leadership style scales have four items, Extra Effort has three items, Effectiveness has four items, and Satisfaction has two items.

Not at all	Once in a while	Sometimes	Fairly often	Frequently, if not always
0	1	2	3	4

*Idealized Influence (Attributed) total/4 =

*Idealized Influence (Behavior) total/4 =

*Inspirational Motivation total/4 =

*Intellectual Stimulation total/4 =

*Individual Consideration total/4 =

\# Contingent Reward total/4 =

\# Management-by-Exception (Active) total/4 =

+Management-by-Exception (Passive) total/4 =

+Laissez-faire Leadership total/4 =

Extra Effort total/3 =

Effectiveness total/4 =

Satisfaction total/2 =

1. Contingent Reward	0	1	2	3	4
2. Intellectual Stimulation	0	1	2	3	4
3. Management-by-Exception (Passive)	0	1	2	3	4
4. Management-by-Exception (Active)	0	1	2	3	4
5. Laissez-faire Leadership	0	1	2	3	4

APPENDIX C

Normative Tables

Percentiles for Individual Scores Based on Lower Level Ratings (US)

	II(A)	II(B)	IM	IS	IC	CR	MBEA	MBEP	LF	EE	EFF	SAT	
N =	12,118	12,118	12,118	12,118	12,118	12,118	12,118	12,118	12,118	12,118	12,118	12,118	
%tile	MLQ Scores									Outcomes			%tile
5	1.25	1.25	1.5	1.5	1	1.29	0.25	0	0	1	1.5	1	5
10	1.75	1.75	2	1.75	1.5	1.75	0.5	0	0	1.33	2	2	10
20	2.25	2.21	2.25	2.25	2	2.25	0.75	0.25	0	2	2	2.5	20
30	2.5	2.5	2.75	2.5	2.5	2.5	1.11	0.5	0.25	2.33	2.5	3	30
40	2.75	2.54	3	2.75	2.75	2.75	1.37	0.75	0.25	2.67	2.75	3	40
50	3	2.75	3	2.75	3	3	1.62	1	0.5	3	3	3.5	50
60	3.25	3	3.25	3	3.17	3.13	1.87	1	0.75	3	3.25	3.5	60
70	3.5	3.25	3.5	3.25	3.25	3.25	2.25	1.25	0.93	3.33	3.5	3.67	70
80	3.75	3.46	3.75	3.5	3.5	3.5	2.5	1.7	1.25	3.67	3.52	4	80
90	4	3.75	4	3.75	3.75	3.75	3	2	1.75	4	4	4	90
95	4	3.75	4	4	4	4	3.25	2.5	2	4	4	4	95

Percentiles for Individual Scores Based on Same Level Ratings (US)

	II(A)	II(B)	IM	IS	IC	CR	MBEA	MBEP	LF	EE	EFF	SAT	
N =	5,185	5,185	5,185	5,185	5,185	5,185	5,185	5,185	5,185	5,185	5,185	5,185	
%tile	**MLQ Scores**									**Outcomes**			**%tile**
5	1.5	1.5	1.5	1.5	1.5	1.75	0.25	0	0	0	1.75	1.5	**5**
10	2	1.75	1.75	1.75	1.75	2	0.5	0.11	0	1.66	2	2	**10**
20	2.25	2.25	2.25	2.25	2.25	2.37	1	0.35	0	2	2.5	2.5	**20**
30	2.67	2.5	2.5	2.5	2.5	2.6	1.25	0.5	0.25	2.23	2.75	2.91	**30**
40	2.75	2.75	2.75	2.75	2.75	2.75	1.5	0.75	0.25	2.67	3	3	**40**
50	3	2.75	3	2.75	3	3.06	1.75	1	0.5	2.73	3.03	3.08	**50**
60	3.25	3	3	3	3	3.25	2	1.04	0.75	3	3.25	3.5	**60**
70	3.5	3.25	3.25	3.25	3.25	3.25	2.25	1.25	1	3.33	3.5	3.5	**70**
80	3.5	3.28	3.28	3.34	3.34	3.5	2.5	1.5	1.17	3.34	3.75	4	**80**
90	3.75	3.75	3.75	3.75	3.75	3.75	2.87	2	1.5	3.67	4	4	**90**
95	4	3.75	4	4	4	4.77	3.25	2.5	2.5	4	4	4	**95**

Percentiles for Individual Scores Based on Higher Level Ratings (US)

	II(A)	II(B)	IM	IS	IC	CR	MBEA	MBEP	LF	EE	EFF	SAT	
N =	4,268	4,268	4,268	4,268	4,268	4,268	4,268	4,268	4,268	4,268	4,268	4,268	
%tile	**MLQ Score s**									**Outcomes**			**%tile**
5	1.75	1.75	1.5	1.5	1.5	1.75	0.25	0	0	1.33	1.75	1.5	**5**
10	2	2	1.75	1.75	2	2	0.5	0.25	0	1.67	2	2	**10**
20	2.5	2.5	2.25	2.18	2.25	2.43	0.95	0.35	0	2	2.5	2.5	**20**
30	2.75	2.75	2.5	2.41	2.5	2.62	1.25	0.5	0.25	2.33	3	3	**30**
40	2.95	2.95	2.75	2.5	2.75	2.75	1.5	0.75	0.25	2.67	3.04	3	**40**
50	3	3	2.9	2.75	2.97	3	1.7	1	0.5	2.74	3.25	3.08	**50**
60	3.25	3.25	3	3	3	3	1.95	1.03	0.75	2.82	3.5	3.5	**60**
70	3.5	3.5	3.25	3	3.25	3.25	2.21	1.25	0.92	3	3.5	3.5	**70**
80	3.5	3.5	3.5	3.25	3.96	3.47	2.5	1.5	1.17	3.33	3.75	3.5	**80**
90	3.75	3.75	3.75	3.5	3.67	3.62	2.88	2	1.5	3.67	4	4	**90**
95	4	4	4	3.75	3.75	3.75	3.25	2.5	2	4	4	4	**95**

LEGEND :

II(B) = IDEALIZED INFLUENCE (BEHAVIOR)
IM = INSPIRATIONAL MOTIVATION
IS = INTELLECTUAL STIMULATION
IC = INDIVIDUALIZED CONSIDERATION
CR = CONTINGENT REWARD
MBEA = MANAGEMENT-BY -EXCEPTION (ACTIVE) MBEP = MANAGEMENT-BY -EXCEPTION (PASSIVE) LF = LAISSEZ-
EE = EXTRA EFFORT EFF = EFFECTIVENESS SAT = SATISFACTION

Note: Percentile tables for the samples listed in Table 1 are available at: www.mindgarden.com/docs/MLQinterna

Key of Frequency:
4.0 = Frequently if not always
3.0 = Fairly often
2.0 = Sometimes
1.0 = Once in a while
0.0 = Not at all

APPENDIX D

Full Range Leadership Theory[1]

TRANSFORMATIONAL LEADERSHIP IS a process of influencing in which leaders change their associates' awareness of what is important and move them to see themselves and the opportunities and challenges of their environment in a new way. Transformational leaders are proactive. They seek to optimize individual, group, and organizational development and innovation, not just achieve performance "at expectations." They convince their associates to strive for higher levels of potential as well as higher levels of moral and ethical standards.

A. Idealized Influence (Attributes and Behaviors)

These leaders are admired, respected, and trusted. Followers identify with and want to emulate their leaders. Among the things leaders do to earn credit with followers is to consider followers' needs over their own needs. Leaders shares risks with followers and are consistent in conduct with underlying ethics, principles, and values.

---

1 For each of these leadership attributes, behaviors, or outcomes, several questions/observation items are included on the selected "rater" form for completion by the rater. Only five (5) of forty-five (45) items are shown on the rater form listed in Appendix B. Due to publisher copyright constraints, those questions/observation items have been excluded from this section. However, they are assumed to have been addressed as referenced by completion of the rater forms throughout this book.

Idealized Attributes (IA)
Idealized Behaviors (IB)

B. Inspirational Motivation (IM)

These leaders behave in ways that motivate those around them by providing meaning and challenge to their followers' work. Individual and team spirit is aroused. Enthusiasm and optimism are displayed. The leader encourages followers to envision attractive future states which they can ultimately envision for themselves.

C. Intellectual Stimulation (IS)

These leaders stimulate their followers' effort to be innovative and creative by questioning assumptions, reframing problems, and approaching old situations in new ways. There is no ridicule or public criticism of individual members' mistakes. New ideas and creative solutions to problems are solicited from followers, who are included in the process of addressing problems and finding solutions.

D. Individual Consideration (IC)

These leaders pay attention to each individual's need for achievement and growth by acting as coaches or mentors. Followers are developed to successfully higher levels of potential. New learning opportunities are created along with a climate in which to grow. Individual differences in terms of needs and desires are recognized.

I. Transactional Leadership

Transactional leaders display behaviors associated with constructive and corrective transactions. The constructive style is labeled contingent-reward and the corrective style is labeled management-by-exception. Transactional leadership defines expectations and promotes performance to achieve these levels. Contingent reward and management-by-exception are two core behaviors associated with management functions in organizations. Full range leaders do this and more.

A. Contingent Reward (CR)

Transactional contingent reward leadership clarifies expectation and offers recognition when goals are achieved. The clarification of goals and objectives and providing of recognition once goals are achieved should result in individuals and groups achieving expected levels of performance.

B. Management-by-Exception: Active (MBEA)

The leader specifies the standards for compliance, as well as what constitutes ineffective performance, and may punish followers for being out of compliance with those standards. This style of leadership implies closely monitoring of deviances, mistakes, and errors, and then taking corrective action as quickly as possible when they occur.

Passive-Avoidant Behavior

Another form of management-by-exception leadership is more passive and reactive. It does not respond to situations and problems systematically. Passive leaders avoid specifying agreements, clarifying expectations, and providing goals and standards to be achieved by followers. This style has a negative effect on desired outcomes—the opposite of what is intended by the leader-manager. In this regard, it is similar to laissez-faire styles of no leadership. Both types of behavior have negative impacts on followers and associates. Accordingly, both styles can be grouped together as passive-avoidant leadership.

II. Management-by-Exception: Passive (MBEP)
III. Laissez-Faire (LF)
IV. Outcomes of Leadership

Transformational and transactional leadership are both related to the success of the group. Success is measured with the MLQ by how often the raters perceive their leader to be motivating, how effective raters perceive their leader to be at interacting at different levels of the organization, and how satisfied raters are with their leader's methods of working with others.

A. Extra Effort
B. Effectiveness
C. Satisfaction with the Leadership

REFERENCES

Antonikas, J., B. Avolio, and N. Savisubrananiam. 2003. "Context and Leadership: An examination of the nine-factor full range leadership theory using the multi-factor leadership questionnaire." *The Leadership Quarterly*, 14, 261–95.

Aguayo, R. 1990. *Dr. Deming: The American Who Taught the Japanese About Quality*. New York: Fireside.

Armstrong, M. 2009. *Armstrong's Handbook of Performance Management—An Evidence-based Guide to Delivering High Performance: Fourth Edition*. London & Philadelphia: Kogan.

Armstrong, A., and M. Nuttawuth. 2008. "Evaluating the Structural Validity of the Multifactor Leadership Questionnaire (MLQ)", *Capturing the Leadership Factors of Transformational-Transactional Leadership Contemporary Management Research* 4(1), 3–14.

Ashkenas, R., S. Kerr, and D. Ulrich. 2002. *GE Work-Out: How to Implement GE's Revolutionary Method for Busting Bureaucracy and Attacking Organizational Problems—Fast!* (R. Narramore, A. Glover, Eds.). New York: McGraw-Hill.

Atwater, L. B., Avolio, and B. Bass. 1996. "The Transformational and Transactional Leadership of Men and Women." *Applied Psychology: An International Review*, 45(1), 5–34.

Avolio, B. J. Lawler, and F. Walumbwa. 2007. "Leadership, Individual Differences, and Work-Related Attitudes: A Cross-Culture Investigation." *Applied Psychology: An International Review,* 56(2), 212–30.

Ayers, R. 2015. "Aligning Individual and Organizational Performance: Goal Alignment in Federal Government Agency Performance Appraisal Programs." *Public Personnel Management*, 44(2) 169 –91.

Baban, A., and L. Ratiu. 2012. "Executive Coaching as a Change Process: An Analysis of the Readiness for Coaching." *Cognition, Brain, Behavior: An Interdisciplinary Journal*, 16(1) 139–64.

Babin, B. J., and W. G. Zikmund. 2007. *Exploring Marketing Research: Ninth Edition*. (Ohlinger Publishing Services, P. Buskey, eds.). USA: Thomson Southwestern.

Barge, J. and D. Schlueter. 1991. "Leadership as Organizing: A Critique of Leadership Instruments." *Management Communication Quarterly*, (4), 541–70.

Bateman, T. S., and C. P. Zeithaml. 1993. *Management: Function and Strategy* (K. Strand, J. Roberts & L. Ruberstein, eds.). Homewood: Irwin.

Belschak, F., N. Deanne, and D. Hartog. 2012. "When Does Transformational Leadership Enhance Employee Proactive Behavior? The Role of Autonomy and Role Breadth Self-Efficacy." *Journal of Applied Psychology*, 97(1), 194–202.

Bennett, T. 2009. "A Study of the Management Leadership Style Preferred by Its Subordinates." *Journal of Organizational Culture*, 13(2), 1–24.

Berk, K. N., and P. Carey. 2010. *Data Analysis with Microsoft Excel*. (M. Taylor, D. Seibert, S. Walsh, C. Ronquillo, eds.) Boston: Books/Cole.

Baye, M. R., and R. O. Beil. 1994. *Managerial Economics and Business Strategy*. (M. Junior, G. Nelson, S. McDonald, L. Baster, eds.). Burr Ridge: Irwin.

Bertrand, R. 1812. *The Problems of Philosophy*. (A. Chrucky, ed.) Oxford University Press.

Bhattacharya, J. 2014. "Root Cause Analysis: A Practice to Understanding and Control the Failure Management in Manufacturing Industry." *International Journal of Business and Management Invention* 3(10), 12–20.

Bogler, R. 2001. "The influence of Leadership Style on Teacher Job Satisfaction." *Educational Administration Quarterly*, 37(5), 662–83.

Boyatzis, R. E., and A. McKee. 2005. "Resonant Leadership: Renewing Yourself and Connecting with Others through Mindfulness, Hope, and Compassion." Boston: Harvard Business School Press.

Brackett, M., S. Rivers, and P. Salovey. 2011. "Emotional Intelligence: Implications for Personal, Social, Academic, and Workplace Success." *Social and Personality Psychology Compass*, 5(1), 88–103.

Brewer, J. L., and K. C. Dittman. 2010. *Methods of IT Project Management*. (B. Joran, S. Yagan, E. Svendsen, K. Loftus, J. Leale, eds.) Boston: Prentice Hall.

Briesch, A., S. Chafouleas, H. Swaminathan, and M. Welsh. 2014. "Generalizability Theory: A Practical Guide to Study Design,

Implementation, and Interpretation." *Journal of School Psychology*, 52, 13–36.

Brigham, E. F., and L. C. Gapenski. 1991. *Financial Management Theory and Practice: Sixth Edition*. (A. Heath, J. Sarwark, K. Hill, J. Perkins, eds.) Fort Worth: The Dryden Press.

Burton, D. 2009. "The Most Hazardous and Dangerous and Greatest Adventure on which Man Has Ever Embarked." *Mechanical Engineering*, 131(7), 28–35.

Carless, S., L. Mann, and A. Wearing. 1998. "Leadership, Managerial Performance and 360-Degree Feedback." *Applied Psychology: An International Review*, 47(4), 481–96.

Carlson, J. G. 1985. "Recent Assessments of the Myers-Briggs Type Indicator." *Journal of Personality Assessment*, 49(4), 356–64.

Chan, C., M. Jalbert, and T. Jalbert. 2012. "Community College and State Rankings by Cost of Living Adjusted Faculty Compensation." *International Journal of Education Research*, 7(2), 25–37.

Chang, C., Johnson, R., Lanaj, K., Mao, C. and Venus, M. 2012. "Leader Identity as an Antecedent of the Frequency and Consistency of Transformational, Consideration, and Abusive Leadership Behaviors." *Applied Psychology*: Advance online publication.

Christopher, H., and E. Weber. 1998. "Cross-Cultural Differences in Risk Perception, But Cross-Cultural Similarities in Attitudes Towards Perceived Risk." *Management Science*, 44(9) 1205–17.

Cilliers, F., V. Deventer, and R. Eeden. 2008. "Leadership Styles and Associated Personality Traits: Support for the Conceptualization of Transactional and Transformational Leadership." *South African Journal of Psychology*, 38(2), 253–57.

Clegg, C., J. Cordery, and T. Wall. 2002. "Empowerment, Performance, and Operational Uncertainty: A Theoretical Integration." *Applied Psychology: An International Review*, 51(1), 146–69.

Copeland, R.D. (ed.). 2007. Merriam-Webster's Dictionary and Thesaurus. Springfield: Merriam-Webster.

Copi, I. M. 2002. *Introduction to Logic*. (C. Owen, R. Miller, S. Lesan, C. Smith, D. O'Connell, D. Chodoff, eds.) Upper Saddle River: Pearson Education.

Creswell, J. W. 2009. *Research Design: Qualitative, Quantitative and Mixed Methods Approaches*. Thousand Oaks: Sage Publications.

Crispo, A, and Y. Sysinger. 2012. “Employee Motivation and 360° Feedback.” *Insights to a Insights to a Changing World Journal*, (9), 1–13.

Daley, J. 2013. *History's Greatest Speeches*. (J. Daley, M. Waldrep, J. Kopito, eds.) Mineola: Dover Thrift Editions.

DeBerg, R., A. Jarzebowski, and J. Palermo. 2012. “When Feedback Is Not Enough: The Impact of Regulatory Fit on Motivation after Positive Feedback.” *International Coaching Psychology Review*, 7(1), 14–32.

Dolan, R. J., T. J. Kosnik, and J. A. Quelch. 1993. *Marketing Management*. (S. Patterson, L. Nordbrock, P. Buschman, eds.) Burr Ridge: Irwin.

Dubrin, A. 2010. *Leadership: Research Findings, Practice, and Skills*. Mason: Southwestern Cengage Learning.

Eckes, G. 2001. *The Six Sigma Revolution: How General Electric and Others Turned Process into Profits*. New York: John Wiley & Sons, Inc.

Ellam-Dyson, V., and S. Palmer. 2011. “Leadership Coaching? No Thanks, I'm Not Worthy.” *The Coaching Psychologist*, 7(2), 108–17.

Elster, C. H. 1995. *Verbal Advantage*. Achievement Dynamics Corporation.

Evans, J., and W. Lindsay. 2005. “An Introduction to Six Sigma and Process Improvement.” (C. McCormick, T. Wilkins, D. Quinn, eds.). Mason: Southwestern Cengage Learning.

Funk and Wagnalls. 1995. *Young Students Learning Library*: Universe—World War I, Volume 22, 2802–03. Shelton: Funk and Wagnalls.

Grant, R. M. 1995. *Contemporary Strategy Analysis: Concepts, Techniques, Applications—Second Edition*. Cambridge: Blackwell Publishers.

Gupta, N., G. Jenkins, A. Mitra, and J. Shaw. 2015. “The Utility of Pay Raises/Cuts: A Simulation Experimental Study.” *Journal of Economic Psychology*, 49, 150–66.

Harvard Business Review. 2004. “The Results Driven Manager: Presentations That Persuade and Motivate.” Boston: Harvard Business School Press.

Hosein, Z., and A. Yousefi. 2012. “The Role of Emotional Intelligence on Workforce Agility in the Workplace.” International Journal of Psychological Studies, 4(3), 48–61.

Hu, J., and R. Liden. 2011. “Antecedents of Team Potency and Team Effectiveness: An Examination of Goal and Process Clarity and Servant Leadership.” *Journal of Applied Psychology*, 96(4), 851–62.

Ivancevich, J., and M. Matteson. 1993. *Organizational Behavior and Management: Third Edition.* (K. Strand, L. Spell, and R. McMullen eds.) Burr: Irwin.

Johns, H. E., and H. R. Moser. 1989. "From Trait to Transformation: The Evolution of Leadership Theories." *Academic Journal Education,* 110(1), 115–23.

Juran, J. M. 1995. *Managerial Breakthrough: The Classical Book on Improving Management Performance.* New York: McGraw-Hill.

Kark, R., and T. Yaffe. 2011. "Leading by Example: The Case of Leader OCB." *Journal of Applied Psychology,* 96(4), 806–26.

Kell, W. G., D. E. Kieso, and J. J. Weygandt. 1990. *Accounting Principles: Second Edition* (G. Scandone, G. Stahl, eds.) New York: John Wiley & Sons.

Ken, S. 1975. "On the Folly of Rewarding A, While Hoping for B." *The Academy of Management Journal,* 18(4)), 769–83.

Kets, V. M. F. R., K. Kortov, and E. Florent-Treacy. 2007. *Coach and Couch: The Psychology of Making Better Leaders* (K. de Vries, K. Korotov, and E. Florent-Treacy, eds.) Basingstoke: Palgrave Macmillan.

Kobel, M. and Zeman. 2012. "Introduction: Relativism about Value." *The Southern Journal of Philosophy,* 50(4), 529–37.

Kouzes, J. M., and B. Z. Posner. 2007. *The Leadership Challenge.* San Francisco: Jossey-Bass.

Korner, H., and H. Nordvik. 2004. "Personality Traits in Leadership Behavior." *Scandinavian Journal of Psychology,* 45, 49–54.

Kussrow, P. 2009. "Brain Based Leadership." *Contemporary Education,* 72(2), 10–15.

Lam, S., A. Peng, and J. Schaubroeck. 2011. "Cognition-Based and Affect-Based Trust as Mediators of Leader Behavior Influences on Team Performance." *Journal of Applied Psychology,* 96(4), 863–71.

Lawrence, P. 2011. "What Leaders Need to Know about Human Evolution and Decision Making." *Leader to Leader,* 60, 12–16.

Leedy, P. and J. Ormond. 2013. *Practical Research Planning and Design.* Upper Saddle River: Pearson Education, Inc.

Levine, H., and D. A. Raynor. 2006. "Associations between the Five-Factor Model of Personality and Health Behaviors among College Students." *Journal of American College Health,* 58(1), 73–82.

Liu, J., O. Siu, and K. Shi. 2010. "Transformational Leadership and Employee Well-Being: The Mediating Role of Trust in the Leader and Self-Efficacy." *Applied Psychology: An International Review*, 59(3), 454–79.

Lo, M., H. W. Min, and T. Ramayah. 2009. "Leadership Styles and Organizational Commitment: A Test on Malaysia Manufacturing Industry." *African Journal of Marketing Management*, 1(6), 133–39.

Lynam, D., and J. D. Miller. 2001. "Structural Models of Personality and Their Relation to Antisocial Behavior: A Meta-Analytic Review." *Academic Journal—Criminology* 39(4), 765–98.

Martin, W., and Schinzinger. 2010. *Introduction to Engineering Ethics: Second Edition.* (D. Hash, D. Schueller, eds.) New York: McGraw-Hill.

McMenamin, P. 2014. "New BLS Data on Staff Nurse Compensation and Inflation Adjusted Wages." *Nursing Economics*, 32(6), 320–22.

Nordhaus, J., and P. Samuelson. 1992. *Economics: Fourteenth Edition*. (J. Bittker, J. Kromm, and I. Roberts, eds.). New York: McGraw-Hill.

Northouse, P. G. 2013. *Leadership: Theory and Practice.* (L. Shaw, P. Quinlin, M. Stanley, M. White, N. Vail, E. Garner, and M. Masson, eds.) Thousand Oaks: Sage.

O'Brien, J. A. 1990. *Management Information Systems: A Managerial End User Perspective.* (L. Alexander, R. Johnson, S. Tretacosti, eds.). Boston: Irwin.

Pichler, S., and A. Teckchandani. 2015. "Quality Results from Performance Appraisals." *Industrial Management Institute of Industrial Engineers*, 16–20.

Plinio, A. J. 2009. "Ethics and Leadership." *International Journal of Disclosure and Governance*, 277–83.

Rock, D., and J. Schwartz. 2007. "The Neuroscience of Leadership." *Reclaiming Childhood and Youth*, 16(3), 10–17.

Reynolds, G. 2008. *Presentationzen: Simple Ideas on Presentation Design and Delivery.* (M. Nolan, M. Justak, and H. Sala, eds.). Berkeley: New Riders.

Sachs, R. T. 1992. *Productive Performance Appraisals.* New York: AMACOM.

Srivastava, S. 2010. "The Five-Factor Model Describes the Structure of Social Perceptions." *Psychology Inquiry*, 21, 69–75.

Steensma, H., and B. van Knippenberg. 2003. "Future Interaction Expectation and the Use of Soft and Hard Influence Tactics." *Applied Psychology: An International Review*, 52(1), 55–67.
Suleyman, Y. 2011. "Relationship between Leader-Member Exchange and Burnout in Professional Football Players." *Journal of Sports Sciences*, 29(14), 1493–1502.
Smith, A. 1776. *The Wealth of Nations* (C. Bullock, ed.). New York: Barns & Noble, Inc.
Vroom, V. 1997. "Loose-Tight Leadership: What Is the Question?" *Applied Psychology: An International Review*, 46(4), 422–27.
Welch, Jack. 2001. "Straight from the Gut." (J. Byrne, ed.) New York: Warner Business Books.

INDEX

D

E

F

M

N

O

P

Q

R

V

W

Z

Printed in the United States
By Bookmasters